CHOOSING TOMORROW'S
GROWTH STOCKS TODAY

By John W. Hazard

CHOOSING TOMORROW'S
GROWTH STOCKS TODAY

•

By JOHN W. HAZARD

DOUBLEDAY & COMPANY, INC.
GARDEN CITY, NEW YORK

*To Helen
and our investments in the future:
Anne
John
Amanda
Thomas
Charlotte
Charles*

CONTENTS

ACKNOWLEDGMENTS

This book, while newly written and updated, is based largely on material derived from articles that have appeared in *Changing Times* magazine. The articles referred to were written by myself with some exceptions, such as those from which I drew information on insurance, trusts, home ownership, and personal savings. I am indebted to the publisher of *Changing Times,* Austin H. Kiplinger, and to the editor, Robert W. Harvey, for permission to make use of this material.

The basic investment philosophy set forth in these pages was developed by Lew G. Coit, for many years investment consultant to *Changing Times* and the Kiplinger Washington Editors. Mr. Coit, in my opinion, is one of the country's most skillful and successful investment counselors, and I am grateful for his judgment, instruction, and help.

I am indebted to the editor of *Barrons National Business and Financial Weekly* for permission to excerpt from several of the excellent *Barrons* articles on the various growth industries described in Chapter 4.

I express my appreciation to two members of the *Changing Times* staff: Andrea Ronhovde, research assistant, for her help in research and editing, and Claire Ann Sullivan, administrative assistant, for help in preparing the manuscript.

JOHN W. HAZARD

CHOOSING TOMORROW'S
GROWTH STOCKS TODAY

CHAPTER 1

The Attractiveness of Common Stocks

Buying and owning common stocks—notably those of strong, growing companies—can be a fascinating and rewarding project. If certain precautionary rules are followed, money thus invested will grow at 6%, 8%, 10%, 12% or even faster. Look at the charts of a few leading growth stocks on pages 91–95. If you had invested in International Business Machines in 1950, your investment would have doubled by 1955. If you had started in 1955 your money would have quadrupled by 1960. If you had started in 1960, your money would have doubled by 1965. If you had started in 1965, you can find where you'd be by glancing at the daily stock quotations. Examine the other charts and you will see that, had you invested at almost any time in a good growth stock and held on for at least five years, your money would have snowballed. And this takes no account of dividends.

This sounds great, but admittedly it involves a lot of hindsight. How do you know that the stock market will continue to rise? Mightn't there be a depression? And how do you pick out stocks that will grow in the future as IBM and the others have grown in the past?

THE NEW ECONOMY—GROWTH WITH INFLATION

These are valid questions. But if you examine the changes that have taken place in our society and in our economy since the great depression of the Thirties, you probably will agree that another such catastrophe is highly unlikely. And if you examine the changes that have taken place since the end of World War II, you probably will agree that the outlook, rather than being gloomy, is quite rosy.

The country appears to be in another great period of growth and boom. Furthermore, if you bear in mind what inflation does to bonds and savings accounts, you probably will agree that for most families investing in stocks not only is desirable but almost a necessity.

Another depression unlikely   First, what about the danger of a depression? There *could* be another one, that's true. But here are some of the arguments that make it seem highly unlikely. Today the federal government has assumed responsibility for keeping employment high and business good. To do the job, it has established various snubbers, cushions, and stabilizers that were not available in the Thirties. Income taxes are vastly higher. When business begins to slide off, a hefty tax cut can put billions of dollars back into the spending stream. Furthermore, the government can borrow tremendous amounts and pump billions into various public programs. Bank deposits and savings accounts are now insured, generally up to $15,000 per account. Farm prices are supported when they decline below certain levels. Home mortgages are amortized monthly, instead of falling due every three to five years as used to be the case. And many mortgages are guaranteed or insured. In contrast to the old days, millions of people now have a floor under their incomes. The older ones draw monthly checks from social security and pension plans. The sick are helped financially by Medicare. Unemployment compensation stands ready to take up slack when unemployment grows. All in all, it would appear that, while we may still have recessions, we probably never again will have a real block buster of a depression. And the recessions we have had since World War II have been relatively mild. History indicates that the stock market can ride out such recessions very well.

Growth probably will continue   Now look at the more positive side—the reasons for thinking that, long-range, the boom will continue. At the end of World War II, when the servicemen came home, a great crop of war babies was born. This bulge in the birth rate lasted ten years. Now statistics show that young families begin spending for houses, furniture, cars, appliances and so on when they reach age twenty-three to twenty-five. Therefore the period twenty-three to twenty-five years after the end of World War II should mark the beginning of a ten-year period of basically good and expanding business. Thus the decade of the Seventies should be a prosperous one for business and for stockholders.

Add another ingredient. More billions have been spent on research, since the beginning of World War II, than in all the previous history of mankind. These research dollars are like seeds. They sprout and produce new seeds. A tremendous wave of new materials, new products, and new methods has swept over the land. You can name a dozen off hand: lasers, satellites, color TV, computerized banking and billing, synthetic fibers, tough new plastics, wonder drugs, artificial heart pacers, kidney machines and so on. Research keeps the industrial and business pot boiling and no end is in sight. In fact, industry finds it increasingly difficult to get the capital and the manpower to do all it wants to. America is on the move. Rich and vigorous companies are inventing, expanding, and prospering. And you can own a share of it via common stock.

More inflation coming Furthermore, you probably *should* own a share in it. Considering the direction our economy is taking, ownership of common stocks has become almost a must. This may sound strange to those brought up to believe that the ideal investment was "money in the bank." In earlier days, back in the 1930's, prices were stable. A sum of money put into savings would buy as much at the end of a ten-year period as at the beginning. And compound interest added a few dollars to the kitty. But times change. Today the universal demand is for growth. Everything, it seems, must grow: production, profits, wages, benefits, even debt. And prices, perforce, are carried along and grow too. Thus the cost of living appears to be in a continuous upward drift. Over the past fifteen years, prices have risen 2% a year. More recently the rise has been over 3%. This creeping inflation may not be very noticeable in the course of day-to-day living; the incomes of people who work tend to move up to meet the rise in daily expenses. But there are two areas where inflation hurts and hurts badly: it bears down hard on people whose income is fixed, and it damages savings set aside for a future goal.

Take the older couple who are retired and living on a flat dollar pension. Each year, as prices rise, each dollar of income buys a little less. This couple need assets that will grow in value and in yield to offset the erosion of their purchasing power.

Now, take a middle-aged couple who hope to retire in ten, fifteen, or twenty years. Their goal is to build up a fund to supplement Social Security or a pension. With high taxes and the high cost of living, and perhaps the expense of sending children to college, it is hard for such a family to save anything. So once money is saved it is poor policy to let it languish where its growth is barely enough to offset inflation. This middle-aged couple need to pay a lot of attention to investments having a powerful growth potential. The savings account route will never get them where they want to be.

A younger couple may be building a fund to send a child to college. This fund, if put into savings, will earn interest at 4% to 5% compounded. But the cost of a college education is rising at the rate of 7% compounded. Think how fast this husband and wife are losing ground. They, too, need to invest in growth.

Really, whatever your age, you probably should have a substantial portion of your assets invested in equities; that is, real estate or common stocks. And stocks in many ways are easier to acquire and manage.

MINIMIZING THE RISKS

There's risk in it, of course. Stocks go down as well as up. There's bound to be some luck in how well your selections turn out. But look at what the careful investor has going for him. For thirty years American industrial output has been growing at a rate of more than 3% a year. And in some recent years the growth has been between 5% and 9%. Many leading companies have grown in value much faster. From 1950 to 1965 the Dow-Jones Industrial Average almost quintupled, showing a growth rate of over 10% a year compounded. This is growth in value only; no account is taken of dividends. Of course, the rise was not steady. The average had its ups and downs. Just the same, if at any time during that fifteen-year period you could have bought the average, your investment would inevitably have shown a profit in five years or less.

Taking advantage of the long-term rise   But, you may say, you can't buy the averages. Well, consider this. Two professors of the University of Michigan made studies of a random selection of stocks listed on the New York Stock Exchange. In the first study, which covered the period from 1937 to 1950, they assumed a regular investment each year on January 15 in each of the ninety-two stocks that had had a trading volume of a million shares or more in 1936. All dividends were assumed to have been reinvested. The portfolio showed a growth over the period of 12.2% compounded. When the professors tried random portfolios of every second stock of the ninety-two, every third stock, every fourth stock, and so on up to every tenth stock, results generally were even better than 12.2%. Later the professors continued the original study through 1960. The compound growth rate of the master list for the whole twenty-five-year period turned out to be 14%. Then a similar study was made covering the same stocks for the period 1950 to 1961. The compound growth rate was 14.2%.

A somewhat similar study by two professors of the University of Chicago Graduate School of Business showed that an investment in all New York Stock Exchange stocks in 1926, with dividends reinvested, held until 1960, would have shown an average growth of 9% a year compounded. And remember that these studies assumed in one case a series of random selections, and in the other a total selection—mechanical methods that are neither practical nor advisable. A careful and informed selection should bring even better results.

Buying into faster growing companies   For example, the economy is growing rapidly. But obviously not all industries are growing at the same pace. Some are expanding faster, some slower than the average. So why not concentrate on the fastest growing fields? Within those industries, some companies have records of steady growth. They have strong financing; they spend heavily on research; they are constantly developing new products and more efficient methods; their management is competent and aggressive. Why pick companies whose earning records have been erratic or which show signs of being unable to forge ahead against fierce competition? Obviously, the smart thing is to pick the leaders, even though their shares may be more expensive in the beginning. All other things being equal, those companies that have been doing well tend to continue to do well. By making this kind of careful selection, and spreading the risk over several companies in different industries, you should be able to keep your money growing faster than the economy as a whole and much faster than the cost of living.

It sounds wonderful but there is a catch. You can't do this by guessing and gambling. Successful investing can be fun but it is not just a lark. You must have a plan and enough self-discipline to stick to it. You need independence and self-confidence to reject the bad advice that's always flying around. And you have to do some homework, some browsing through facts and statistics. Even if you don't want to make the basic decisions yourself, but prefer to entrust your money to professionals, it takes some study to discover which professionals are really top notch. How to start an investment program and minimize the risks will be covered in early chapters of this book.

BUT FIRST—MONEY RESERVES AND INSURANCE

First, here are a few preliminaries. You need some capital to start with, and a continuous flow, or at least a trickle to put into the stocks you select. Unless you are lucky enough to have received an inheritance, you need to save. And saving requires careful money management, something that is becoming a lost art.

There is another ingredient that goes into successful investing. You must have a certain freedom from pressure. You can't play a good game of golf or tennis if you are playing against the clock. If you buy stocks with money that your subconscious tells you may be needed for something else, this gnawing knowledge will warp your judgment and cramp your style. Stock prices appear to be in a long upward trend, but the short-term movements are erratic. Even if you own a stock that promises to triple in five years, you can't possibly forecast where it will be in six months or one year. A sharp downward movement of the market as a whole may drag down the price of your stock even though its potential never looked brighter. So if you buy stocks with money that you are going to need for purchase of a new car, or for some other important expenditure or an emergency, then fate may well decree that you will need the money just when the market is in one of its periodic dips. You must guard against being forced to sell at a time NOT of your own choosing.

This means that before you start an investment program you should have a savings fund that will get you through any reasonably expectable emergency such as temporary loss of your job. Also, before the family's money is put at risk in the stock market, three other financial defenses should be in place: life insurance, liability insurance, and what used to be called "catastrophe" health insurance. The last is designed to protect, not against expectable, common ailments, but against the staggering, once-in-a-lifetime medical expenses that can drain a family's resources.

The investing part of a financial program may be the most glamorous, but like all good and beautiful structures it must be built on strong underpinnings. In this case, the foundations are sound money management and adequate savings and insurance. That is why these less glamorous, but very important subjects—money management, savings, and insurance—will be covered in early chapters of this book.

CHAPTER 2

Money Management

If you are the head of a family, you are in fact a businessman. The family has all the elements of a business. It makes and sells something—usually in the form of the services of the breadwinner. It has income, expenses, overhead, invested capital, working capital, and surplus. This may seem a dull and mundane way of looking at a family, with its wealth of relationships that are not merely material or financial. And yet, whether it irks you or not, you cannot escape from the reality that any family is a form of small business.

A family is probably tougher than a business. A family can survive and even prosper with slovenly internal methods that would send any other business to the wall. The family is more flexible. For this reason it is actually not necessary for a family to manage its business p's and q's as carefully as a regular business must. But it is desirable. It is a way of getting along better, and making the available family money go farther.

In this discussion an attempt is made to show any head of any family how to stretch the money and make it do more. The methods are essentially business methods. Some may be too complex for the average family or unsuited to the nature of the family head. In this case, the full dose of guidance may be cut to half a dose. The whole thing need not be swallowed, but it would do no harm to swallow a little bit of it.

Young men, especially, face the problem of learning how to finance a family. Eventually they learn it, usually by trial and error. When young men get to be older men, they think in arrears of how much better off they would have been if they had followed certain stricter financial courses in their younger years. That's the benefit of hindsight.

Even older men, even businessmen, do not always run their family affairs on a "businesslike basis." They may be crack administrators at the office, but they often are loose with the personal and family budget.

BUSINESS METHODS FOR THE FAMILY

First, then, take a look at the way a business is run. It must make a profit or die. So at the beginning of each year it estimates its gross income, expenses, and net profits, and then plans on how to use the profit most effectively. Month by month during the year, the businessman eagerly compares his accomplishments with his forecast. If he is doing better than expected, he may expand; if worse, he may have to trim his sails and set a new course. But at all times he knows where he is and what he is aiming for.

The same cannot be said for many families. Their finances are run on a hit-or-miss basis. The hit-or-miss family, Mr. and Mrs. Homf, always have to strain to get the things they really want because they have let their money leak away on less essential stuff bought on impulse. Mr. Homf gets a good salary, but he tries to operate on too little working capital. This causes him to worry and fuss at Mrs. Homf and the children. Often he has to borrow to tide the family over a crisis, and this causes unnecessary fees and interest.

Mrs. Homf sees plenty of bargains in clothes and appliances, but seldom takes advantage of them because she knows only in the vaguest way what items she is going to need and when. Eventually necessity forces her to buy in a hurry without much chance to shop around.

Mr. Homf always thinks things are going to be better next month, and this causes him to start investment programs which he usually has to give up. The last time he bought stock it was not long before he needed the money. Unfortunately, at that particular time the market was down. He had to sell, although if he could have held on he would eventually have had a nice profit.

Several times the Homfs have gotten a little ahead and bought savings bonds only to have to cash them in within a few years. The interest they received was thus only a per cent or so instead of the more than 4% they would have received had they held on for the full seven years.

CHART 1: CASH FORECAST*

	January			February		
	Last year	Estimated for this year	Actual for this year	Last year	Estimated for this year	Actual for this year
Cash on hand and in checking						
account, end of previous period	$167	$150		$ 78	$165	
Receipts:						
Net pay	518	552		518	552	
Borrowed	100					
Other				26	26	
Total cash available during period	$785	$702		$622	$743	
Fixed Payments:						
Mortgage	$ 70	$ 70		$ 70	$ 70	
Life insurance				191	191	
Fire insurance	26	26				
Auto liability insurance						
Savings bond	19	19		19	19	
Real estate taxes						
Loan		8		8		
TOTAL	$115	$123		$288	$280	
Variable Payments:						
Light	$ 7	$ 7		$ 6	$ 6	
Gas	23	23		28	28	
Telephone	7	7		6	6	
Medical	12	5		8	8	
Car	17	17		15	15	
Food	140	140		132	132	
Clothing	25	25		40	40	
Nonrecurring large payments						
Airline tickets	193					
Christmas bills	80	100				
Other	88	90		75	75	
TOTAL	$592	$414		$310	$310	
Total payments	$707	$537		$598	$590	
Recapitulation:						
Total cash available	$785	$702		$622	$743	
Total payments	707	537		598	590	
Cash balance, end of period	$ 78	$165		$ 24	$153	

* Copyright by *Changing Times*.

Net worth and cash forecast charts It is not hard to see that a little financial planning would do the Homfs a world of good. Maybe it would do your family some good too. Are you game? If so, here is the way to start. Examine the sample charts on pages 32 and 33. They may look a bit complicated at first glance, but don't let that worry you. The theory is very simple. You are going to make one chart to keep track of your net worth. Your net worth, of course, is the value of your major assets, such as savings, stocks, bonds, real estate, etc., minus your debts. If you are getting anywhere, your net worth should be increasing a little bit each month. Your net worth chart is going to show you how much.

The other chart is to be a cash forecast. It will show you how the cash is going to flow through the family coffers during the coming year, with no regard to whether it goes toward increasing your net worth. It may show that in certain months you will be pinched and that in others you will be loaded with cash. But in the latter case it may be cash that will be sorely needed for heavy obligations later on.

An example will show the difference between the two charts. Say that you know that in February you will pay a life insurance premium

CHART 2: NET WORTH FORECAST*

	January 31			February 28		
	Last year	*Estimated for this year*	*Actual*	*Last year*	*Estimated for this year*	*Actual*
Assets:						
House	$16,000	$15,750		$16,000	$15,750	
Car	1,138	875		1,116	857	
Life insurance cash value	354	472		472	590	
Savings bonds	220	440		240	460	
Cash	78	165		24	153	
TOTAL ASSETS	$17,790	$17,702		$17,852	$17,810	
Liabilities:						
Mortgage	$ 8,750	$ 8,450		$ 8,725	$ 8,425	
Loans	100			92		
TOTAL LIABILITIES	$ 8,850	$ 8,450		$ 8,817	$ 8,425	
Net Worth	$ 8,940	$ 9,252		$ 9,035	$ 9,385	

* Copyright by *Changing Times*.

of $191, which will cause the surrender value of the policy to increase by $118. This $118 is a saving and will show up as an increase in net worth. The remaining $73 is an expense and will not appear on the net worth chart. Your cash forecast, on the other hand, will show an outgo of the whole $191.

Now note that each chart has one wide column for each month. Each wide column is divided into three narrow columns labeled *Last year, Estimate for this year* and *Actual*. This is a device to help you estimate the figures for twelve months ahead, then compare actual results with your estimates. The reason for recording last year's figures is that they are usually the best basis for making estimates for this year.

Cash forecast   The cash forecast is the one to do first. Take a big sheet of drawing paper, leave a three-inch margin on the left, then divide the rest of the sheet into twelve wide columns, and finally divide each wide column into three narrow columns. Or you can buy sheets with columns already marked. They are obtainable at a stationery store and are known as accountants' work sheets or ruled columnar sheets. Another method is to use one 8½ × 11″ notebook sheet for each month. Divide it into three columns.

Label the columns as indicated in the sample, one wide column for each month, and the first narrow column for the same month a year earlier, the second for this year's estimate, the third (to be filled in later) for this year's actual figures.

The cash forecast, in its simplest form, is going to enable you to look ahead at the coming months and make four estimates about each one: how much cash you will have on hand at the beginning of the month; how much money you will take in during the month; how much you will spend; and how much you will have at the end of the month. Just how detailed you want to make those estimates is up to you. The number of categories used in the sample cash forecast on page 32 has proved about right for many people. But yours can have either more or less, depending on your needs. Here is a warning, however: Don't try for too much detail at first. A simple work sheet kept up to date is better than an elaborate one abandoned.

The next step is to label the horizontal spaces in the left-hand margin. The top line should be *Cash on hand and in checking account, end of previous period.* That shows what you start each month with. On the next lines list receipts during the month including all cash coming in, paycheck, money borrowed, gifts, and so on. The total of all the first few lines, then, will give you all the money available during that month.

The next section covers fixed payments, the ones you can positively expect to be a certain amount. They will include rent or payments on the mortgage, various insurance premiums, regular savings, and so on.

Then come variable payments, the ones you know are coming but can't tell exactly in what amount. They will be bills for telephone, light, gas, doctors, food, clothing, and so on. In this section, inevitably, there will be a large sum of money spent but not easily accounted for. It will include all kinds of cash payments and incidentals too numerous and bothersome to record. This item is probably going to look pretty big, but don't worry about it and don't try to break it down—at least not at first. You will only involve yourself in needless paper work. Label it *Other*.

Here also leave a few lines for large nonrecurring payments such as Christmas bills, vacations, out-of-town trips, and so on. If you threw these into the *Other* category, it would distort it and make it jump around from month to month. You want it to be stable so you can estimate it accurately.

Now come the critical spaces. Devote the bottom of the sheet to a recapitulation. Label one line *Total cash available,* the next, *Total payments,* the last *Cash balance, end of period.* That, of course, will be the amount with which you will head the column for the next month.

Your blank cash forecast is now ready and you can start entering figures. If you have never done it before, this is going to be very revealing. Before you start, here is a trick that is strongly recommended. Use three differently colored pencils: red, green, and blue. Red will always be used for last year's figures. Green will be used for future estimates. Then blue will be used later for actual results.

The way to start is to get out your checkbook stubs and receipted bills for the past twelve months and whatever other financial records you keep. Start with whatever month it happens to be when you read this. If it is June, all right, start with your records for last June and enter them in red. Probably you won't have accurate figures for every category for last June, but fill in every category anyway, guessing where you have to. Your check stubs should give you most of the data you need.

This is the time to take up your green pencil and begin making estimates for this month. You know how much you had at the beginning of the month, so enter that. You also know what the monthly paycheck is and you can figure the fixed expenses. The variable expenses you can't know, but here is where last year's figures come in handy. If you don't know the size of the electric bill you'll get this month, just assume it's going to be the same as the one you got a year ago. When it comes in you can pay it and then enter the correct amount in blue under *Actual*. And that will give you help in making the estimate for next month.

Don't stop now, however. Still going through your old check stubs, fill in the red figures for the other eleven months. All twelve months will then have a column of red figures filled in. Next, begin filling in the rest of the green estimates. Keep in mind that they are only estimates and don't rack your brain too fiercely. And by all means resist the temptation to decide right now that you are going to change your normal pattern of spending. This is a forecast, not a New Year's resolution. You are trying to make a hardheaded judgment on what lies ahead.

As you go forward in your estimate, you will spot in such upcoming items as mortgage payments, insurance premiums, tax bills, Christmas spending. Each month you should have about the same big *Other* item. And you will be able to see pretty clearly how much cash you will have on hand at the beginning and end of each period. The average of these two figures for any month is your average working capital. If it is under $100, it is probably too low.

Here are a few tips that will make record keeping easy in the future. When you come home from a shopping trip, throw store receipts for cash payments into a box. Collect them and tot them up at the end of the month. Pay by check whenever you can. Make sure all family income goes first into the checking account, then out into other channels by check. Use charge accounts and credit cards if you can handle them conservatively.

Net worth forecast   The net worth forecast comes next. It is comparatively easy to make because, unfortunately, most people have very few items to list. Forget about your income and your living expenses. A pipe doesn't care how much water flows through it. All you are interested in now is what you are catching in the reservoir.

Take your net worth forecast sheet and list in the left-hand margin your major assets. Omit minor items such as personal possessions, clothes, and furniture. Stick to such things as the market value of your house, car, stocks and bonds, the amount in savings accounts, the cash value of life insurance policies, and the actual cash you have on hand at the end of the period. Use the sample on page 33 as a guide.

Next list your liabilities. These will include the balance you owe on the mortgage, the balance you owe on other debts such as the loan on your car, and bank loans. Again use red pencil for last year's figures, green pencil for this year's estimates, and blue pencil for actual results.

To get your net worth at the end of each month, simply subtract total liabilities from total assets. The month-to-month increase probably won't look very large, but let's face it, that's all it was. Maybe you can do better, but don't yield to the temptation to start a brand-new savings program on the spur of the moment.

There are a couple of tricky things about your net worth. Theoretically your house is depreciating, losing value because of increasing age. But maybe over the past years the actual market value has gone up because of inflation. Here is the way to handle this part of your net worth forecast. For all last year's months simply list what you consider the market value to have been at the beginning of last year. To get this year's figure, make a new estimate in the light of the condition of the house and the real estate market today. Use this figure for all months of this year, and plan to revalue again at the beginning of next year.

Your car is another item somewhat hard to assess. A car loses value much faster than a house. Depreciation plus obsolescence (going out of style) reduces a new car's value by 30% to 40% the first year, 15% to 20% the second year, 10% to 15% the third year, and around 10%, 9%, and 6% in the years succeeding. The man who buys a new car every year has an average annual depreciation expense about twice that of the man who keeps his car four years. This is a real decrease in net worth, which shows up unmistakably in the trade-in allowance.

Figure how much your car has depreciated from its original cost. If it is two years old, it has depreciated 45% to 60%. So for its present worth put down between 40% and 55%. The exact figure will depend on the condition of the car. At the beginning of next year its value will have dropped another 12½% on the average. So during this year lower the value by one twelfth of this amount each month. Say you figure it is worth $875 now, but will be worth only $656 in a year. Each month its value will drop around $18.

Using your records effectively When you have completed your cash and net worth forecasts, you are in business. Maybe it has taken a couple of afternoons to get everything figured and entered, but it will be worth it. You have created a wonderful tool that has many uses.

First of all, you now have a pretty good idea of where the money has been going. And as months go by, you can begin to form a pretty shrewd guess as to where it will go in the future. By anticipating future demands, you should be able to cut overhead. All life insurance premiums can be put on an annual basis. Bank service charges can be cut. Borrowing can be kept to a minimum. Maybe in the months ahead you will be saving a bit more. If so, fine. If, on the other hand, you are spending more, you should be able to spot where it is going.

HOW TO GET THE FUNDS YOU NEED

If you want to invest or build a reserve fund, you must have money, and, to get money, most people have to save. Saving in this sense means the building up of a cash fund that can be invested or stashed away in a reserve fund. Broadly speaking, an increase in the cash value of a life insurance policy or a decrease in the size of the mortgage on your house is also a saving. But for the purposes of this chapter, saving means accumulating cash or the equivalent.

Saving isn't easy and it isn't much fun. Basically there's only one way to do it: hold down your outgo and keep up your income. There are, however, some tricks that make the job a little more intriguing and less of a chore. Here are half a dozen of the most common.

The marked-money method is the oldest known to man and is nothing more than a piggy bank with a rule book built in. Pick a coin, anything from a penny to a half dollar. Say you decide on nickels; from then on, nickels are unspendable. Every nickel you get goes into the sugar bowl. Keep this up for a little while and it easily becomes a habit. And you'd be surprised at how quickly small-change savings can mount.

The short-take method is based on the theory that it's easy to be strong-willed for a week or two at a time. You can manage a lot of economies for a few months that you couldn't stand indefinitely. So, many families have successfully used the technique of setting a brief period, say three months, and just saving their heads off. They'll cut expenses to the bone, knowing that the end is always in sight, and sock away a tidy sum of cash. When it's over, they blow themselves to a celebration and resume their unthrifty living (but with cash in the bank) until they feel strong enough for a repeat.

The windfall method is one for which the circumstances have to be just right. Every once in a while you are likely to "find" some money. Perhaps you get a raise. Perhaps you finish paying an installment debt. Perhaps the doctor orders you to quit smoking, or the cleaning woman quits and you can't find a replacement. Wherever it comes from, there's suddenly a certain amount of money lying loose. Grab it quick, or part of it, for savings, before it gets absorbed by living expenses. You got along without it before, and you can continue to.

The even-swap method requires real determination. Pick one specific regular expense. Trade it for savings money. Make it a sacrificial lamb and deposit its cost in the bank each month. This is a bit easier than more general kinds of budget-cutting because the dramatic twist helps morale. Managing a cut in the entertainment budget, for some mysterious reason, is generally harder than depositing the price of the midweek movie in a tin can as you settle down to a quiet evening at home.

The self-service method calls for discovering a job you pay other people to do that you might do yourself. Laundry? Car washing? Lawn mowing? Repair work? Kids' clothing? Do it yourself and bank the saving.

The elbow-grease method means you save more by earning more. It's not as hard as it sounds. If your goals are modest enough, say ten or twenty dollars a month, there may be plenty of opportunities for a little spare-time earning. For example, the apartment developments of the country are full of housewives who save up for this or that by baby-sitting for their neighbors. Look around. If you can spare a couple of days or evenings a week, there may well be a way to cash them in.

None of these tricks contains any magic. But any one—or another of your own invention—might prove a shot in the arm to make the flesh as willing as the spirit.

PROGRAMS TO HELP YOU SAVE

The financial people who make a business of safekeeping other people's money have devised a number of more formal schemes to add a zip to thrift. Here are some samples of how they work.

Some savings banks offer packaged plans designed to help the saver reach any goal. For residents of the bank's own state the package can include savings bank life insurance, E bonds, and a savings account.

Suppose a state resident, aged thirty-five, decides that in ten years he wants to have $1000 in E bonds, $1000 in a savings account, and, during the whole period, $3000 of ordinary life insurance. All he has to do is to send this information to the savings bank and its statisticians will figure out how much he should send the bank each week. In this case it comes to about five dollars. The bank will take the money, make the deposits, and buy the insurance and E bonds, all in the customer's name.

The statistician of such a bank will figure out a similar package plan for anyone anywhere. Tell him how much you want to have in E bonds and a savings account at the end of x number of years, and he will figure the correct weekly or monthly rate of savings. You can also state how much you want to save each week or month, and the bank will tell you how much you can expect to have at any given time. All computations cover interest on savings at the current rate. One advantage of this plan is that there are no commission or service charges. Also, there is no penalty if you miss a payment.

Commercial banks, with their variety of services, make it possible for a bit-at-a-time investor to work out several interesting programs. For example, a good many banks now issue savings certificates similar to E bonds but maturing in a shorter period of time. You could deposit so many dollars a month in a savings account and, every time you get up to $100, buy a savings certificate. These certificates vary from bank to bank. One type is payable on a certain date; another after a certain length of time; a third only after the owner has given written notice of intention to cash it in. These certificates pay 4%, 5% or more, if held for the full term but less if cashed prior to maturity. You can also instruct your bank to buy you an E bond at any regular interval, deducting the money from your checking account.

Ordinarily banks will not agree to deduct money from your account for any other purpose unless you are a good customer and have a special problem stemming from a trip abroad or something of that sort. The reason is, obviously, that the bookkeeping is expensive, requiring the use of a tickler file to remind the bookkeeper to make each deduction. In some cases, however, banks have agreed to deduct a fixed amount periodically from a depositor's checking account and send it to a designated place. If this appeals to you, it is worth looking into.

Thousands of large companies have also made it possible for employees to have money deducted from their paychecks and invested in E bonds and Freedom Shares. The advantage is that what you don't see you won't miss. Some companies will make similar deductions for the purchase of their own stock or shares of mutual funds.

There are several other ways by which you can invest a small amount each month in common or preferred stock or the shares of mutual funds. These are discussed in Chapter 10, titled "Dollar Cost Averaging."

An interesting but expensive way to save is to make an installment loan at your bank, use the money to buy an E bond or to make some other investment, and then pay back the loan out of current income. The advantage is that the bank will put the heat on more strongly to make you pay back the loan than you would to make yourself save. The man behind the note teller's window is a more compelling personage than the one behind the window marked "Savings."

Some people have even borrowed from a bank and used the money to buy stocks. You have to be careful here to stick to the rules. You cannot put up listed stocks as collateral and use the proceeds to buy more listed stocks. This would be a violation of the Federal Reserve Board's margin requirements. For this reason, when you borrow on listed stocks you must fill out a form stating the purpose of the loan. These requirements, however, do not apply to unlisted stocks. And you can put up as collateral assets other than listed stocks—a life insurance policy, for example—or borrow on your signature, and use the money to buy stocks whether they are listed or unlisted.

Choosing a goal   One great way to help yourself save is to keep continually in mind the goal that lies ahead with all its glittering promises and feeling of security. It is also comforting to note your

CHART 3: REGULAR SAVINGS NEEDED TO REACH
A GIVEN GOAL

Find your savings goal in this column	Here is the regular monthly saving needed to reach that goal if your money is invested at . . .							
	1½%	2%	2½%	3%	3½%	4%	5%	6%
$1000 in 5 years	$16.04	$15.84	$15.64	$15.44	$15.24	$15.05	$14.66	$14.29
10 "	7.72	7.53	7.33	7.15	6.96	6.78	6.43	6.10
15 "	4.95	4.76	4.58	4.40	4.23	4.06	3.74	3.44
20 "	3.57	3.39	3.21	3.05	2.88	2.73	2.44	2.17
30 "	2.20	2.03	1.87	1.72	1.58	1.44	1.21	1.00
$1500 in 5 years	$24.06	$23.76	$23.45	$23.16	$22.86	$22.57	$21.99	$21.43
10 "	11.58	11.29	11.00	10.72	10.44	10.17	9.65	9.14
15 "	7.43	7.15	6.87	6.60	6.34	6.09	5.61	5.16
20 "	5.36	5.09	4.82	4.57	4.32	4.09	3.66	3.26
30 "	3.30	3.04	2.80	2.58	2.36	2.17	1.81	1.51
$2000 in 5 years	$32.08	$31.68	$31.27	$30.87	$30.48	$30.09	$29.33	$28.58
10 "	15.44	15.05	14.67	14.29	13.92	13.56	12.86	12.19
15 "	9.91	9.53	9.16	8.80	8.46	8.12	7.48	6.89
20 "	7.15	6.78	6.43	6.09	5.76	5.48	4.88	4.34
30 "	4.40	4.06	3.74	3.43	3.15	2.89	2.41	2.01
$3000 in 5 years	$48.12	$47.51	$46.91	$46.31	$45.72	$45.14	$43.99	$42.86
10 "	23.16	22.58	22.00	21.44	20.88	20.34	19.29	18.29
15 "	14.86	14.29	13.74	13.20	12.69	12.18	11.23	10.33
20 "	10.72	10.17	9.64	9.14	8.65	8.18	7.31	6.52
30 "	6.60	6.08	5.60	5.15	4.73	4.33	3.62	3.01
$4000 in 5 years	$64.17	$63.35	$62.54	$61.75	$60.96	$60.18	$58.65	$57.15
10 "	30.88	30.10	29.33	28.58	27.84	27.12	25.72	24.39
15 "	19.81	19.06	18.32	17.61	16.91	16.24	14.97	13.77
20 "	14.29	13.56	12.85	12.18	11.53	10.91	9.75	8.69
30 "	8.80	8.11	7.47	6.87	6.30	5.78	4.83	4.02
$5000 in 5 years	$80.21	$79.19	$78.18	$77.18	$76.20	$75.23	$73.31	$71.44
10 "	38.61	37.63	36.67	35.73	34.80	33.90	32.16	30.48
15 "	24.77	23.82	22.90	22.01	21.14	20.30	18.71	17.22
20 "	17.86	16.95	16.07	15.23	14.41	13.64	12.19	10.86
30 "	11.00	10.14	9.34	8.58	7.88	7.22	6.04	5.02
$7500 in 5 years	$120.31	$118.78	$117.27	$115.77	$114.31	$112.84	$109.97	$107.16
10 "	57.91	56.45	55.00	53.59	52.20	50.86	48.23	45.72
15 "	37.15	35.73	34.35	33.01	31.71	30.46	28.07	25.82
20 "	26.80	25.43	24.10	22.84	21.62	20.46	18.28	16.29
30 "	16.50	15.21	14.01	12.88	11.82	10.84	9.06	7.53

progress from month to month. Here, then, are two tables, one to tell you how much to put away each month in order to reach a particular goal, the other to show you how a certain amount put away faithfully twice a year will snowball.

Chart 3 is for use in setting up a regular monthly saving program, and it shows the sum you must put aside each month, at various rates of interest, to build up a given amount in a given time. If your goal is larger than $7500 or is an in-between amount and you want to avoid multiplying or moving decimal points, split your objective into two or three smaller ones. Treat a $9000 goal, for example, as a $4000 one plus a $5000 one.

The required monthly investments have been figured as exactly as possible and will hit your objective almost on the nose. Therefore you're safe in rounding them off a bit or in using them as minimums. *Note:*

The table is based on two assumptions: 1. Interest is compounded semiannually, 2. Money starts to earn interest the same month it is deposited or invested.

Chart 4 shows how regularly deposited savings grow over the years. The assumption is that deposits are made in two equal amounts, one at the beginning of each six-month period. Interest is compounded semiannually.

RAINY DAY MONEY—WHERE TO INVEST IT

One of the first precepts in investing is: Don't use money that you may need for something else, because even the most carefully selected investment probably won't appreciate in value all at once. It may take years for it to fulfill your hopes. In the meantime, as the stock market fluctuates, the value of your stock may at times be below what you paid for it. Now, if during such a dip in price you happened to need money desperately and had no reserves for emergencies, you might be forced to sell out at the worst time.

That's the reason that the first thing to do with your savings is to sock away a certain amount of money in an emergency fund. If you have such a fund, plus adequate insurance, you can approach the problems of investing with a freedom from pressure and worry that will enhance your good judgment.

Strictly speaking, an emergency fund is not an investment, since investing implies converting money into stocks, real estate, or

Chart 4: How Regular Savings Grow Over the Years

Yearly Savings	After 1 Year		After 3 Years		After 5 Years		After 7 Years		After 10 Years		After 15 Years		After 25 Years	
	Earnings to date	Total	Earnings to date	Total	Earnings to date	Total	Earnings to date	Total	Earnings to date	Total	Earnings to date	Total	Earnings to date	Total
$100 at 1%	.75	100.75	5.29	305.29	13.95	513.95	26.82	726.82	54.20	1054.20	122.07	1622.07	346.41	2846.41
$100 at 1½%	1.12	101.12	7.97	307.97	21.95	521.95	40.68	740.68	82.62	1082.62	187.70	1687.70	542.36	3042.34
$100 at 2%	1.50	101.50	10.67	310.67	28.34	528.34	54.84	754.84	111.95	1111.95	256.63	1756.63	755.39	3255.39
$100 at 2½%	1.88	101.88	13.40	313.40	35.69	535.69	69.31	769.31	142.25	1142.25	329.03	1829.03	987.14	3487.14
$100 at 3%	2.26	102.26	16.14	316.14	43.16	543.16	84.10	784.10	173.52	1173.52	405.08	1905.08	1239.40	3739.40
$100 at 3½%	2.64	102.64	18.92	318.92	50.74	550.74	99.22	799.22	205.81	1205.81	484.99	1984.99	1514.15	4014.15
$100 at 4%	3.02	103.02	21.71	321.71	58.43	558.43	114.67	814.67	239.16	1239.16	568.97	2068.97	1813.54	4313.54
$100 at 4½%	3.40	103.40	24.53	324.53	66.25	566.25	130.45	830.45	273.60	1273.60	657.23	2157.23	2089.98	4589.98
$100 at 5%	3.78	103.78	27.37	327.37	74.17	574.17	146.60	846.60	309.16	1309.16	725.01	2250.01	2446.07	4946.07
$100 at 5½%	4.16	104.16	30.23	330.23	82.22	582.22	163.08	863.08	345.89	1345.89	847.56	2347.56	2884.70	5384.70
$100 at 6%	4.54	104.54	33.12	333.12	90.38	590.38	179.94	879.94	383.82	1383.82	950.13	2450.13	3309.03	5809.03
$200 at 1%	1.50	201.50	10.58	610.58	27.91	1027.91	53.65	1453.65	108.40	2108.40	244.14	3244.14	692.83	5692.83
$200 at 1½%	2.25	202.25	15.94	615.94	42.19	1042.19	81.36	1481.36	165.24	2165.24	375.41	3375.41	1084.72	6084.72
$200 at 2%	3.01	203.01	21.35	621.35	56.68	1056.68	109.68	1509.68	223.91	2223.91	513.27	3513.27	1510.78	6510.78
$200 at 2½%	3.76	203.76	26.80	626.80	71.39	1071.39	138.63	1538.63	284.50	2284.50	658.06	3658.06	1974.28	6974.28
$200 at 3%	4.52	204.52	32.29	632.29	86.32	1086.32	168.21	1568.21	347.05	2347.05	810.17	3810.17	2478.80	7478.80
$200 at 3½%	5.28	205.28	37.84	637.84	101.48	1101.48	198.44	1598.44	411.63	2411.63	969.99	3969.99	3028.30	8028.30
$200 at 4%	6.04	206.04	43.42	643.42	116.87	1116.87	229.34	1629.34	478.33	2478.33	1137.94	4137.94	3627.09	8627.09
$200 at 4½%	6.80	206.80	49.06	649.06	132.49	1132.49	260.91	1660.91	547.20	2547.20	1314.46	4314.46	4279.96	9279.96
$200 at 5%	7.56	207.56	54.74	654.74	148.34	1148.34	293.19	1693.19	618.32	2618.32	1500.02	4500.02	4992.14	9992.14
$200 at 5½%	8.32	208.32	60.47	660.47	164.44	1164.44	326.17	1726.17	691.78	2691.78	1695.12	4695.12	5769.40	10769.40
$200 at 6%	9.09	209.09	66.24	666.24	180.70	1180.70	359.89	1759.89	767.64	2767.64	1900.26	4900.26	6618.07	11618.07

$300 at 1%	2.25	302.25	15.87	915.87	41.86	1541.86	80.47	2180.47	162.60	3162.60	386.21	4866.21	1039.24	8539.24
$300 at 1½%	3.37	303.37	23.21	923.21	63.28	1563.28	122.04	2222.04	247.86	3247.86	563.11	5063.11	1627.08	9127.08
$300 at 2%	4.51	304.51	32.02	932.02	85.02	1585.02	164.52	2264.52	335.86	3335.86	769.90	5269.90	2266.17	9766.17
$300 at 2½%	5.64	305.64	40.20	940.20	107.08	1607.08	207.94	2307.94	426.75	3426.75	987.09	5487.09	2961.42	10461.42
$300 at 3%	6.78	306.78	48.43	948.43	129.48	1629.48	252.31	2352.31	520.57	3520.57	1215.25	5715.25	3718.20	11218.20
$300 at 3½%	7.92	307.92	56.76	956.76	152.22	1652.22	297.66	2397.66	617.44	3617.44	1454.98	5954.98	4542.45	12042.45
$300 at 4%	9.06	309.06	65.13	965.13	175.30	1675.30	344.01	2444.01	717.49	3717.49	1706.91	6206.91	5440.63	12940.63
$300 at 4½%	10.20	310.20	73.59	973.59	198.75	1698.75	391.35	2491.35	820.80	3820.80	1971.69	6471.69	6269.94	13769.94
$300 at 5%	11.34	311.34	82.11	982.11	222.51	1722.51	439.80	2539.80	927.48	3927.48	2175.03	6750.03	7338.21	14838.21
$300 at 5½%	12.48	312.48	90.69	990.69	246.66	1746.66	489.24	2589.24	1037.67	4037.67	2542.68	7042.68	8654.10	16154.10
$300 at 6%	13.62	313.62	99.36	999.36	271.14	1771.14	539.82	2639.82	1151.46	4151.46	2850.39	7350.39	9927.09	17427.09
$600 at 1%	4.50	604.50	31.74	1831.74	83.73	3083.73	160.95	4360.95	325.20	6325.20	732.42	9732.42	2078.49	17078.49
$600 at 1½%	6.75	606.75	47.82	1847.82	126.57	3126.57	244.08	4444.08	495.72	6495.72	1126.23	10126.23	3254.16	18254.16
$600 at 2%	9.03	609.03	64.05	1864.05	170.04	3170.04	329.04	4529.04	671.73	6671.73	1539.81	10539.81	4532.34	19532.34
$600 at 2½%	11.28	611.28	80.40	1880.40	214.17	3214.17	415.89	4615.89	853.50	6853.50	1974.18	10974.18	5922.84	20922.84
$600 at 3%	13.56	613.56	96.87	1896.87	258.96	3258.96	504.63	4704.63	1041.15	7041.15	2430.51	11430.51	7436.40	22436.40
$600 at 3½%	15.84	615.84	113.52	1913.52	304.44	3304.44	595.32	4795.32	1234.89	7234.89	2909.97	11090.97	9084.90	24084.90
$600 at 4%	18.12	618.12	130.26	1930.26	350.61	3350.61	688.02	4888.02	1434.99	7434.99	3413.82	12413.82	10881.27	25881.27
$600 at 4½%	20.40	620.40	147.18	1947.18	397.50	3397.50	782.70	4982.70	1641.60	7641.60	3943.38	12943.38	12539.88	27539.88
$600 at 5%	22.68	622.68	164.22	1964.22	445.02	3445.02	879.60	5079.60	1854.96	7854.96	4350.06	13500.06	14676.42	29676.42
$600 at 5½%	24.96	624.96	187.38	1981.38	493.32	3493.32	978.48	5178.48	2075.34	8075.34	5085.36	14085.36	17308.20	32308.20
$600 at 6%	27.24	627.24	198.72	1998.72	542.28	3542.28	1079.64	5279.64	2302.92	8302.92	5700.78	14700.78	19854.18	34854.18
$1000 at 1%	7.50	1007.50	52.90	3052.90	139.55	5139.55	268.25	7268.25	542.00	10542.00	1220.70	16220.70	3464.15	28464.15
$1000 at 1½%	11.25	1011.25	79.70	3079.70	210.95	5210.95	406.80	7406.80	826.20	10826.20	1877.05	16877.05	5423.60	30423.60
$1000 at 2%	15.05	1015.05	106.75	3106.75	283.40	5283.40	548.40	7548.40	1119.55	11119.55	2566.35	17566.35	7553.90	32553.90
$1000 at 2½%	18.80	1018.80	134.00	3134.00	356.95	5356.95	693.15	7693.15	1422.50	11422.50	3290.30	18290.30	9871.40	34871.40
$1000 at 3%	22.60	1022.60	161.45	3161.45	431.60	5431.60	841.05	7841.05	1735.25	11735.25	4050.85	19050.85	12394.00	37394.00
$1000 at 3½%	26.40	1026.40	189.20	3189.20	507.40	5507.40	992.20	7992.20	2058.15	12058.15	4849.95	19849.95	15141.50	40141.50
$1000 at 4%	30.20	1030.20	217.10	3217.10	584.35	5584.35	1146.70	8146.70	2391.65	12391.65	5689.70	20689.70	18135.45	43135.45
$1000 at 4½%	34.00	1034.00	245.30	3245.30	662.50	5662.50	1304.50	8304.50	2736.00	12736.00	6752.30	21572.30	20899.80	45899.80
$1000 at 5%	37.80	1037.80	273.70	3273.70	741.70	5741.70	1466.00	8466.00	3091.60	13091.60	7250.10	22500.10	24460.70	49460.70
$1000 at 5½%	41.60	1041.60	302.30	3302.30	822.20	5822.20	1630.80	8630.80	3458.90	13458.90	8475.60	23475.60	28847.00	53847.00
$1000 at 6%	45.40	1045.40	331.20	3331.20	903.80	5903.80	1799.40	8799.40	3838.20	13838.20	9501.30	24501.30	33090.30	58090.30

something other than cash. Nevertheless, an emergency fund can earn interest or dividends and grow in value. So it is an investment in a sense. Several questions arise about a fund of this kind. What's it for? How much do you need? Where do you put it?

How big a reserve?   An emergency fund should obviously be reserved for bona fide emergencies: serious illness, loss of job, and so on. It should never be borrowed for such relatively unimportant uses as the purchase of a car, house, or TV set. It should not be loaned even to close relatives except in cases of dire need.

As to how big the fund should be, an old rule of thumb says a family should be able to live for six months if its regular income were cut off. Interpreted conservatively, that would mean that a family's liquid savings, minus its short-term debt, would equal one half its annual take-home pay. Interpreted very liberally, it might mean that a family should be able to lay its hand on enough cash by various means to live six months. In addition to liquid savings, certain other assets might be counted: cash value of life insurance policies, stocks conservatively valued, the amount fully vested in a company pension plan. Note the dangers of this practice. The cash value of a life insurance policy might be needed to keep up premium payments. Stocks might go so low, in a recession for example, that it would be a shame to sell them. The amount vested in a company pension fund might be obtainable only by quitting. So for defense against a financial crisis, a family should certainly rely largely, if not wholly, on liquid savings.

There are four qualities you want your savings to have. These qualities will pretty well determine where the money is to be kept. Listed in order of importance, they are:

Safety—You want your money to be reasonably secure against depression, panic, and theft.

Liquidity—You want to know that you can withdraw your savings without too much delay or red tape even during a possible banking crisis like that of 1933.

High earnings rate—You want your money to earn interest at as high a rate as possible consistent with safety and liquidity.

Convenience—You want your savings to be located where you can take care of them with minimum trouble.

No one institution provides the maximum safety, liquidity, earning rate, and convenience all in one package. It would be nice to have a place right across the street that would keep your savings completely safe and entirely liquid while paying 6% interest. Naturally there is no such place. To get a high interest rate, you must sacrifice some other advantages, such as liquidity. To have your savings instantly available, you must be prepared to accept a lower interest rate.

It may be best, therefore, to split up your cash and put it in several places.

In making a choice, keep in the back of your mind the two different relationships possible between you and a savings institution. There is a debtor-creditor relationship, as for example when you open an account with a commercial bank. There is also an ownership relation, such as when you buy a share in a savings and loan association. The difference may sound technical, but it could be important under certain conditions. (More on this later.)

Here are the most common places where you can put your savings. Note the particular advantages and disadvantages of each.

Savings account in a commercial bank   Convenient, safe, liquid, low rate of interest.

A handy place to keep savings is in the same bank where you have your checking account. The interest rate on savings accounts is relatively low. To keep the money liquid so that it can be paid out on short notice, banks must invest it in liquid short-term notes which earn a low rate of interest.

Technically, you could be required to give a written notice, usually thirty days, before you can withdraw your savings. This notice is not generally required. But in times of sudden depression or business panic, the bank could require you to wait the full period.

The banks reserve the right to make you give thirty days' notice because of sad experience in the big depression. In the 1920's there were many more banks than there are today. Naturally they were competing to attract money, so they paid high interest rates on both checking and savings accounts, sometimes as high as 4%. To earn these rates, the banks invested the money in longer-term securities, some of which were not of too high quality or readily convertible into cash. When the bank runs started, many banks could not get these securities and their loans converted into cash fast enough to suit depositors.

As a result, the government now prohibits any bank over which it has control from paying interest on *demand deposits,* or deposits that can be withdrawn without advance notice.

Are your savings safe in a bank? Yes, because almost all commercial banks in the country are insured by the Federal Deposit Insurance Corporation. Each insured bank contributes a small amount to the fund each year. In return the bank gets insurance up to $15,000 for each depositor. If an insured bank fails, the depositor either gets cash or else he gets another account opened in his name in a going bank. The money in this new account may be withdrawn at once without notice.

When you open a savings account in a commercial bank, you establish a debtor-creditor relationship. You are not entitled to any of the bank's profits. The stockholders get the profits. The bank merely owes you your money plus interest. If you demand your money after giving the required notice and the bank cannot or will not pay, then you, as a creditor, can get the banking authority to close the bank.

Mutual savings bank   Safe, liquid, medium rate of interest, but not locally available in most parts of the country.

Mutual savings banks were started over a hundred years ago by public-spirited men who were not seeking profit but who wished to encourage the habit of thrift among workers. At first, most of the expenses of operation were paid out of the pockets of the founders and all earnings went to the depositors. Even today the trustees of mutual savings banks receive no salaries. All earnings, after deduction of expenses and additions to surplus, go to depositors in interest dividends.

Mutual savings banks accept only savings, no checking accounts. When you open an account in a mutual savings bank, you are both a creditor and to some extent an owner. You get the profits, just as a stockholder does in a commercial bank. But if the bank cannot pay you your money, you can also get the supervisory authority to close the bank.

There are over five hundred savings banks, mostly located in the Northeast. During most times a depositor can walk into any of them and withdraw his money without giving advance notice. But all mutual savings banks have provisions on the books requiring thirty, sixty, or ninety days' written notice, and these regulations could be put into effect at any time.

Your money is safe in mutual savings banks. A great many of them are insured by the Federal Deposit Insurance Corporation, and most others are insured by a similar arrangement with the state in which they are located.

Savings and loan association   Good rate of dividend, safe, might not be as liquid as a bank in times of business panic.

Savings and loan associations were founded to help people save a nest egg to buy a home. Many are still called building associations or building and loan associations. In Massachusetts they are known as co-operative banks, in Louisiana as homestead associations.

When you put your money in a savings and loan association, you are buying a share. You can do it by buying $100 certificates, in which case you receive a dividend check every six months. Or you can open a savings share account of any size, in which case your dividends are added to your account. In any event, the size of your share is simply your account divided by the total of all accounts. When you want to withdraw, the association repurchases a part or all of your share. Thirty days' written notice could be required but usually is not enforced. The point is, you are a shareholder, an owner. You and the association do not have a debtor-creditor relationship.

Note the difference. A bank owes you your deposited money, and if you don't get it, you can have the bank closed. But in the case of a savings and loan association, it is recognized that home mortgages cannot be liquidated all at once. So the association has the privilege of paying off a little at a time.

If that sounds like a disadvantage, note the advantage. Eighty-five per cent of savings and loan association assets are invested in first mortgages on homes. This investment pays a high rate of interest. So the associations in turn can pay high dividends.

Of the 6200 savings and loan associations, some two thousand are small neighborhood associations, some of which do not have regular office hours or full-time employees. Sometimes they pay higher rates of dividend than the big city associations that are larger and more elaborately organized. Before investing in a small neighborhood association, check on its record. Many are very old and profitable. But all depend on the judgment of the directors. Most of the larger associations are insured by the Federal Savings and Loan Insurance Corporation, a government agency. The insurance covers up to $15,000 for each investor. In general, the small neighborhood associations are not insured.

If an insured savings and loan association defaults, the shareholders get new accounts in another association not in default.

U.S. Savings Bonds   Safe, liquid, convenient, but do not pay much interest unless held several years.

Savings bonds, series E, may be bought at almost any financial institution or post office. They are highly liquid. Once you have held a savings bond for sixty days you can cash it at any bank.

For short periods, however, savings bonds will not pay as much interest as other types of savings. The interest rate starts out low and becomes gradually higher the longer you hold the bond. For example, in the first year it averages 3.02%. If you hold it the whole seven years, of course, you receive 4.15%.

Those are the four places to put your cash. There are only three if you live in a town that has no mutual savings bank. Each place has a unique combination of the qualities you want—safety, liquidity, earnings rate, and convenience. If you are smart, you probably won't leave all your cash in a place where it is earning little or no interest. But neither will you put it all where it might be frozen if a recession should hit.

Measuring your reserves   Now, what if you want to count as part of your emergency fund certain other assets which can be borrowed on or converted readily into cash? These might be money in a checking account, or money invested in stocks, or the cash reserves built up in life insurance policies.

The way you make up your mind on these borderline cases will depend on how conservative you want to be. Money in your checking account, strictly speaking, is working capital which you continually turn over as you pay bills. Still, there is a residual amount below which you seldom go, say $100 or $200. If you maintain such a minimum, this could be included in an emergency fund.

When you buy stock, you buy a share of a business for better or worse and take your chances on whether or not it thrives. Of course, most stocks are extremely liquid, so you can always get back cash. How much cash, however, is never predictable. It always seems to turn out that, when you have to sell a stock in order to obtain cash, the market is down at that particular time. Stocks, therefore, should probably not be considered as part of an emergency fund. But if they are, they should never be carried at 100% of their current price. Banks will lend only 60% to 70% on stocks. So carry them, if at all, only at some percentage of their market value. This percentage might be higher for good preferreds than for speculative commons.

Cash reserves in life insurance policies are savings in one sense, since you can get them back at any time. To do so, however, you either have to borrow the money back, usually at 5% to 6% interest, or you have to cash in the policy and lose its protection.

There are other hard-to-measure assets that many families have that might be included in an emergency fund, for example, money built up in a company pension plan. This is definitely an asset under certain conditions. Perhaps the best way to measure it is to count only the amount that is vested in you, that is, the amount of money you would get if you left your job.

If you don't know exactly how much of these assets to include in your emergency fund, try making up a report on your available resources. You might arrive at two figures, the first being bona fide cash reserves readily available, the second being your ultimate resources available in extreme emergencies. Use the form below as a guide.

YOUR RESOURCES TO MEET EMERGENCIES	
Savings	$_____
MINUS	
Short-term Debts	$_____
Difference	$_____
(amount available for emergencies)	
PLUS	
Stocks (75% of Market Value)	$_____
Life Insurance (cash value)	$_____
Pension Fund (amount vested)	$_____
TOTAL	$_____
(ultimate amount available for extreme emergency)	

Building up an emergency fund before you start to invest will save you worry and probably save you money. With such protection you can buy good quality growth stocks, sit back, and let them appreciate in their own good time. You won't have the haunting thought that you might have to dump them at a moment's notice.

CHAPTER 3

Insurance: A Prerequisite to Investing

There are two basic reasons why a man works hard and tries to accumulate money. First, he wants to acquire wealth for himself. It may be that he desires to use it to obtain an independent income, luxuries, a business, or the wherewithal to retire in his old age. Second, he wants to provide an estate to leave to his family upon his death.

LIFE INSURANCE

Building up wealth is a slow and arduous process. But creating an estate can be done overnight. Life insurance does it. So life insurance should definitely be acquired before a man plunges into the long and hazardous task of saving and investing money. After he has made his pile, his insurance needs will change. But until then he should cling to enough to take care of his dependents in case "something happens to him."

Buying life insurance is not always easy because the buyer is apt to let his emotions sway his judgment. Some life insurance salesmen deliberately, or unwittingly, play on these emotions and cause the buyer to get more insurance than he can afford or the wrong kind for his particular purposes.

The young man in the market for life insurance and also the family man who already may have some protection should know the fundamentals of insurance and how it works. They should understand the different kinds of insurance. They must be able to get and use expert advice. They must know how to build a program of family security, tailored to fit their individual needs.

Get these things clear in your mind to start with:

The basic job of life insurance is protection. It has certain investment features that should be remembered. But concentrate on safeguarding your family against possible loss of your earning power. Don't take on such things as retirement and college educational plans, at least not in the beginning.

The subject of death should not be evaded. Some people, including a lot of young wives, are squeamish about dealing bluntly and openly with the chances of death. That attitude is a luxury you can't afford. Sit down and explore your problem thoroughly and rationally.

How insurance works   Insurance is highly technical. You can't expect to be an expert and you don't need to be. It will help, though, if you understand the underlying theory.

First, picture a set of statistics known as a "mortality experience table." It takes a million persons at the age of one year and then proceeds to tell you approximately how many of them are going to die every year from age one to ninety-nine.

This table is the precision tool that makes life insurance possible. You, as a buyer, are concerned with *who* is going to die; all the insurance company cares about is *how many.*

To see how this works, imagine a group of ten thousand young married men, all twenty-nine years old. These men realize that some of them will die during the coming year, leaving widows without income. Why not get together and raise a fund to guarantee each widow a $5000 nest egg?

A glance at the mortality table shows that twenty-one of their number will probably not live out the year. That means that twenty-one widows will need $5000 apiece—so the fund must contain $105,000. Each man puts $10.50 into the kitty and is assured that his wife will not be left destitute if he should be one of the twenty-one.

The association will have to tack on a little extra to pay for time and paper work. On the other hand it will also allow for the fact that some money can be invested for a while and produce income.

There you have the equivalent of a life insurance company writing one-year-term life insurance policies.

The basic pattern is as simple as that. A big national insurance company works with a varying number of people of all ages and walks of life. The investment of collected funds plays a big role in its operations. Most insurance is not written on the simple, one-year, revolving-fund basis. But the theory is the same.

Study the above example and you will see that if you live you cannot expect to get back all the money you have paid in unless you have a type of policy specifically designed for investment values. Some or all of your premium has gone into the common fund to pay beneficiaries. You have not thrown this money away, however, for you received something in return. It paid for protection against something that might have happened but didn't.

Kinds of insurance There are four basic kinds of life insurance policy, but no one can tell you which kind to buy without a careful look at your individual case. Each has its special uses.

Term insurance You buy it for a specified period only—usually one, five, or ten years. At the end of that time you stop paying and the protection stops too. You get nothing back if you are still living at the end of the term, and little or nothing if you drop the policy before that. As you grow older, the cost of term insurance gets higher. Term insurance is relatively cheap, as far as annual expense is concerned. It is usually recommended when temporary protection is needed, or when the buyer needs protection but just can't afford higher-priced insurance that might be more desirable for the long pull. Note that some kinds of term insurance are convertible during the life of the policy into more permanent types. The insured person can convert without the necessity of taking another physical exam and thus is guaranteed insurability.

Ordinary life This is a permanent, lifetime policy. You must pay an annual premium as long as you live, or at least until you are about eighty-five, to keep the full amount of protection. The premium is higher than for a term policy bought at the same age, but the premium always stays the same, instead of going up periodically, as on term insurance. Part of what you pay goes to build an increasing cash value. You can borrow against this cash value. If you cancel the policy, you get the cash value back or exchange it for a certain amount of paid-up protection or you can use the cash value to extend your full protection for a specified number of years.

Ordinary life—often called straight life—is the standard, most popular kind of insurance. It gives permanent protection and contains an element of saving. It does, in a smaller way, all the things that fancier, costlier policies do.

Limited payment   This policy is like ordinary life, except that you pay premiums only for a fixed number of years—usually twenty or thirty. After that the full amount of insurance remains in force without further cost to you. In effect, you simply telescope the payments on an ordinary life policy into a fixed period of time. While you *are* paying, therefore, the premium is higher than for ordinary life. The cash values are higher, too.

Endowment   The policy is written for a fixed number of years—say twenty—and a certain amount, say $10,000. If you die before the policy matures, your beneficiary gets the $10,000. If you live out the full period, you get it—in a lump sum or in monthly installments. The cost is necessarily heavy. At age thirty, for instance, you must pay over twice as much for a twenty-year endowment policy as for ordinary life in order to give your family the same amount of protection.

Chart 5: WHAT VARIOUS POLICIES COST

Here are premiums and cash values per $1000 of insurance to show how they vary with the type of policy. (Figures are for nonparticipating—guaranteed price, no dividend—policies issued by one company and, of course, would not be the same for all companies.)

AGE AT WHICH POLICY
IS ISSUED:

	25		35		45	
	Annual premium	*20th yr. cash value*	*Annual premium*	*20th yr. cash value*	*Annual premium*	*20th yr. cash value*
Five-yr. renewable term	$ 3.46	—	$ 4.30	—	$ 8.43	—
Term to 65	8.10	$ 79	11.24	$ 79	16.27	—
Whole life	12.44	236	17.81	325	26.94	$ 427
20-payment life	21.27	459	27.48	574	36.51	690
20-yr. endowment	42.45	1000	43.81	1000	46.31	1000

There are special policies that are combinations or adaptations of these four.

A family-income policy, for example, is an ordinary life policy (or some other permanent policy) with term insurance on top of it. The amount of term insurance coverage starts high and gets smaller every year until it finally runs out. The whole thing is rigged to guarantee that, if you die while your children are young, the policy will pay a certain income until they are grown. Then your wife will collect the full value of the permanent policy.

Sometimes special policies of this type are what you want, sometimes not. The trick is to understand just how they work. The most frustrating thing of all about this subject is the discovery that there is no real answer to the fundamental question, How much insurance does a man need? It has been said—not at all helpfully—that the man who died yesterday didn't have nearly enough, while the man who will die next week needs none at all today. You hear of families being "insurance poor," meaning that so much goes for premiums that living standards actually suffer. Yet the late Mayo Adams Shattuck, a lawyer who was a top authority on estate planning, once wrote, "I have yet to see my first client who has enough life insurance."

How much is enough?   A number of formulas have been offered as solutions to the riddle of how much is enough, but none are really useful. The most familiar is the one that says 10% of your income should go into insurance premiums. Another says a man should carry at least $10,000 for a wife and $5000 for each child. Another says he should provide enough to assure half of his present income.

The fanciest ones are those that treat Pop as though he were a capital sum, hired out at interest. Estimate his probable future earnings over his life span, says one such theory, and subtract his personal expenses. Calculate the sum of money that, if invested at a reasonable rate of interest, would produce the same sums in yearly payments of principal plus interest. Buy that much insurance.

Most of these attempted formulas ignore your budget. All ignore the fact that every family is in some way different from all others. And all ignore the fact that there is no such thing as "enough" insurance for the same reason that there is no such thing as "enough" income or "enough" years to a lifetime.

The best way to decide how much insurance you need is to forget all such systems and work on your own individual situation.

First, estimate how much immediate cash would be needed to wind up your affairs. This amount should include: funeral and medical bills, unpaid income and property taxes, death taxes if any, outstanding bills and debts, estate costs, the general expenses of getting the family re-established.

Next, work out an estimated budget. This will involve some long, sober husband-and-wife talks—for the basis of such a budget is what she and the kids would most likely do should something happen to him. Reckon, item by item, the minimum amount the family would probably need for housing, clothes, food, and so on.

Third, fix the amount desired for special lump sum needs or goals. For example: the mortgage, an emergency fund, college educations.

Then go back and find out how much of this ready cash and steady income your present resources will provide. Social security will, in most cases, provide a good chunk of income while children are around and, later on, after the wife reaches sixty-two or sixty-five. Social security will pay a small lump sum benefit, too. You may have group insurance where you work. You may have health insurance to provide cash or produce income, or to do both. If you are a veteran, your widow and minor children may be entitled to benefits. The family may have or be due to inherit an independent income of some sort.

Between the sum you have figured the family would need and the sum your present resources would supply there will be a gap. The amount of insurance you need is the amount it will take to fill that gap. Your insurance agent or broker can help you calculate the monthly income that a given face amount of insurance could provide your family.

Don't be surprised if you have to compromise. You may very likely find that you can't afford enough insurance to fill in the entire picture all at once. You may have to let one item slide for now, concentrate on another, weigh one need against the other. You're the only one who can say what your household budget can and should absorb.

There are over seventeen hundred companies that write life insurance in the United States. Which one should you buy from?

Don't buy from a small or relatively new company unless you are thoroughly familiar with it. That may sound tough on young and struggling outfits, but the prudent thing is to make them prove they can give you the economy, safety, and experience of the large, well-established, and well-known organizations. Strength, not size, is important. Check out a small company in *Best's* or some other rating manual.

Don't buy by mail. Many companies advertise by mail. Some special operations—for ministers, for example—are conducted by mail. But a regular mail-order outfit probably just isn't licensed to have offices in your state, and a prudent buyer deals with one that is. Also, you don't get the services of an agent.

Do take group insurance if eligible for it or the special insurance that is sometimes available to such groups as teachers and ministers. Also, if you live in Connecticut, Massachusetts, or New York, look into the advantages of insurance sold by savings banks in those states. There are no salesmen, therefore no sales commissions to be deducted from premiums.

Do ask around among your friends and relatives and find out how they feel about companies with which they have had experience. When they are dissatisfied, find out why. Remember those companies that are consistently praised or recommended.

Companies vary in the premiums they charge for their insurance, in the benefits their policies provide, and in various practices connected with the sale and execution of their contracts.

If you shop costs, be guided for the most part by general reputation; look upon cost estimates as approximate, don't fuss over slight differences, and don't think in terms of price tags only.

Life insurance may be either "participating" or "nonparticipating." In the former case, the annual premium contains a considerable safety margin which will ordinarily be returned to the policyholder at the end of the year as a so-called dividend. How much will be returned can't be foretold, however, since the amount depends on such factors as investment yields, expenses, and death rates during the course of the year. Participating insurance is sold by mutual companies, those owned co-operatively by policyholders, and sometimes by stock companies, those owned privately by stockholders.

Nonparticipating insurance is sold by all stock companies, and many sell only that. The premium is noticeably lower than that on participating policies, but no dividends are paid to reduce it.

How to buy insurance The fact is that you will probably do best to choose an agent rather than a company. Again go after the word-of-mouth recommendation. If an agent comes to you cold without being sent by a mutual acquaintance, ask for references—that is, get the names of clients who can tell you how they have fared in the agent's hands, what kind of job of analysis and planning he has done for them.

Most agents (who like to be called "underwriters," by the way) are both honest and competent. But they are also salesmen. They have a special knowledge of and a natural bias for the policies of their own company. If you buy from an agent you will probably have to rely on his advice and counsel to a very great extent, even though you are well aware that he is no "impartial expert." There are also "brokers" who do not represent one company exclusively. They can sell you a policy from any one of several companies, depending on your individual needs.

Don't be pushed, pressured, or rushed. Make sure that the agent or broker takes time enough to examine your needs and resources carefully, time enough to work out an individual solution to your individual problem. Make sure that you take time enough to furnish him all the information he needs, as well as time enough to think long and carefully before you sign up.

The transaction is not over when you have decided to sign. You should expect your agent or broker to furnish you with a written summary of the plan you and he have worked out for using the insurance proceeds in case anything happens. You should expect him to handle or guide you through any routine paper work that may be required. It may be necessary, for example, to fill out various settlement agreement forms in connection with the policies of other companies which you have bought in the past. He should also be able to supply information on your social security benefits.

And finally, you and he should go over your program at least once every five years to see what adjustments or additions may have become advisable.

The day may come when you have accumulated enough wealth by hard work and shrewd investing to enable you to begin cutting down on your insurance, or to change your coverage to meet different needs such as estate taxes, etc. That will be a happy day if it comes. But the truth is, even the men who make the big fortunes seldom find it advisable to dispense with their insurance.

HEALTH INSURANCE

Today there is a wider variety of good health insurance available than ever before. And the policies themselves are easier to understand, containing less of the old-time "fine print" of which the comedian said, "The big print gives it to you and the little print takes it away."

Nevertheless, a good bit of this excellent coverage is wasted because too many people insist on insuring against expenses they could pay themselves. At the same time, they fail to cover themselves against the shattering, once-in-a-lifetime expense that could use up years of savings and wreck the family finances.

Partly this is due to a misunderstanding of what constitutes real insurance. Think of fire insurance as an example. Thousands of people in a community pay premiums year after year, and once in a while someone's house burns down and he is fully compensated. The others don't expect anything back from the insurance company. They are happy that their houses didn't burn down.

Ideally, health insurance should operate the same way. A family with good coverage should pay in without expecting anything back unless the worst happens—some huge expense that couldn't possibly be handled by the family's regular finances. Medical expenses caused by appendicitis operations, having babies, a week or two in the hospital certainly could be handled as easily as an automobile is bought or a vacation paid for.

Unfortunately, however, millions of people tend to measure their health insurance coverage by how much they can get back from the insurance company. They want policies that will consistently pay them back as much as they have paid in—more if possible.

This attitude defeats the insurance principle. If everyone in an insurance pool of this type gets his money back in benefits, no one, in the long run, can get more than he contributed. This kind of insurance policy, then, must have severe limitations that prevent it from covering the heaviest expenses that, logically, should be insured against. Buy such a policy and you are merely paying the insurance company to handle your medical budgeting. The company collects, deducts expenses and overhead, and regularly pays you back 80% or 90%. That simply isn't insurance.

Test your insurance So to test the adequacy of your own health insurance, dream up a couple of very serious health situations, then figure out whether your insurance would take care of them. Suppose, for example, the breadwinner in the family was injured or became seriously ill and was unable to work for 18 months. What would happen? Or suppose that another member of the family, wife or child, had a mental breakdown, required many months in a sanitarium, the total bill running to $3000. Where would the money come from? These situations, you might say, are improbable. Yet it is these very improbable events that should be insured against. Probable events should be budgeted for.

Failure to make this distinction between the role of insurance and the role of budgeting has caused millions of families to waste part of their insurance dollars. So the first, great principle in health insurance is to have *real* insurance that will handle the worst health problems you can think of.

The second principle, just as important, is to know exactly what you have. Know what your policy does and does not cover, who in your family is eligible, whether it will ever expire or its benefits be narrowed. Although most policies nowadays are clear and explicit, too many people don't even bother to read them carefully. Group policyholders especially are negligent.

One man recently retired after working for years in a company that had a group health insurance plan covering employees and their families. Upon retirement he was informed that he was still covered. He assumed that his wife also was still covered, but she wasn't. Very shortly after this man's retirement, his wife became seriously ill and spent the remainder of her life in a hospital. The resulting financial strain could have been averted if the couple had realized the facts. But they had never read the company's policy carefully.

Even Blue Cross or Blue Shield basic plans can be full of surprises if you don't read the policy. There are dozens of Blue Cross plans in effect across the country. They vary widely in coverage. One will pay for a semiprivate room for 180 days, if needed. Another cuts you off after 31 days. So no matter what kind of coverage you think you have, know for sure by reading the policy. If necessary, ask questions.

Income protection   Protection against loss of the breadwinner's income is thought by insurance men to be the most important kind of health insurance a family can have. The vice-president of a large company puts it this way, "Even the individual of limited means can eventually pay big bills and big debts if only he retains the ability to work and earn a living. When that is lost, all is lost unless funds are available to replace the earnings."

Disability income insurance, as it is called, protects the policyholder by guaranteeing to pay him so much a month while he is disabled. A variety of policies is available. The program most often recommended would pay the insured something less than his regular income. The amount, generally ranging from 75% to 50%, is based on the belief that most families can get along on less than full pay if they have to, particularly since the first $100 a week, after thirty consecutive days of disability, is not subject to income tax.

Two important considerations in disability insurance are the waiting period and the maximum period during which the policies pay. The longer the waiting period, within reason, the more economical this kind of insurance becomes. If the waiting period is only one week, the insured person will be putting in a claim every time he is sick for more than seven days. Small claims cost insurance companies money in paper work and overhead. If the waiting period is one month, the insured person handles the shorter periods of disability himself. His premiums then will pay for a larger monthly income during any long period when he is unable to work. Many people work for companies that will pay for a certain period of disability so that the waiting period is no hardship.

The longer the policy guarantees to pay for disability, the better. Some guarantee to pay only up to one year per disability; others guarantee five years, and so on. Note in this connection that social security now provides some disability benefits. The best policies, of course, pay to age sixty-five, when pension benefits normally begin. These long-term policies cost the most, but then if a man were to be disabled for life, he would want a continuous income. Your own disability policy should, of course, be merged into social security and/ or any plan your employer may have. Professional men often can get coverage through their professional association.

It is particularly important that disability policies be noncancelable and guaranteed renewable up until the day the policyholder retires. Otherwise, if the insured person becomes a poor risk because of deterioration of health or because of having been through a disabling illness or having suffered an accident, the company can refuse to renew the policy on some anniversary date.

"When you have a policy that is noncancelable and guaranteed renewable," one insurance company executive says, "you own the policy and regardless of the number of claims you may have, you still exercise policy control. But when a policy is renewable at the option of the company, it means you rent the policy and you can be evicted any time the company wishes."

Guard against the big bills Catastrophe insurance, or major medical, also is the kind of "real insurance" that most insurance experts think it important to have. A wide variety of policies is available.

The principle of major medical is that it leaves the smaller medical expenses to be handled by the individual himself. There usually is a deductible, say $100, $200, or $500 or more. The deductible is least when major medical is bought along with a "basic" hospital and surgical policy. Unless the medical expenses rise above the deductible, the policy does not begin to pay. But when medical bills soar above the deductible, the major medical policy pays 75%, 80% or sometimes 100%, depending on the terms, of all legitimate expenses.

A good, broad major medical policy covers hospital bills, doctors' bills, nursing bills, treatment for mental illness and just about every medical expense. It may have a coinsurance feature, which means that the company pays 75% or 80% of all covered expenses, while the insured pays the other 25% or 20%. The purpose of this is to give the policyholder an incentive to keep bills to a reasonable level. Also note that coverage for out-of-hospital expenses for psychiatric treatment usually is limited.

Although most major medical policies are good and broad, each policy should be read carefully. There are always some limitations and exclusions. Some limit the amount to be paid for hospital room; some exclude mental illness; most exclude expenses for practical nursing, and so on.

Here are some criteria for purchasing major medical coverage.

—Get broad coverage with the fewest possible exclusions. Don't buy a policy that covers you only against certain named diseases. Buy one that covers you in general. Be sure that mental illness is not excluded.

—Have the limit per illness plenty high, say $10,000. The whole purpose of this kind of insurance is to keep you prepared for the worst. Also know the cut-off period for any one illness if there is one. Three years is not any too long.

—Make sure members of the family are covered. It's just as expensive for a wife to be sick as for a husband.

—Get a policy that will be noncancelable and guaranteed renewable until Medicare would take over.

—Buy fairly early in life. Many policies can be first purchased only at ages below 50.

—If you have a group policy, check to make sure that all members of your family are covered and can continue to be covered if you leave the group or retire. Those who leave the group should have the privilege of converting their policies to nongroup policies without medical examination. The premiums in this case, of course, are higher. Many group policies, too, continue coverage on employees and their families even after retirement, although the coverage may be somewhat narrowed.

Hospital bills and surgery   Hospital and surgical insurance are number three in importance on most insurance men's list. The reason is that these policies generally begin repaying the first dollar that the insured person spends. Usually there is no deductible. "First dollar" policies are designed to help pay for even short stays in the hospital, for obstetrical care, or for operations that do not result in prolonged expense. In effect, these policies perform a budgeting task. But apparently millions of people are willing to pay to have someone do the budgeting for them.

The truth is that people tend to be lax about providing even for routine medical expenses. Doctors' bills often go unpaid; patients go to the hospital unprepared to settle up in cash. So years ago doctors and hospitals joined together to make what amounts to a budgeting service available. Today it is very widely used.

Blue Cross and Blue Shield plans differ from other coverage in that the benefit payments are made to the hospital or participating surgeon, not to the insured. The terms of these policies should be read carefully. Most Blue Shield plans pay full surgical costs if the insured person is in a low income bracket, because the participating doctor will accept as his full fee the amount that the Blue Shield payment schedule allows for the particular operation. But for those in higher brackets, the plan usually pays only part of the cost because the doctor is free to charge his regular fee, which is ordinarily higher than the allowances made by Blue Shield.

Even those not in a group can buy Blue Cross or Blue Shield plans, but enrollment may be open only at certain periods during the year, and applicants must prove they are in good health. Those who cannot get into group plans can buy individual hospital or surgical policies from insurance companies, but a health examination or medical questionnaire is required. These plans are more economical if bought with a deductible.

What should you spend?   How much should a family logically spend on health insurance? The vice-president of one company says,

"I would think that the average family should spend somewhere between 2½% and 4% of its income on health insurance, depending on the amount of group insurance provided by the employer, salary-continuance policies of the employer, and the amount of other assets that might be called upon to meet emergency costs." Another company says that a family in the $7500 to $15,000 income bracket might spend 3½% to 5%.

A family's health insurance needs vary during its life span. In early and middle years the family should guard the breadwinner's earning power with disability income insurance, noncancelable and guaranteed renewable up to retirement. There should be broad catastrophe insurance on all members of the family, renewable at least to the point where Medicare begins. When the family approaches retirement age, the need for disability insurance disappears. Catastrophe insurance, though, definitely should be continued at least until Medicare takes over. If it is not available, good basic hospitalization and medical coverage are musts.

At any age, the maxim should be: Buy real insurance to cover real emergencies and know exactly what you have.

LIABILITY INSURANCE

Big damage suits have become so common, and juries have become so prone to award large sums to the complainant, that a prudent family is obliged to carry a certain amount of liability insurance. Otherwise, a successful suit might wipe out the family's entire financial assets—home, savings, investments, and all.

Usually the most needed type is auto liability insurance. Most states require a minimum coverage of $10,000 per person injured, $20,000 per accident, and $5000 property damages, but this is hardly enough in the light of the size of award often made by a modern jury. Awards of $100,000 have become common. The extra cost for raising the minimums to $100,000 per person, $300,000 per accident, and $10,000 property damage is well worth the relatively small additional premium.

Perhaps the second most dangerous area is around the home. If a visitor or even a stranger stepped into a hole in your yard or fell on a broken step, he could sue you for plenty. Fortunately, your homeowner's insurance policy, which covers fire, windstorm, and other damage, probably carries a $25,000 liability clause covering bodily injury and property damage. It probably would not cover you, however, if you were sued for libel or for causing a false arrest or if you are a professional man and were sued in connection with professional activities. If there's any likelihood of this happening, you can buy what is known as an "excess liability" policy, which will cover you up to a million dollars. Normally such coverage will cost $65 to $70 a year. For most people the auto and homeowner's policies, if the minimum amounts are high enough, provide all the coverage that's reasonably necessary. But the extra coverage could be worth the cost if you have any doubts.

The main thing to remember in all three kinds of insurance, life, health, and liability, is to avoid the gimmicks and stick to coverage against the most likely *big* losses. In other words, buy real insurance against expenses that you never could manage to pay yourself.

CHAPTER 4

A Stake in an Expanding America

If you believe that America is a vigorous and expanding country, then you probably would like to have a monetary stake in its growth. Everybody can't participate directly by starting a new factory or inventing a new drug or synthetic fiber. But here is one thing you can do. Buy the common stock and thereby become part owner of certain wellmanaged companies that themselves seem destined to share largely in America's next period of expansion.

Growth stocks, these are called. To make a wise investment in them you need do only three things:

1. Believe that America has a glowing future and be willing to bet on it.

2. Have the good sense to select sound companies in industries that are expanding.

3. Be coolheaded enough not to plunk down all your money when prices are unreasonably high and nervy enough to keep buying when prices dip.

THE COUNTRY'S FUTURE GROWTH

Taking first things first, how does anyone know that America will continue to grow? You can't say positively that it will, of course, but economists can tick off some pretty good supporting arguments. These include such things as the increases in population and the billions of dollars being spent to develop new methods, materials, and products. If you are skeptical, remember that Americans, even though they are notorious for their optimism, have consistently underrated their own future. Benjamin Franklin thought it would take hundreds of years to settle the American continent. Thomas Jefferson figured on twenty-five generations for the occupation of the Louisiana Purchase.

Even the forecasts made but a few years ago have already fallen short. In 1947 the scholarly researchers of the Twentieth Century Fund looked at the rising curve of economic activity and projected it into the future. Their calculations caused a sensation. By 1960 population would be 155,000,000 and employment 60,000,000.

Even before 1955 all those marks were passed and the Fund had to do its 1960 forecast over again. Instead of 155,000,000 people in 1960, there were 155,000,000 in 1952. There were more than 60,-000,000 employed soon after the original forecast. As early as 1950 national income and gross production went beyond the 60% increase predicted for ten years later.

So don't shrug off the economists when they see expansion. They may even be too conservative. Over the past twenty years, the long-term trend of American production and consumption has been upward, the rise averaging 3¾% a year. Sometimes the actual rate is higher for a while, and sometimes lower, which makes a peak-and-valley curve. But the straight line representing the trend has a definite upward tilt. For example, in 1966, the gain in Gross National Product, which is the retail value of all goods and services produced, was 8½%, of which 5% represented a real gain in production, and 3½% represented a rise in prices.

In 1967, the Joint Economic Committee of Congress, after an exhaustive study, stated that the U.S. economy had a potential economic growth rate of 5½% or 6½% a year from 1965 to 1975. The 5½% assumption was based on a real growth of 4% a year in GNP coupled with 1½% annual rise in prices; the 6½% growth rate, on a real growth of 4½% a year in GNP with a 2% annual rise in prices. It should be pointed out that these rates were not predictions or forecasts, but projections based on a set of fairly optimistic assumptions concerning the public and private sectors of the economy. Nevertheless, in the past, such projections have proved to be conservative. So there is good reason to expect that this rate of growth, or a higher one, actually will be achieved. Look at Chart 6 on page 70 to see the steep rise in Gross National Product that these projections would produce. The chart portrays real production only and has been adjusted to eliminate inflation due to past and projected price rises.

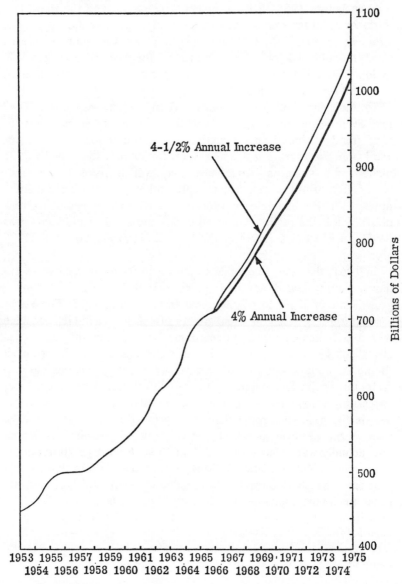

CHART 6: GROSS NATIONAL PRODUCT
1953 to 1966 and projected to 1975

(In Constant 1965 Dollars—Adjusted to Eliminate Distortion Due to Price Rises)

4-1/2% Annual Increase

4% Annual Increase

Billions of Dollars

1100
1000
900
800
700
600
500
400

1953 1955 1957 1959 1961 1963 1965 1967 1969 1971 1973 1975
1954 1956 1958 1960 1962 1964 1966 1968 1970 1972 1974

POPULATION, INCOME, EDUCATION

Let us now take a look at the big prime movers that give evidence that the economy will forge ahead through the Seventies.

Population growth The first one is population. For ten years after World War II, the tremendous crop of war babies made a recognizable hump in the population curve. During the 1960 to 1970 decade, the postwar babies were 10 to 14 years old. During the present decade—1965 to 1975—they are 15 to 19. During the 1970 to 1980 decade they will be 20 to 24. And that is the age at which these young people are married, holding down jobs, setting up households, and beginning to invest in all the houses, furniture, autos, and other appurtenances so necessary to today's families. And as they begin to have their own children, a new wave of babies will begin its course through the population curves.

A fast-growing population does not guarantee prosperity, of course, as demonstrated by India and China. But in a country where business is aggressively seeking new customers under a system of free enterprise, and constantly devising new products to sell, a population rise spells business activity.

Rise in real income Here is another angle. Not only are there more families, but in recent years their "real" income has increased tremendously. Real income is measured in terms of what it will buy rather than in terms of inflated dollars. Obviously it is no good to double your income if prices also double. But actually the average income per person in the United States has increased a good deal more than prices.

Families also are moving upward into higher income groups—and by higher income is meant "real" income in "constant" dollars which have been corrected to eliminate the effect of rising prices. Look at the chart on page 72 and you will see that in 1947 61% of the population was in the lowest group with real incomes under $5000. By 1965 the figure had dropped to 33%. But the number having incomes in the $5000 to $10,000 range rose from 31% to 42%. The number in the $10,000 to $15,000 group rose from 8% to 17%. And the number with incomes of over $15,000 increased from 1% to 8%.

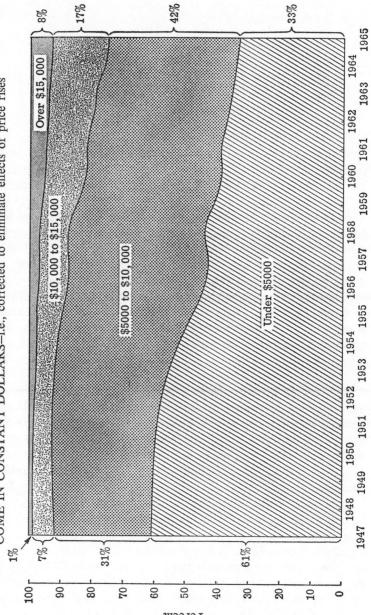

CHART 7: PERCENTAGE OF FAMILIES RECEIVING VARIOUS LEVELS OF IN-COME IN CONSTANT DOLLARS—i.e., corrected to eliminate effects of price rises

As families increase their real income and move into a higher group, they also tend to move to the suburbs. It all fits into a pattern that bodes good for business in the years ahead: families growing in numbers, moving up into the middle-income bracket, and spreading to the suburbs to buy homes and all the paraphernalia that go with them.

Better education   Education goes hand and hand with prosperity. Consider now only Americans over the age of twenty-five. Twenty years ago only 33% had completed high school; today 50% have. Twenty years ago 5% had completed four years of college; today 10% have.

These trends toward "more" will continue as far ahead as anyone can see. There will be more young families starting out, more families in the middle and upper income levels. They will be buying more color TV sets, more medicines, more autos, more houses; taking more vacations and trips abroad; traveling faster; communicating more rapidly. There will be more education and more brain power multiplied by computers, to apply to the problems of the day and the future. There will be change, innovation, new methods of achieving goals, new ways of behavior.

NEW PRODUCTS, MATERIALS, AND METHODS

The other big prime mover that is storing up energy for another big boom is research and development, known in industry as R & D. Consider that only a few years ago there were no lasers, cordless electric tools, color TV, birth control pills, silicon solar cells, hydrofoil boats, communication satellites, supersonic jet aircraft, or electrostatic printing. Go back a few years further and there were no nylon, dacron, orlon, synthetic rubber, titanium, television, transistors, antibiotics, jet planes, radioactive isotopes, radar, DDT, instant photography, or atomic energy.

There is no pause for breath as far as research goes. Industry, government, and the universities together spend over twenty billion dollars a year hunting for new products, new materials, new methods and just doing pure research for the sake of knowledge. As an example of a pure research project, physicists are bombarding the nucleus of the

CHART 8: MONEY INVESTED IN SCIENTIFIC RESEARCH
AND DEVELOPMENT BY GOVERNMENT, BUSINESS,
AND UNIVERSITIES

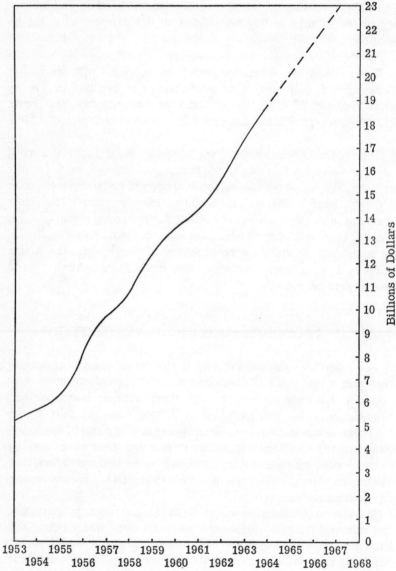

atom with higher and higher energies in hopes of discovering its ultimate composition. Although no usable application of such a project
is apparent, similar pure research in the past almost always has led
to tremendous breakthroughs resulting in useful materials, products,
or methods.

Look at Chart 8 on page 74 to see how expenditures on research
are soaring. In the Fifties they were doubling every five years. Even
though expenditures have reached a tremendous size, they still are
doubling every ten years. The potential is unlimited. Each new discovery opens up new unexplored vistas. Sumner Slichter, eminent
professor of Harvard Business School, has predicted that in most
years ahead investment opportunities created by research will exceed
the supply of investment-seeking funds.

Here are some of the areas where tremendous changes are being
seen, and will continue to be seen over the coming decades. So un-
believably wide and complex is this technological explosion that it is
only possible to mention brief and random samples.

Systems analysis Perhaps the most significant and least understood innovation is a new method by which industry, government,
science, and the military attack today's vast and complex problems.
Instead of plugging along, one step at a time, with hunches and the
old fashioned "cut-and-try" approach, management may start with
the ultimate desired goal, or several theoretical goals. By use of computers and "mathematical models," the problem is worked backward
through all its ramifications. The resulting analysis gives a much
clearer picture of alternatives than any methods in use heretofore.
Different approaches to complex problems can be pretested, sometimes in a matter of minutes. Once an approach is embarked on,
results can be measured against goals with lightning speed. Secretary
of Defense Robert McNamara introduced the method to solve the
complicated problems of missile development. It is coming into wide-
spread use, not only in the Department of Defense, but in other
branches of government, as well as in industry and science. As an
example, scientists at Princeton University's physics lab were working on ways to control the energy released by thermonuclear fission;
in other words, slow release of the energy of a hydrogen bomb.
Needed was a new and powerful kind of electron gun and magnetic
field to focus its beam. In the old days, years of experimentation
might have been required. But by use of computers, simulated tubes

were invented and tested without the actual production of a single one. Thus the long process of building and experimenting with real models was eliminated and a working device was obtained in a matter of weeks.

The use of systems analysis, or systems planning, is not confined to problems of scientific development or financial analysis. Such methods may eventually be used to attack the most complex social and economic problems, city slums, the tangled interrelationship between federal, state, and local governments, poverty, air and water pollution, and even foreign affairs. Thus systems analysis may solve complicated problems that cut across all elements of society by intricately matching and fitting efforts of federal and local governments, industry, science, and universities.

Health   Since the powerful combination of progestin and estrogen steroids were combined into "The Pill," ten to twelve million women have begun taking oral contraceptives. And dozens of more advanced pills are now being tested. In addition, drug companies are trying out injectible contraceptives that will last for months.

The Lippes Loop, a uterine device, proved its effectiveness by cutting the population growth in Korea from 3% to 1.9%. New types of uterine devices are under development along with male contraceptives.

Researchers are working on a "morning after" pill which a woman could take following intercourse. Another possibility is a tiny silastic capsule to be injected under the skin which, working by osmosis, could send small doses of progestin into the blood stream and prevent conception for twenty years. The market is immense. There are estimated to be 650,000,000 women of childbearing age in the world, only 5% of whom are practicing birth control. And approximately 300,000 babies are born each day, two-thirds of them into families that are poor, hungry, ignorant, or ill. UN Secretary-General U Thant called unplanned population growth as serious a problem as world peace.

Heart trouble is the number one killer of Americans. Those who survive the first attack are extremely susceptible to a second, which often comes within days. Thus medical engineers have developed measuring devices attached to the patient's body that give an early warning of recurring trouble. Twenty hospital patients at a time can be kept under observation by closed-circuit TV. If a warning signal is flashed, a nurse can administer electric shock treatment by remote control, sending the heart back into its normal beat.

Heart block is a common ailment which occurs when the muscle that activates the heart simply gives up. Electronic pacemakers can send electric shock signals into the heart to keep it beating evenly. At present these are battery-operated and must be replaced every eighteen months or so. Engineers are working on several improvements: one would be powered by radio-frequency waves, another by nuclear power which hopefully would operate for ten years without replacement; a third would operate on a battery recharged by body chemicals. Other experiments look toward a "demand pacer" that would operate only when the heartbeat actually stopped; still another would be synchronized so as to speed up the heartbeat when the patient exercised. Scientists also are working on artificial pumps that would take over some of the work of the heart itself and permit it to rest and regain strength. One such pump has circulated a patient's blood for ten days.

The cardiac pacemaker is being adapted to other ailments, such as high blood pressure. Scientists are experimenting with a device to be implanted in the neck that would do the work of the nerve that regulates blood pressure in healthy persons. A battery-operated pancreas regulator theoretically can be hooked up to a diabetic patient's circulatory system so as to release insulin automatically when the blood-sugar level rises above normal. Pacemakers also are being tested for malfunctioning bladders. Under development is a cheap artificial kidney that could be mass produced and used conveniently in the home. Artificial devices may someday send impulses to a leg muscle atrophied by disease or age so that a crippled person could again be able to walk. An aerospace company has developed a moonwalker ambulating chair for crippled children that can travel over uneven ground and climb curbstones on its spiderlike legs.

Ultrasonic, or high frequency sound waves, sent into the human body can detect ills that X-rays do not always show. Ultrasonics can tell whether a woman is pregnant or has a tumor; can differentiate between a malignant and a benign eye tumor. High frequency sound waves can speed healing of wounds and cut hospital stays by 50%. They can break up the calcium deposits that cause bursitis.

Computers and other electronic devices are changing the whole concept of diagnosis and treatment. Medical researchers have constructed a mathematical model made up of thirty-one equations that simulate the action of the human lung and aid in diagnoses. Another possibility is a system of mass electrocardiograms. Specialists have separated the human heart into fourteen thousand components and programmed the data into a master computer. Eventually, this central system could be linked to doctors' offices, clinics, and hospitals everywhere. When a patient had an EKG taken, results could be put on magnetic tape and sent by telephone line to the computer, which would read the data and in seconds determine whether the heart is normal or defective, print out the diagnosis, and flash it back. A research group has recorded and programmed every case of cancer in El Paso County, Texas, in the past eighteen years. This statistical profile will be used to analyze the common characteristics of the disease and the effectiveness of radiation treatment.

In some hospitals electronic sensors monitor the health of patients, relaying impulses of heart, brain, and blood pressure to a central console. A patient can walk around, exercise, take drugs and even undergo surgery, and all the while the system keeps tabs on his condition. When a physician arrives at a hospital in the morning, before making his rounds, he will be able to press a button and see flashed on a screen the data on all his patients. Electronic pain killers, now being tested on animals, may replace chemical anesthetics and one day ease the pain of cancer and other diseases.

Communications   The Picturephone permits callers to see, as well as talk to one another. Letters, drawings, and pictures can be sent and reproduced over ordinary telephone circuits. But more significant by far is the unbelievable speed at which computers can absorb information, transmit it over wires, and print it out. Scanners can read typewritten data at over two thousand characters per second and store the information in a computer. It can be printed out by computer, but the output is relatively slow, some one thousand characters per second, and the type is that of the typewriter or teletype. Lines can be "justified"; that is, spaced out so that the right-hand margin is even. Under development are electronic phototypesetters that will be able to take data from a computer, set it in any style of type, justifying the lines, all at phenomenal speeds.

Phototypesetters are not new, but present-day models are relatively slow. They are activated by punched or magnetic tapes that come from computers. Instead of forming type from hot metal, they make a photographic picture of the characters. Any number of type fonts can be stored in a memory system. A person can even write out the alphabet in his own handwriting and have the typesetter print a manuscript in that style. When computer tape comes to the typesetter, it takes each letter out of its memory and tells a cathode ray tube scanner to reproduce it. The image of the letter then is projected through a lens system onto photographic paper or film. It is expected that eventually phototypesetters will be speeded up to where they can print whole pages at a time and produce book quality printing at the rate of thousands of characters per second.

Education The automated classroom is already here. Textbooks and blackboards are giving way to computers and other electronic devices such as the cathode ray tube. The Ford Foundation has proposed a noncommercial TV network beamed coast-to-coast via communication satellites providing live classroom instructional programs to sixty million students at all levels of education. At the Brentwood School in East Palo Alto, California, first graders spend an hour a day engaging in a "tutorial dialogue" with a high-speed IBM computer. Each student wears earphones and watches a TV-type screen. In response to instructions of a tape-recorded voice he touches a light pen to an image on the screen, then types the name of the object on an electronic keyboard. Tirelessly and with infinite patience the machine guides the learner through the alphabet, to word recognition, and the constructing of sentences.

Computer-programmed instruction for older pupils feeds them information in small, easily digested bites, quizzing them after each bite. A fast learner, who may become bored by this "linear" approach, is fed information in bigger bites. As long as he digests the material he can go at his own pace. But if he slips on a quiz he is "branched" onto remedial material which he must master before he goes on. In another method pupils respond to instruction by pushing buttons at "learner stations," which are wired to the teacher's control panel. She can present taped or filmed material or her own lecture, using questions as she goes along and branching when the lights on her panel indicate a need.

Four hundred schools in New York State are hooked up to a central studio via closed circuit TV. Whole libraries of video tapes can be built up and used in such systems. Already in use is "Select-a-Lesson," whereby a university student can enjoy a filmed or tape-recorded lecture in his own dormitory. He simply sits down at a listening-viewer station equipped with headphones and a TV screen. From a catalogue he orders the film or tape he desires by spinning what looks like a telephone dial. At a library a computer retrieves and plays back the program without human intervention. At Harvard Business School, students can emulate the actual operation of a business, making all necessary decisions as they are presented by the computer. Or the computer can be used as a simulated science laboratory, permitting the student to "discover" for himself all the laws of nature from gravity to relativity.

Electronics Integrated circuits (IC's) still offer the most exciting possibilities. The IC, like the transistor, begins with pure silicon. Crystals are grown in special furnaces to provide the raw material. It is sliced into thin, half-dollar-size wafers which are polished to a mirrorlike finish and covered with a layer of photosensitive material. The wafers next are masked with a series of microscopic stencils and exposed to ultraviolet light. An acid bath then etches the pattern into the surface. What emerges is a tiny chip (each wafer yields hundreds of chips) bearing a microscopic network of circuits. The silicon, which retards the flow of electrical current, furnishes the basic resistance. By doing a little insulating here, a little connecting there, the producers can build a complete circuit that rectifies, simplifies, switches, and stores current, or, in short, performs all the functions handled by an assembly of transistors, capacitors, and resistors. It is routine to put the equivalent of fifty devices on a chip. And a special-purpose chip measuring only eighty-six by seventy-two thousandths of an inch can pack the equivalent of two hundred transistors. Large-scale integration can produce chips that carry the equivalent of a million transistors per square inch. Eventually engineers will be able to put the equivalent of a whole computer on a chip.

IC's are expected to do almost every job now done electromechanically. Household appliances and switches will be controlled by a panel that will fit into a pocket. TV sets with flat screens will hang on the wall. Autos will have electronic power plants. Control devices at intersections will regulate traffic flow. By turning to his wrist-watch transmitter, a New Yorker will be able to speak instantly to associates in London, Paris, or Rome. Computers will be everywhere, as common and as easy to use as telephones. Lawyers will be able to gain immediate access to every prior case and decision in history. Doctors will feed symptoms into a machine, then sit back and await the computer's diagnosis. And in the home computers will plan, schedule, and operate robot vacuum cleaners, washing machines, and ranges. Computers will prepare income tax returns, pay the bills, and even do the kids' homework.

Agriculture Surging demand from a hungry world has changed the outlook for farmers and turned surpluses to shortages. Hybrid corn and other seeds, antibiotics in animal feed, new insecticides are an old story. Today the emphasis is on new and more powerful machinery. Tractors of over fifty horsepower now outsell smaller machines and permit faster plowing and harvesting, reduce vulnerability due to adverse weather, and lengthen the growing season. One company has an experimental small helicopter that may someday be used as an airborne tractor. Versatile new machines can pick the most delicate crops. Some pests can be controlled by trapping females of species, treating them with a steroid, and releasing them.

Birth control devices are being used to prevent ovulation in ewes until the exact desired time. Then the device is removed, permitting pinpoint breeding and a precise schedule of lambing. A progestational agent used in the feed of cows makes mass breedings and other efficiencies possible.

New kinds of cheap foods are under development. Soybeans which, pound for pound, are the cheapest source of edible protein, can be transformed into a frozen food that tastes like fried chicken.

Oceanography Scientists know less about what's under the ocean than they do about what's in outer space. Only the most primitive kind of explorations have been made, but progress is picking up. A twenty-two-foot submarine *Alvin,* equipped with floodlights, portholes, and a mechanical "claw," has carried a two-man crew to the bottom of a six-thousand-foot canyon in the Bahamas. *Aluminaut,* a fifty-foot vessel carrying two or three men, is capable of going to depths of fifteen thousand feet which will make it possible to explore the Great Abyssal Plains, or the very floor of the ocean. The ship is equipped with floodlights, two robot arms and can map the bottom and take core samplings. The U. S. Navy is testing a torpedo-like vessel called *Moray* which will be able to descend to six thousand feet and cruise at fifteen knots. The bathyscaphe *Trieste* has reached the deepest known place on the ocean floor—

35,800 feet or 6¾ miles in the Mariana Trench off Guam. There the crew found flatfish and red shrimp scuttling about on the bottom. The ocean is teeming with valuable minerals. The research vessel *Spencer F. Baird* has dredged potato-sized nodules of almost pure manganese from a depth of twelve thousand feet off the coast of California. Hush-hush reports tell of a vast gold beach under nineteen feet of water off the coast of Alaska.

Aquanauts are already living for extended periods on the ocean floor. Jon Lindbergh and Robert Stenuit spent forty-nine hours in a rubber tent at a depth of 432 feet near Nassau. They breathed special mixtures of exotic gases. In the Navy's Sealab II project, three groups of ten men each lived at 205 feet for fifteen days and Astronaut Scott Carpenter stayed down thirty days. SPID, for "submerged, portable, inflatable dwelling," was used as a base of operations by two men who lived two days on the Continental Shelf at a depth of 432 feet.

Transportation Supersonic passenger planes, high-speed trains perhaps running in tubes, fast hydrofoil passenger ships are widely discussed. Los Angeles is considering a plan to ease traffic congestion at its busy international airport by using giant crane-type helicopters that would pick up specially designed passenger buses in the downtown area and set them down a few minutes later near the loading ramps at the field. Similar helicopters may soon be unloading ships where dock facilities are crowded or nonexistent.

New power sources for automobiles and trucks that would eliminate gasoline engines with their air-polluting fumes are under intense study. One company has a prototype of an electric car powered by four silver-zinc batteries from an F105 fighter plane. It accelerates like a drag racer, sneaks along in absolute silence at fifty-five miles per hour and has a range of 75 miles without recharging. Operating cost is less than one-half cent a mile. The obstacles to commercial production are short range and the high cost of zinc, but these difficulties may be overcome. Ford is working with a sodium and sulphur battery; GM with lithium and chloride; other companies with lithium-fluoride and zinc and air. Fork lift trucks already are being converted to electric power and the Edison Electric Institute expects electric delivery trucks to be plying city streets in the early Seventies.

The fuel cell is another potential power source. It reverses the process of electrolysis, whereby an electric current passing through a container of water separates it into its elements of hydrogen and oxygen. In the cell, hydrogen and oxygen are fed in and with the aid of a catalyst yield water and electric current. Other chemicals can be used, for example, hydrazine, made from ammonia, and air, which produce electricity, water, and nitrogen.

Power   Nuclear-powered electric generating plants have come into being faster than most people expected ten years ago. Lesser known developments include, for example, the gasification of coal. A pilot plant in the Dakotas is expected shortly to be producing 500,000 to 1,000,000 cubic feet of gas per day from just forty-eight tons of coal. And the United States has recoverable reserves of coal amounting to 830,000,000,000 tons. During New York City's power blackout in November 1965, one ultramodern Manhattan apartment remained lighted and heated. It draws its power from a "total energy installation." A gas turbine, or it can be a gas or Diesel engine, is used for on-site generation of electricity. The heat produced by the unit, normally wasted, is used to make steam or hot water for space-heating and air-conditioning.

Automation   All kinds of operations in manufacturing and transportation are being taken over by automatic controls, often in connection with computers. As one small example, the entire water system of San Jose, California—consisting of 154 wells, 138 booster pumps, 35 reservoirs and tanks, 2 filter plants, several chlorination stations and other pressure and flow controls—is operated and monitored by a central console.

*   *   *

The above sketchy recital of developments only scratches the surface. Scientists and engineers are preparing to explore and use the depths of the oceans; to draw fresh water cheaply from salt water; to eliminate pollution in the air; to clean up rivers and streams; to rebuild America's cities.

It is a wonderful thing that you can buy a stake in all this. You do it by buying common stock in some of the companies that are the leaders in the frenzied race to create, innovate, and grow. But the problem of selection is formidable. Competition is fierce. Amid all the welter of change and progress, many ventures will fail and many companies fall by the way. How to avoid these, and to spot the strongest, fastest-growing, and eventually the most profitable, will be the subject of the following chapters.

CHAPTER 5

Selecting Industries and Companies

"Selectivity" as used on Wall Street means choosing just the right stocks from among the thousands that are available. To the trader or speculator, the right stock is one that he thinks is due for a big rise. Maybe he has heard rumors of an impending merger, a stock split, or a dazzling new product. For most people, however, such a method of selection is unprofitable. The day-to-day rumors and tips in the financial community are unreliable, and the short-term movements of individual stocks and the market as a whole are unpredictable even by the so-called experts. A far better method is to block out a set of long-range investment goals, then begin narrowing down choices, first to the most suitable industries, then to the best companies within those industries.

AN INVESTMENT PHILOSOPHY

Here is a method of selection that has been successful. First pick industries that are growing faster than the economy as a whole and that may be expected to continue such growth rate for at least five or ten years. Second, from within such industries, select top quality companies with aggressive management and with earnings that have a record of doubling every five to eight years. Here are some of the arguments in favor of this investment philosophy.

Fast-growing companies usually are plowing back a large part of their earnings into research, development of new products and new markets. This means that the dividend payout is small, but this is not a disadvantage. Most investors, notably those who have not yet reached retirement age, do not need, and should not want, dividend income. Dividends are taxable and what's left after taxes easily can be frittered away. Earnings put to work by the company, on the other hand, are being reinvested by the best brains in American industry.

The stockholder pays no taxes on such earnings, even though he owns a pro-rata share of them. He will be taxed on his profits when he sells his stock, but at that time only a capital gains tax will be due. The rate will be half the stockholder's top income tax rate and in no event will it be more than 25% of his gain.

The above is based on the assumption that the stockholder does not plan to trade in and out of the market but intends to keep his stock for a period of years. There are two reasons why a growth stock should be held and not sold unless and until the company's business definitely turns sour. First, in a sense Newton's law of gravitation applies to growth stocks. If a company has been increasing its earnings for some years, chances are it will continue to do so until something definite stops it. So even when the investor has a large paper profit, he should resist the temptation to nail it down by selling. If he lets his investment ride, it probably will continue to grow in value at least as fast as anything else he might buy. Second, if he sells his stock when he finds he has a paper profit, he incurs a capital gain and must pay the gains tax. Only a part of his profit then is left to reinvest. In addition, he suffers all the original headaches of making another good selection.

FAST-GROWING INDUSTRIES

The first step in selection, then, is to pick fast-growing industries. That means avoiding nongrowth or "cyclical" industries. Cyclical companies tend to prosper when business as a whole is good. When business contracts, their earnings tend to decline, sometimes rather sharply. Thus prices of cyclical stocks rise and fall within a limited range. Growth stocks also rise and fall irregularly, but there is a strong upward tilt to the trend line of earnings and prices.

Look at Charts 9 and 10 to see a contrast between the cyclical steel and iron industry and the rapidly growing drug industry. While steel companies do make innovations and improvements, their output basically is geared to the level of manufacturing as a whole. Despite some automation, wages still make up a large percentage of costs, and rapid rises in wage rates have kept earnings down.

The drug industry, on the other hand, is boiling over with new products and has almost unlimited possibilities for developing medicines and devices to prevent or cure the diseases and ailments of

CHART 9: STEEL AND IRON STOCKS*

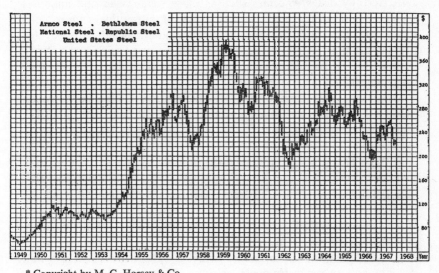

Armco Steel . Bethlehem Steel
National Steel . Republic Steel
United States Steel

* Copyright by M. C. Horsey & Co.

CHART 10: DRUG STOCKS*

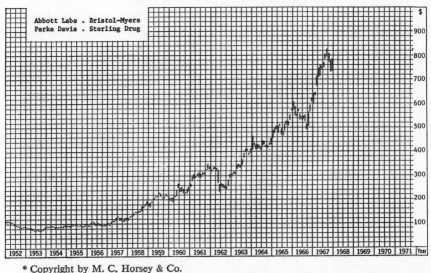

Abbott Labs . Bristol-Myers
Parke Davis . Sterling Drug

* Copyright by M. C. Horsey & Co.

mankind. Intensive research is going on in the fields of contraceptives, fertility drugs, vaccines such as those for measles and mumps, mental health drugs, and possible ways of alleviating cancer and heart and circulatory diseases. Medicare and Medicaid will provide a great stimulus. While the restrictive policies of the Food and Drug Administration are dampening profit prospects to some extent, the long-range effect may not be great.

Drugs are one example of a growth industry. There are a good many others. Each one is unique, but in general, a growth industry will have several, if not all, of the following characteristics:

A vigorous program of research and development   Large expenditures on R & D are the underpinning of most sustained growth. The National Industrial Conference Board lists the following industries as those that spend an above average percentage of income from sales on R & D: aircraft and missiles, 18%; communication equipment and electronic components, 12½%; scientific and mechanical measuring instruments, 9½%; optical, surgical, photographic and other instruments, 7½%; other electrical equipment, 7%; industrial chemicals, 5%; drugs and medicines, nearly 5%.

How this R & D money is spent is important. Generally speaking, money spent on developing new products gives more zip to growth than money spent on improving methods or existing products. Most iron and steel companies, for example, say the main purpose of their R & D spending is to improve existing products. But 70% of chemical companies say the main object of their programs is to create new products. As an extreme example of the value of new products, consider the companies that developed electronic computers. They have found that they have a development as revolutionary as was the auto in the Twenties.

One measure of the effectiveness of R & D, then, might be the proportion of a company's sales accounted for by new products. A survey by McGraw-Hill Publications shows that the following industries expect a very large percentage of 1969 sales to be in new products that did not exist in 1965: aerospace, 40%; electrical machinery, 24%; machinery, 23%; "other transportation equipment," which includes ships and railroad equipment, 23%; autos, trucks and parts, 22%; chemicals, 18%; fabricated metals and instruments, 17%, and stone, clay and glass, 17%.

While these figures give some interesting ideas on industries that are spending heavily on R & D, other factors also must be considered. Following are examples.

Freedom from competition   No company is completely free from competition, but a fast-growing, imaginative company often can develop so many new products and ideas that it can keep out ahead of similar companies. Such a company is like a football player that manages to get into the clear with the ball. On the other hand, some of the most outstanding innovating companies are in industries that for one reason or another are fiercely competitive. The aerospace industry, for example, is outstanding in research. But it also suffers from the fact that there is only one large customer and that is the federal government. In other fields, such as drugs, chemicals, electrical machinery, electronics, etc., the potential range of customers is much wider and there is more room to compete.

Once a company comes up with a brand new product, it may have some years to exploit it before competition catches up. By this time, it must be ready to bring other rabbits out of the hat. It's a never-ending race.

Profiting from growth   Some areas of the country and some parts of the economy are growing faster than the country or the economy as a whole. And some industries, or parts of industries, are taking advantage of this "super growth." The crop of war babies born in 1946 and 1947, when the servicemen came home from World War II, forms a bulge in the population. These young people, now in their early twenties, are in demand as workers by a booming economy, earn good money, and make prime prospects for life insurance. This situation, plus the rising standard of living of the population as a whole, has made life insurance, odd as it may seem, into an interesting growth industry.

Where growth of population and industry is concentrated in a particular geographic area, electric utilities serving that area surge ahead faster than the industry as a whole.

Increasing leisure combined with a long period of prosperity has made a growth industry out of companies that cater to recreation needs.

Low labor costs   An industry in which wages make up a large percentage of costs has trouble spurting ahead. The reason, of course, is that the cost of labor is one of the fastest rising costs that industry must cope with. Hence in most growth industries labor costs are a relatively small percentage of the whole. A logical extension of this development is that a whole growth industry has been built up to fill industry's demand for labor-saving machinery.

Freedom from government control   Regardless of the investor's personal feelings about government control over private industry, he will be well advised to invest in industries that are least subject to such control. Note the fate of the railroads, which have been so long under the dead hand of the Interstate Commerce Commission. The threat of increasingly heavy-handed interference by the Federal Communications Commission sent the stock of A T & T into a decline which, during the years 1964 to 1966, caused it to lose one third of its value. Utilities, although closely regulated, usually are under the control of state utility commissions. Growing states, in their efforts to attract new industry, generally allow utilities earnings large enough to finance expansion. But one of the problems of the drug industry is the growing interest that the federal government is taking in its operations.

THE MOST PROMISING COMPANIES

Selecting fast-growing industries with some or all of the above-described characteristics is only half the battle. The other half consists of combing those industries and finding the most promising companies. Even in a prime growth industry, where many companies are expanding and increasing profits by leaps and bounds, there are always others that may sound just as glamorous when described but that are actually spinning their wheels and getting nowhere. Glance ahead at the charts on the next few pages to see contrasts between companies in the same business. Each pair of companies is in what is generally considered to be a growth industry.

Outstanding past performance   This is one of the best clues to the future. Companies that have been doubling their per share earnings every five to eight years, which means a good growth rate, will continue to do so unless something stops them. If you can't find evidence of the existence of that "something," then the stock has

BUSINESS MACHINES

FAST GROWTH
CHART 11: INTERNATIONAL BUSINESS MACHINES*

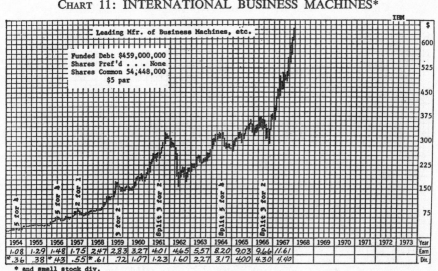

Leading Mfr. of Business Machines, etc.

Funded Debt $459,000,000
Shares Pref'd . . . None
Shares Common 54,448,000
$5 par

Year	1954	1955	1956	1957	1958	1959	1960	1961	1962	1963	1964	1965	1966	1967	1968	1969	1970	1971	1972	1973
Earn	1.08	1.29	1.48	1.75	2.47	2.83	3.27	4.01	4.65	5.57	8.20	9.03	9.66	11.61						
Div.	*.36	.38	*.43	.55	*.61	.72	1.07	1.23	1.60	2.27	3.17	4.00	4.30	4.40						

* and small stock div.

SLOW OR NO GROWTH
CHART 12: SPERRY RAND CORPORATION*

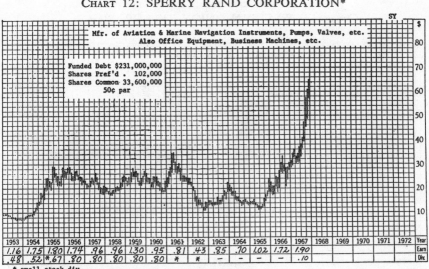

Mfr. of Aviation & Marine Navigation Instruments, Pumps, Valves, etc.
Also Office Equipment, Business Machines, etc.

Funded Debt $231,000,000
Shares Pref'd . 102,000
Shares Common 33,600,000
50¢ par

Year	1953	1954	1955	1956	1957	1958	1959	1960	1961	1962	1963	1964	1965	1966	1967	1968	1969	1970	1971	1972
Earn	1.16	1.75	1.80	1.74	.96	.96	1.30	.95	.81	.43	.85	.70	1.02	1.72	1.90					
Div.	.48	.52	*.67	.80	.80	.80	.80	.80	*	*	—	—	—	—	.10					

* small stock div.

COMMUNICATIONS

FAST GROWTH
CHART 13: GENERAL TELEPHONE AND ELECTRONICS

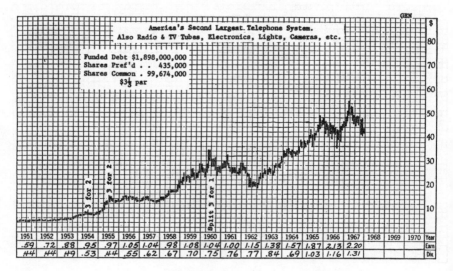

	1951	1952	1953	1954	1955	1956	1957	1958	1959	1960	1961	1962	1963	1964	1965	1966	1967	1968	1969	1970	Year
Earn	.59	.72	.88	.95	.97	1.05	1.04	.98	1.08	1.04	1.00	1.15	1.38	1.57	1.87	2.13	2.20				Earn
Div.	.44	.44	.49	.53	.44	.55	.62	.67	.70	.75	.76	.77	.84	.69	1.03	1.16	1.31				Div.

SLOW OR NO GROWTH
CHART 14: WESTERN UNION TELEGRAPH CO.

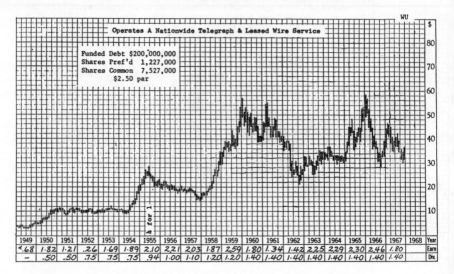

	1949	1950	1951	1952	1953	1954	1955	1956	1957	1958	1959	1960	1961	1962	1963	1964	1965	1966	1967	1968	Year
Earn	<.68	1.82	1.21	.26	1.69	1.89	2.10	2.21	2.03	1.87	2.59	1.80	1.34	1.42	2.25	2.29	2.30	2.46	1.80		Earn
Div.	—	.50	.50	.75	.75	.75	.94	1.00	1.10	1.20	1.20	1.40	1.40	1.40	1.40	1.40	1.40	1.40	1.40		Div.

DRUGS

FAST GROWTH
CHART 15: PFIZER (CHARLES) & COMPANY, INC.

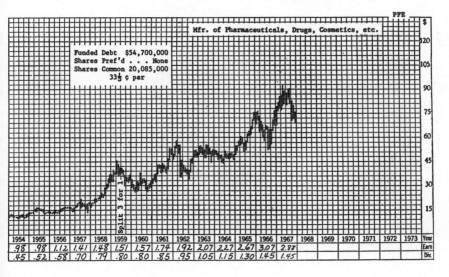

PFE

Mfr. of Pharmaceuticals, Drugs, Cosmetics, etc.

Funded Debt $54,700,000
Shares Pref'd . . . None
Shares Common 20,085,000
33⅓ ¢ par

Split 3 for 1

	1954	1955	1956	1957	1958	1959	1960	1961	1962	1963	1964	1965	1966	1967	1968	1969	1970	1971	1972	1973	Year
	.98	.98	1.12	1.41	1.48	1.51	1.57	1.74	1.92	2.07	2.27	2.67	3.07	2.87							Earn
	.45	.52	.58	.70	.79	.80	.80	.85	.95	1.05	1.15	1.30	1.45	1.45							Div.

SLOW OR NO GROWTH
CHART 16: PARKE, DAVIS & COMPANY

PDC

Mfr. of Pharmaceuticals, Surgical Dressings, etc.

Funded Debt . . . . None
Shares Pref'd . . . None
Shares Common 14,831,000
No par

Split 3 for 1

	1951	1952	1953	1954	1955	1956	1957	1958	1959	1960	1961	1962	1963	1964	1965	1966	1967	1968	1969	1970	Year
	1.30	1.11	.64	.71	.97	1.20	1.89	1.89	2.09	2.05	1.50	1.28	1.49	1.76	2.20	2.14	1.25				Earn
	.63	.63	.53	.47	.47	.57	.67	1.00	1.30	1.40	1.40	1.15	1.00	1.00	1.15	1.45	1.40				Div.

GLASS

FAST GROWTH
CHART 17: CORNING GLASS WORKS

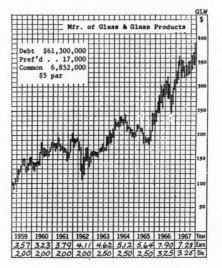

GLW
$

Mfr. of Glass & Glass Products

Debt $61,300,000
Pref'd . . 17,000
Common 6,852,000
    $5 par

	1959	1960	1961	1962	1963	1964	1965	1966	1967	Year
Earn.	3.57	3.23	3.79	4.11	4.62	5.12	5.64	7.90	7.28	
Div.	2.00	2.00	2.00	2.00	2.50	2.50	2.50	3.25	3.25	

SLOW OR NO GROWTH
CHART 18: PITTSBURGH PLATE GLASS CO.

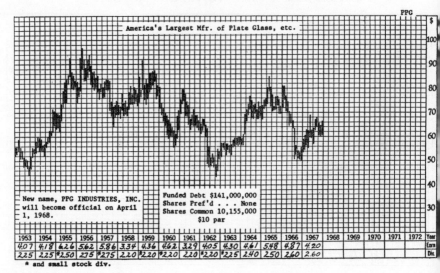

PPG
$

America's Largest Mfr. of Plate Glass, etc.

New name, PPG INDUSTRIES, INC.
will become official on April
1, 1968.

Funded Debt $141,000,000
Shares Pref'd . . . None
Shares Common 10,155,000
    $10 par

	1953	1954	1955	1956	1957	1958	1959	1960	1961	1962	1963	1964	1965	1966	1967	1968	1969	1970	1971	1972	Year
Earn.	4.07	4.18	4.26	5.62	5.86	3.34	4.36	4.62	3.29	4.05	4.30	4.61	5.48	4.87	4.20						
Div.	2.25	2.25	*2.50	2.75	*2.75	2.20	*2.20	2.20	2.20	*2.20	*2.25	2.40	2.50	2.60	2.60						

* and small stock div.

TOOLS

FAST GROWTH
CHART 19: BLACK & DECKER MFG. COMPANY

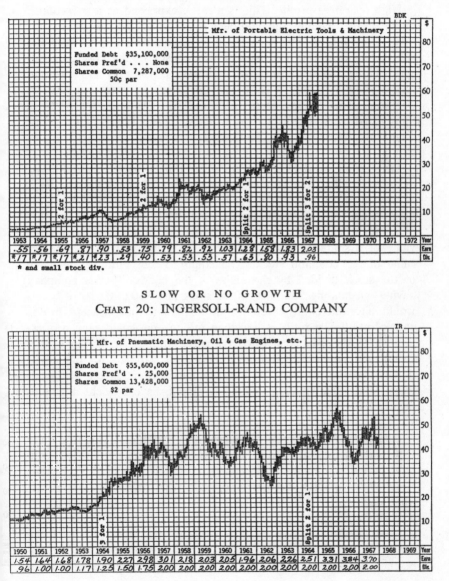

Mfr. of Portable Electric Tools & Machinery

Funded Debt $35,100,000
Shares Pref'd . . . None
Shares Common 7,287,000
50¢ par

2 for 1
2 for 1
Split 2 for 1
Split 3 for 2

Year	1953	1954	1955	1956	1957	1958	1959	1960	1961	1962	1963	1964	1965	1966	1967	1968	1969	1970	1971	1972
Earn	.55	.56	.69	.87	.90	.53	.75	.79	.82	.92	1.03	1.28	1.58	1.83	2.03					
Div.	*.17	*.17	*.17	*.21	*.23	.29	.40	.53	.53	.53	.57	.63	.80	.93	.96					

* and small stock div.

SLOW OR NO GROWTH
CHART 20: INGERSOLL-RAND COMPANY

Mfr. of Pneumatic Machinery, Oil & Gas Engines, etc.

Funded Debt $55,600,000
Shares Pref'd . . 25,000
Shares Common 13,428,000
$2 par

3 for 1
Split 2 for 1

Year	1950	1951	1952	1953	1954	1955	1956	1957	1958	1959	1960	1961	1962	1963	1964	1965	1966	1967	1968	1969
Earn	1.54	1.64	1.48	1.78	1.90	2.27	2.98	3.01	2.18	2.03	2.05	1.96	2.06	2.26	2.51	3.31	3.84	3.70		
Div.	.96	1.00	1.00	1.17	1.25	1.50	1.75	2.00	2.00	2.00	2.00	2.00	2.00	2.00	2.00	2.00	2.00	2.00		

passed one test. To find growth rates, all that's necessary is to look at the record of per share earnings back ten years. Or examine the charts similar to those used in these pages.

High operating profit   This is a ratio, expressed as a percentage, obtained by dividing the company's operating income by its net sales. Operating income is obtained by taking income from sales and subtracting operating expenses, which consist of the cost of goods sold, selling and administrative expenses. Top quality growth companies show not only a sales increase over the years but also an operating profit of, say, from 15% to 30%. The operating profit of most listed companies is shown in Standard and Poor's *Listed Stock Reports* under the heading "% Oper. Inc. of Sales."

Large equity-to-debt ratio   All other things being equal, the less debt outstanding, the better for the holders of the common stock. A way to measure the debt burden of a company is to look up the dollar value of any bonds outstanding. Then look up the number of common shares outstanding, multiply this number by the market value of a share of stock. The resulting figure will be the market value of the common stock. The equity-to-debt ratio is the value of the stock divided by the value of the bonds. Thus a company having outstanding $50,000,000 of stock and $10,000,000 of bonds would have an equity-to-debt ratio of five to one. Except in the case of utilities, a ratio of less than five to one would raise a question as to the quality of the company. Utilities, which have very steady and predictable income, habitually sell bonds for expansion money and the interest cost is taken into account in the setting of rates. Many companies, it should be noted, have no debt outstanding at all.

Adequate current assets versus current liabilities   This is a ratio that analysts look at automatically. It is shown in most stock manuals. Sound companies usually have a ratio of two or three to one. Here again, utilities can safely operate with ratios that are somewhat smaller.

Good quality   A top quality company has most or all of the characteristics mentioned above, plus an indefinable aura of competence and success. This means, among other things, that the management is aggressive and young-thinking. The officers need not be young in years. At one time, several years ago, the top officers and heads of the research and other departments of the Minnesota Mining and Manufacturing Company were all in their sixties and seventies. But they were young in brain power and imagination, as proven by the tremendous growth of the company and the amazing list of new products it continuously has on the market.

As an aid in judging quality in a company read one or more of the investment services. Standard and Poor's *Listed Stock Reports* and *American Stock Reports* give a good succinct account of most companies listed on the New York and American Stock exchanges. Also Standard and Poor's more abbreviated *Security Owner's Stock Guide,* published monthly, rates companies as to stability and growth of earnings and dividends. There are seven marks as follows: A plus (highest); A (high); A minus (above average); B plus (average); B (below average); B minus (low); C (lowest).

EXAMPLES OF INDUSTRIES AND COMPANIES

Today there is a ferment in industry. Companies that are famous for making one product are, for one reason or another, entering completely new fields. Through mergers and acquisitions cigarette companies are going into the liquor business, auto companies into farm machinery, sugar companies into pleasure boats, and so on. Thus it is hard to make a pat assignment of companies into a particular industry. There is too much overlapping, too many companies that are so diversified that they are not assignable to any one industry. Therefore the following section should be considered as illustrative of what has been said earlier in this chapter. The industries and companies are not recommendations but rather examples. And they are not the only ones, by any means. The interested reader can find many others.

CHEMICALS

This amazing industry that makes new and fascinating products out of the leftovers of other industries has had a record of rapid growth and its vigor seems undiminished. According to compilations by the U. S. Department of Commerce, the annual growth rate in the production of certain chemicals over the past eighteen years has been almost unbelievable: polyethylene 35%; helium 31%; argon 26%; noncellulose fibers 22%; styrene plastics and polyester resins 17%; penicillin salts 17%; oxygen 16%; polyvinyl resins 15%; phosphoric acid 14%. Plastics, synthetic fibers, fertilizers, agricultural chemicals are the basic ingredients of this industry's success. New "engineering" plastics are being developed such as Lexan of General Electric and PPO; new synthetic fibers such as DuPont's Corfam. Liquid nitrogen is being used for food freezing. Fuel cells, lasers, new kinds of batteries, and direct energy conversion devices are interesting possibilities.

This industry, like some others, is subject to periods of overproduction and price cutting in certain products. The companies affected, however, always seem to come back strong, and such periods of price weakness may be used to acquire good companies at a bargain.

Here are some examples of companies worth looking at.

Dow Chemical   Producer of plastics, resins, epoxies, solvents, cleaners, insulating materials, packaging wraps and films, synthetic fibers, bioproducts such as herbicides, insecticides, animal feed supplements and veterinary drugs, vaccines, antihistamines, decongestants, as well as ammonia, caustic soda, chlorine, ethylene, glycols, magnesium, and aluminum mill products. Labor and raw material costs are low. Eleven per cent of employees are engaged in full-time research. The company developed the measles vaccine Lirugen and a new fuel that cuts and welds like acetylene. Work is going ahead on air and water pollution control, new plastics, resins, insecticides, and herbicides.

National Starch and Chemical Corporation   Manufacturer of packaging and structural adhesives, cornstarches by the wet milling process, vinyl acetate polymers and copolymers, pressure sensitive coated papers and tapes. Principal markets are paper and paper converting, packaging, food, textile, protective coatings, nonwoven fabrics, furniture, construction materials, and other industrial markets. The company spends about 4½% of sales on research and development.

American Cyanamid Worldwide producer of a broad line of industrial chemicals including explosives and mining chemicals; catalysts; water treatment, refinery, rubber, textile and paper chemicals; plastics and resins; pigments; ethical drugs including antibiotics; agricultural products including fertilizers, medicated feed supplements, animal health products, systemic insecticides (which work up through the plant when applied to the soil) and low toxicity insecticides; hair shampoos, household waxes, cleaners, and disinfectants; building materials including Formica laminated plastic and acrylic clear plastic sheet. The company recently developed a measles vaccine, a nonaddicting pain reliever, and a drug for treatment of tuberculosis.

DRUGS

This industry, spending nearly 5% of sales on research and development, probably is on the threshold of vital breakthroughs in the war against disease.

American Home Products Worldwide manufacturer of drugs including tranquilizers, vitamins, analgesics, antibiotics, estrogens, steroids, cold remedies and Sabin oral polio vaccine; veterinary drugs; household products such as Griffin shoe polishes, Black Flag insecticides, 3-in-1 Oil, and packaged foods such as Chef Boy-Ar-Dee Italian style food specialties and Gulden mustard. The company is carrying out studies on the use of DMSO on humans.

Johnson & Johnson The world's largest producer of surgical dressings, sutures, cotton, and disposable diapers, baby powders and creams, sanitary napkins, and mouthwashes. Earnings doubled in a recent four-year period.

Merck Producer of fine chemicals and drugs including antibiotics, diuretics, antihypertensives, cortisone, steroids, antidepressants, sulphas, antiarthritics, influenza, measles, and other types of vaccines; veterinary drugs, and chemicals for the food, cosmetic, rubber, leather, and other industries. The company spends 10% of its sales dollars on research and about 75% of its business is in products developed within the past ten years. Among its later innovations are drugs that act like hormones but without the usual side effects, as well as a live-virus mumps vaccine.

Pfizer Leading producer of antibiotics, many of which it discovered and developed, including Terramycin and the new Rondomycin; mental health drugs, tranquilizers, oral antidiabetic drugs, diuretics, and medicines to combat ulcers and asthma; inorganic materials such as minerals, pigments, and metals; bulk organic chemicals such as food preservatives, vitamins, acidulants, synthetic sweeteners, and enzymes; consumer products such as Pacquins hand creams and lotions, Ben-Gay ointments and lotion, Desitin baby care products, Barbasol shave products, and the Coty line of fragrances and cosmetics; and animal health products including vaccines. Foreign sales are the largest of any U.S. drug manufacturer.

Plough This widely diversified company produces proprietary medicines, household products, and cosmetics and operates five radio stations in Atlanta, Baltimore, Boston, Chicago, and Memphis. Among its products are St. Joseph aspirin, nose drops, vitamins, etc., diuretic pills, antihistamines, Coppertone suntan products, Mexsana powder, Penetro and Mistol preparation for colds, Di-Gel antacid, Paas Easter egg dyes, shellac, wood fillers, Dap adhesives, sealants, and caulking compounds. Its products are sold throughout the free world.

ELECTRONICS AND ELECTRICAL EQUIPMENT

Tremendous military and space expenditures in this industry are financing breakthroughs that eventually will bring wonderful peacetime applications. At the present, color TV, tape recorders, and microelectronic products hold the stage in electronics. Under development are electro-optics including lasers, holography, and infrared rays.

The electrical equipment industry includes the generation, transformation, and distribution of electrical power, the controls by which it is applied to consumer and industrial uses, and the machines that it operates. Extra-high-voltage transmission involving eight hundred kilovolt systems are due to be in operation in 1969.

By 1969, also, it is expected that 24% of the sales of the electrical machinery and communications industry will be in new products.

International Tel and Tel   This is the largest American international enterprise engaged in the development, manufacture, installation, and service of electronic and telecommunications equipment. It operates domestically and heavily in Europe and Latin America. It turns out telephone equipment, satellite and other space equipment, television sets, record players, refrigerators, underground cable, computers and office machines, military and space age communications equipment, as well as providing such diverse consumer services as rent-a-car, life insurance, small loans, mutual funds, and educational publishing. It set up the Hot Line to Moscow and developed the first transportable "earth station" which, installed aboard the carrier *Wasp,* gave the world the first live television pictures of the splashdown and recovery of astronauts. For seven years per share earnings have grown at the rate of 10% to 12% and the company expects that this growth will continue in the foreseeable future.

General Telephone & Electronics   This is a holding company controlling the largest group of telephone companies in the United States outside of the Bell System. Controlling interest is also owned by General Telephone & Electronics in Canadian telephone companies operating in British Columbia and Quebec. The company also owns domestic and international subsidiaries which manufacture and sell a broad line of telecommunications equipment, industrial relays, control systems, and other communications equipment. Its Sylvania subsidiary manufactures radio and television receiving tubes and sets, picture tubes, lighting and photoflash products, defense electronics systems, and semiconductor products.

Honeywell   Leading producer of automation systems and controls for homes and buildings, including controls for heating, air-conditioning, humidity and appliances, and electronic air cleaners; instruments for industry, medicine, and science; switches and meters; systems management, applied research and product development for defense and aerospace, including guidance and control systems for aircraft, spacecraft, and missiles; design and production of air, ground, and underwater armament systems, including torpedoes, rocket and missile warheads, and munitions; a complete line of electronic data processing systems for industry, commerce, science, and government, including small, medium, and large computers, and special purpose scientific and industrial control computer systems and components; and a complete line of photographic products, including still and movie cameras, projectors, and electronic flash equipment.

Emerson Electric Emerson serves commercial, industrial, residential, and government space and defense markets with production of fractional-horsepower motors for appliances, large motors and drives, measurement and control systems, heat/light/air/sound electrical built-ins, construction tools, bench power tools for Sears, Roebuck "Craftsman" line, and automatic test equipment, heat shields, and defensive weapons systems for military application. Per share earnings have been growing about 20% compounded.

Square D Company Major manufacturer of broad line of electrical distribution and motor control equipment for residential, commercial, and industrial applications. Products range from small, standard circuit breakers to large, custom-designed automated solid state control systems and include starters, panelboards, busways, switchboards, control centers, unit substations, relays, lifting magnets, and safety switchers.

Litton Industries Produces typewriters, copying equipment, electronic calculators and accounting machines, business data processing equipment, retail data registers, office furniture, and revenue control systems. Aerospace products include inertial guidance systems, communication, command and control equipment. Litton's expanding shipbuilding activity builds nuclear submarines and other military and commercial vessels. Other products are industrial unit and material handling systems, electronic and electromechanical components, microwave cooking equipment, and medical electronic measurement and monitoring units. Litton provides resource survey and exploration services and has formed a subsidiary for international economic development projects.

RCA Has diverse and far-ranging domestic and international enterprises. Consumer products include TV sets, radios, phonographs and records, and tape recorders. NBC, a subsidiary, provides nationwide broadcasting. For industry, the company offers computers and electronic data processing systems. Communications products and services include international telegraphic facilities, mobile two-way radios and microwave systems, airborne radar and communications, broadcast equipment, and electronic equipment for shipping. For the graphic industry, the company develops and provides electronic composition, typesetting, and printing systems. For defense, RCA makes radar, fire control systems, missile tracking and warning systems, battlefield radios, and military communications systems. In space, RCA contributes weather satellites and electronic systems for manned space flights and lunar exploration. The company is engaged in educational electronics, including computerized instruction, and is collaborating with a pharmaceutical company to develop new medical electronic apparatus. It is a leader in rental and leasing services through the Hertz Corporation, a subsidiary, and is in the publishing business through Random House, Inc., also a subsidiary. RCA employs about six thousand scientists and engineers, and its research extends across a broad range of basic and applied programs involving new materials, such as superconductors, and new devices and systems such as laser communications.

OFFICE MACHINES

This industry produces, sells, and rents computers, duplicating and copying equipment. The versatility and speed of computers are almost unbelievable and their ability to handle intricate business and engineering chores and problems is increasing so fast that it is expected that the use of computers will triple in ten years. Research is going on into new methods of getting words, figures, and images onto paper at much faster speeds by means of scanners. Electronic copying also may soon be competing with older forms of duplicating such as multilith printing.

IBM World's largest manufacturer of business machines. Customers are using its computing systems to help build bridges, process bank checks, speed airline reservations, schedule freight trains, improve cattle breeds, study the weather, investigate the planets—as well as solve a vast number of other business and scientific problems. At NASA's Manned Spacecraft Center in Houston, IBM computers performed over forty billion calculations a day during each of the Gemini flights. IBM has pioneered in the creation of microcircuitry and has produced experimental monolithic chips one-eighteenth of an inch square, each containing 150 electronic elements making up sixteen circuits. An optical reader can read hand-printed numbers and five different hand-printed alphabetic characters and feed the information directly into a computer for processing. Other data processing equipment is helping hospitals increase their efficiency. One new system records laboratory test data on punched cards and feeds it into a computer for processing so that a physician can obtain test results quickly. Work also is being done on an experimental system which allows electrocardiograms to be recorded and then read and analyzed by a computer. IBM has two new composing units utilizing typewriter-like keyboards which can produce text for reproduction in more than fifty type styles. One of the units uses magnetic tape to record material as it is typed out, adjusting the spacing between words so that both margins are straight. The unit prints out camera-ready copy at the rate of fourteen characters per second. The company also is experimenting with lasers and is working on the development of computer-assisted instruction techniques for use in classroom instruction and industrial training programs. In one year, company scientists and engineers produced more than 1500 inventions.

Addressograph Multigraph   Offers products and systems to originate and communicate information for all types of business, governments, and institutions. Produces data-processing systems, addressing and duplicating equipment and supplies, electrostatic copying machines, type and photo composing equipment, plastic cards, machines, and supplies for engineering drawings, carbon papers, and business machine ribbons. In source data collection, for example, AM methods provide direct input for computer processing from scattered reporting sources using embossed plastic cards, data recorders, and low cost optical code readers. A combined copier-duplicator method extends the advantages of electrostatic copying. The company operates in many countries.

Xerox   Xerography is a fast, dry, electrophotographic copying process and accounts for the bulk of this company's business. The firm offers a variety of copiers and duplicators, one of which will produce a copy of a document every second. Another will automatically make reduced-size copies of computer print-out fanfold material. The company spends around fifty million dollars a year on research and is expanding its efforts in many fields, including education and graphic communications. Other research involves such curious phenomena as the production of holograms by Xerography. When a laser is beamed through them, a three-dimensional image appears.

Pitney-Bowes   This originator of the postage meter manufactures mailing and business machines here and abroad and markets them worldwide through its own sales-service network and through dealers. Postage meter and mailing center equipment includes scales and mail openers. Other products are copiers, collators, addresser-printers, folders, inserters, counters and imprinters, post office equipment, and tax-stamping machines. The company spends about six million dollars a year on research and development and is continuing to expand its product lines and manufacturing and marketing capacity.

LABOR-SAVING TOOLS AND MACHINES

Americans are an impatient lot. They want to get things done fast. This trait, combined with ever-rising costs of manpower, has led to the design and production of labor-saving tools from the householder's quarter-inch drill to the mighty machines that move tons of earth at a time. The market potential seems unlimited.

Black and Decker   This leading manufacturer of portable power tools started business in a Baltimore loft in 1910, producing a portable electric air compressor for inflating tires. Today it produces a line of more than three hundred different tools powered either by electricity or compressed air, including drills, saws, sanders, fastening and valve reconditioning tools, vacuum cleaning systems, and lawn and garden tools. The company is very research-minded and on the average introduces a new or redesigned product every seven days. Recent innovations include a three-speed jigsaw for home hobbyists; a line of variable-speed, double-insulated drills; a one-half-inch electric impact wrench that reverses with a squeeze of the fingers; four new electric belt sanders; three new vacuum cleaners for home shop use; a quarter-inch compact air drill; a new air sander for contour sanding in the automotive repair field; a low-cost pneumatic stud gun capable of inserting studs in snow tires; two new electric lawn mowers; a cordless electric screwdriver, and an experimental battery-powered drill for a lunar tool kit, designed to obtain core samples from the moon's crust.

Skil   Producer of a line of industrial power tools, drills, grinders, rotary hammers, sanders, polishers, saws, wrenches, and drivers. The company also makes heavy portable construction tools such as concrete vibrators, generators, breaker hammers, soil compactors, and power concrete trowels and screeds. In addition it produces auto repair tools such as grinders, polishers, sanders, and wrenches and a line of consumer items including lawn and garden tools. About 40% of the company's business is in products that were not in the product line five years ago. A recent innovation was a reversible, speed-control drill.

Signode   One of the great industrial changes in recent years has involved the ability to "unitize" loads of materials or products. Only a relatively few years ago such products as bricks, lumber, tires, crates, and boxes of all kinds were loaded loosely onto carriers. Today such items are tightly strapped in large units, often attached to a pallet, so that they can be handled swiftly and easily by fork lift trucks and other equipment. Signode is a leader in such unitizing and packaging. It makes steel and plastic strapping, the machines to apply the strapping under tension and automatic nailing and stapling tools. The company is strong on innovation. New products include: a machine that tightens twenty-ton steel coils like a watch spring, and then straps them while they are still at red heat; a tool that makes a strong welded joint in nylon plastic strapping without metal seals or adhesives and without applied heat or electricity; an air-powered, magazine-loaded nailer that can drive at the rate of one hundred a minute, the 16d or 3½-inch nails commonly used in house construction; a machine for automatically stacking and strapping bricks, resulting in handling cost savings for the mason contractor about one-fourth of the cost of the brick.

Caterpillar Tractor   Within the memory of men aged fifty or more, earth moving was done by horses pulling hand-controlled scoops. Today powerful crawlers and wheeled vehicles move tons of earth in a matter of minutes. Caterpillar produces these great Diesel-powered tractors, scrapers, graders, and loaders, as well as Diesel and gas turbine engines. The equipment is used in construction of highways, dams, railways, pipelines, port facilities, airports, reservoirs, canals, farm ponds, and terraces. Large crawlers clear jungle and brush to make land tillable and till farmland. Crawler loaders remove red-hot slag from metal melting furnaces, handle refuse in sanitary land-fill operations. A subsidiary, Towmotor Corporation, produces lift trucks and carriers used in warehouse operations and stevedoring. Caterpillar "total energy" sets supply electric power, heat and air-conditioning to office and apartment buildings, schools, shopping centers, hospitals, and motels. The company sells principally through independently owned dealerships with 816 worldwide sales and service locations.

PETROLEUM INDUSTRY

Worldwide demand for petroleum products has been rising at a rate of around 7% a year compounded and, despite experiments with electric automobiles, it probably will be a long time before gasoline is supplanted as a fuel. Oil companies continue to find sufficient reserves to keep this rate of expansion going. In addition, companies are diversifying by acquiring coal and nuclear fuel reserves and by getting into the production of petrochemicals and fertilizers. The industry has low labor costs and its reserves in the ground may be expected to rise in value at least as fast as the general price level and thus provide a hedge against inflation.

Texaco   A leading international oil company that sells directly through its own retail outlets the full range of petroleum products it refines from each barrel of crude oil. Thus the company retains within its own organization the profits from production and sale of each refined product from gasolines and lubricants to jet fuels and fuel oils. It is one of the few companies to serve the motoring public in every one of the fifty states. Texaco also produces petrochemicals, fertilizers, and, in Western Europe, coal. Company research is going ahead on more efficient methods of recovering oil from shale.

Gulf Oil   This large, integrated, worldwide producer and marketer of petroleum products traditionally produces more crude oil than it refines and sells through its own facilities, making it one of the largest marketers of crude oil. It owns half of Kuwait Oil Company, Ltd., which operates one of the largest oil fields in the world. Recently Gulf has brought its production and marketing into better balance by raising the number of U.S. service stations to 33,600, located in forty-eight contiguous states and the District of Columbia. Gulf owns coal mines that produce eight million tons yearly of bituminous coal. The company also is a major supplier of chemical, petrochemical, agricultural, and plastic products and, through joint operations with other companies, produces synthetic rubber, vinyl chloride, and fertilizers. In addition to oil and gas production and exploration, Gulf also has active exploration programs under way for deposits of such minerals as phosphate, potash, sulfur, and uranium.

Phillips Petroleum   This company is one of the industry's most diversified low-cost producers and marketers. It now markets gasoline in all fifty states. It is the largest producer on liquefied petroleum and a leader in petrochemicals and plastics. It also produces synthetic rubber, Philblack, an oil furnace carbon black, butadiene, fertilizers, synthetic fibers, helium, and other chemicals. The company recently has gone into the paperboard and plastic container field. It conducts a broad petroleum and petrochemical research program that also includes textiles and air purification. It also conducts atomic energy research for the AEC.

Continental Oil   Once largely a domestic company, Conoco has expanded into an international organization with production facilities in Libya and the Arabian gulf, Canada, Latin America, Europe, and Australia. Through its ownership of Consolidation Coal Company, Continental holds an important position in supplying fuel for the generation of electric power. It produces natural gas liquids, chemical raw materials such as ethylene and vinyl chloride monomer, and is a top fertilizer marketer under the brand name Agrico.

ELECTRIC UTILITIES

The Federal Power Commission has estimated that by 1980 electric power consumption in the U.S. will be three times the 1964 level, which would mean an annual growth rate for the industry of 7% compounded. By 1980 the number of electrically heated homes in the U.S. is expected to rise to 18,000,000 from the 2,500,000 of 1965. Customers for space heating alone are expected to rise from around 2,000,000 to 20,000,000. The labor factor of the electric power industry is relatively low, being around 15% compared to 30% for average industrial companies. Larger and more efficient generating plants are being constructed, many using nuclear power. Economies are being effected by increased use of automation and the purchase of coal on contract by the trainload.

Tampa Electric   Florida population is growing twice as fast as the population of the U.S. The Tampa area shares in this growth as indicated by the fact that in a recent year Tampa Electric's sales to residential customers increased by 14%. Industrial growth around the Tampa area is equally impressive. Sales of electricity to industry other than phosphate production has been growing at 12% a year, while sales to the fast-expanding phosphate industry has grown at about 18% annually. Fuel costs have been cut as transportation companies have begun booking bulk cargo from Tampa Bay to the Mississippi Valley area and passing on part of the cost savings in reduced charges for bulk coal shipped down from the Western Kentucky coal fields.

Houston Lighting & Power   Houston is booming to such an extent that it has been predicted that by the end of this century the metropolitan area may be the largest in the country. As a result of the locating of the Manned Spacecraft Center near Houston, some one hundred space-oriented firms have sprung up nearby. Houston Lighting & Power, in addition to serving these companies and a rapidly growing population, serves fast-growing manufacturers of chemicals, petroleum products, steel, petrochemicals, paper, oil tools, food products, cement, building materials, ships, aluminum products, synthetic rubber, natural gas, and petroleum, sulfur, salt, magnesium, tin, and agriculture including cotton, rice, livestock feeds, and cattle raising. The industries are served by the busy ports of Houston and Galveston. In the last ten years the per share earnings of this utility have grown at a rate of 8% compounded annually.

Iowa-Illinois Gas and Electric   This company, located in the heartland of American agriculture, supplies electricity and gas to important processing centers for corn and other grains and livestock. Industrial and commercial activity in the area also is expanding. The company owns a one-quarter interest in the Quad-Cities Nuclear Generating Station, the balance being owned by Commonwealth Edison.

Florida Power   This utility serves an area from the Georgia-Florida line along the Gulf Coast to St. Petersburg and through the central part of Florida including the Disney Park, various space age companies associated with activities at Cape Kennedy, as well as phosphate- and citrus-producing enterprises.

Gulf States Utilities   One of the major petrochemical centers of the world is served by this utility. The area includes southeastern Texas and south-central Louisiana, encompassing the cities of Port Arthur, Beaumont, Baton Rouge, and Lake Charles. The industry in the area, besides chemicals and synthetic rubber, includes shipping, production, and distribution of oil and gas, oil refining, production of rice, cotton, sugar, cattle, lumber, paper, and cardboard.

American Electric Power   This utility supplies power to the industrial heartland of America and does it at low cost and with high efficiency. It serves sections of Michigan, Indiana, Ohio, Virginia, Kentucky, West Virginia, and Tennessee, in which are located industries such as auto manufacturing, coal mining, production of ceramics, steel, textiles, plastics, paper, chemicals, glass, cement, and rubber. Natural resources are plentiful, including coal, gas, oil, limestone, clay, molding sand, salt, and iron ore. American Electric Power is the largest producer of electric energy among the investor-owned electric utilities in the United States.

LIFE INSURANCE

Policies sold and in force over a twelve-year period have tripled, a fact that makes this one of the faster-growing industries—certainly the fastest in the financial field. A new period of growth is at hand as the war babies born in the late 1940's reach the age at which they begin to raise families and feel the need for insurance protection. The industry well may grow at a rate of 8% compounded over the next decade due to increasing population and marriages and a higher standard of living. Another favorable factor stems from the fact that the vast U.S. program to improve the nation's health probably will result in future death claims being less than those predicted by present mortality tables. The industry has largely been automated so that rising labor costs are not a large factor. It also enjoys certain tax advantages. Stocks of life insurance companies have ranged rather widely up and down in response to investor enthusiasm and apathy.

Aetna Life & Casualty   This is the nation's largest multiple-line company in terms of premium income, assets, and life insurance in force. In 1966 its sales of new individual life insurance policies was at twice the industry average. The company's casualty and surety subsidiary has one of the lowest expense ratios in the industry. Aetna was one of the first two insurance companies to be named to participate in Medicare. Through association with its European affiliate, it has begun writing insurance on an international basis. The company also has entered the field of variable annuities.

The Travelers   This is the second largest multiple line stock insurance group in the United States. It has the largest amount of life insurance in force of the stock companies, and in one recent year the rate of increase in the sale of individual life insurance was twice that for the industry. The company writes all lines of insurance. It has pioneered in the use of a central computer system to serve agents and customers.

Franklin Life   This is one of the top ten U.S. stock companies in size, and is the world's largest legal reserve stock life insurance company engaged solely in the underwriting of individual ordinary life insurance policies and annuity contracts. Insurance in force has tripled over a ten-year period. Continental, a fire and casualty company, in recent years has acquired a substantial ownership of Franklin Life and should bring to the latter company, through Continental's large agency system, considerable life insurance business.

Continental Insurance Companies This group has concentrated on fire and allied lines, auto, general liability, workmen's compensation, accident and health, and fidelity and surety insurance. Recently, however, it acquired a substantial interest in the Franklin Life Insurance Company. Continental also has a growing insurance business overseas. The company currently enjoys a large annual net income from its well-managed investment portfolio. The Continental Insurance Company, the parent, has paid dividends every year since its organization in 1853.

RECREATION

As the work week shortens, vacation time lengthens, retirement comes sooner, and discretionary income increases, Americans find more time and money for recreation. And the companies that cater to leisure pursuits are benefiting.

Eastman Kodak For ten years the photographic industry has grown on average at more than twice the rate of growth of the Gross National Product. In more recent years, the industry's growth has been about 18% a year. Kodak, traditional leader in amateur photography, participates also in the growing fields of plastics, chemicals, and fibers. The company produces audio-visual teaching aids, printing and publishing materials, X-ray film and processors, office copiers and duplicating products, microfilm and information handling equipment, film for Hollywood and the television industry, vitamin concentrates, and food additives. Kodak spent about $100,-000,000 in 1967 on research and development and about $210,-000,000 to improve and enlarge manufacturing facilities in the U.S.

Howard Johnson's This company and its licensees operate one of the largest and best known restaurant and motor lodge chains in the world. In addition to Howard Johnson's restaurants and motor lodges, the company operates Red Coach Grills, markets HoJo Cola, and sells Howard Johnson's take-home foods and packaged ice cream through supermarkets and groceries. In recent years it has established a chain of self-service, no-tip HoJo Junction restaurants. By 1970 it expects to have in operation 1000 restaurants and from 450 to 500 motor lodges.

GLASS

Glass, which once was only a brittle and fragile material for windows and bottles, today has myriad applications in the home and industry. The material has been given strength and heat resistance undreamed of a generation ago. Glass fibers are in use as insulation, in textiles, and as reinforcements for plastic boat and auto bodies, radar domes, and other industrial and aerospace products.

Corning Glass Works   This company makes some fifty thousand different glass products and the list keeps growing. Included are consumer products such as heat-resistant kitchenware, lamp bulbs, fluorescent tubing, Steuben crystal, glassware for laboratories and for the chemical industry; windows for Gemini and other space capsules, tubes for color television and integrated circuit chips and microcircuitry modules for the electronics industry. Recent developments include photochromic glass that darkens in sunlight and clears in shade. Research is being conducted in fluidics. The company owns 31% of Owens-Corning Fiberglas, the leading producer of fibrous glass, 50% of Pittsburgh Corning, maker of glass building blocks and cellular glass, and 50% of Dow-Corning, manufacturer of silicone products.

MISCELLANEOUS

Minnesota Mining and Manufacturing   This is one of the most spectacular growth companies in the world. In some forty years its sales have risen from five million dollars a year to well over a billion. Its earnings per share have grown at an average rate of 13% compounded for more than twenty-five years. The company produces some thirty-five thousand different products including the following: Scotch brand pressure-sensitive tapes, coated abrasives, adhesives, magnetic recording, computer and video tapes, tape recorders, reflective sheeting, roofing granules, photographic film, presensitized lithographic plates, electrical insulation materials, medical products, office copying machines and copying papers, microfilm systems, and wood-grained laminates for automotive and furniture markets. A new product is an electronic beam recorder for recording black and white TV signals directly on motion picture film.

The above examples give only an abbreviated idea of the tremendous variety of well-managed, fast-growing companies available to the serious investor. Browse through Standard & Poor's Stock Reports or some other advisory service and you will find many, many more. Their versatility and vitality are such that you'll probably find more attractive opportunities than your money will cover. If you pick the best of those that appeal to you, using the criteria outlined in this chapter, you should have an investment that will grow very satisfactorily over the years ahead.

CHAPTER 6

The Stock Market

One of the wonders of modern business organization and communication is the ease with which you can buy or sell a stake in any one of some fifty thousand publicly held companies. Actually, anyone with established credit who can get to a telephone can buy or sell shares in the smallest or the largest publicly owned company in less time than it ordinarily would take to buy a ready-made suit or a week's supply of groceries. The stock market, in fact, is like a huge department store. The investor in stocks can have a charge account, can order by phone, and have the goods delivered or held in "will call." The "goods," of course, consist of part ownership in some manufacturing company, a railroad, or a company that engages in any one of a thousand different kinds of business. Thus for a given number of dollars you can become part owner of the company that produces your electricity or that made your auto, your television set, or the popcorn vending machine at the neighborhood movie theater. You should remember, though, that the price tags aren't fixed. You can return the goods but you will not get back exactly the amount you paid. You may get less or you may get more. This is because once a company has sold a big block of stock to the public, the shares keep circulating around. People buy them, hold them for a while, then sell them to someone else for whatever happens to be the going price. The amount of this buying and selling is almost unbelievable. In one day, fifty thousand shares of one company's stock can change hands. And remember that there are thousands of these stocks being traded every day.

THE MARKET PLACES

The New York Stock Exchange   Stocks are traded pretty much everywhere in the country. But the best known market place is the

New York Stock Exchange. On its floor, which is two-thirds the size of a football field, about a thousand men mill about all day buying and selling, sometimes for their own accounts but mostly for customers all over the country who have sent in orders via brokerage houses. Another thousand men on the floor are busily engaged in keeping track of the transactions and seeing that a record of each is kept and the price put onto the ticker tape for everyone else to see.

Not just any old stock can be bought or sold through the New York Stock Exchange. It limits its trading to the stocks of about 1300 of the largest and most widely owned companies. Nevertheless, each weekday except Saturday, some six million to ten million, and sometimes more, shares of these stocks change hands on the floor of the exchange. The floor itself resembles the floor of an armory or convention hall except that scattered across it are small horseshoe-shaped islands. Each island is a trading post, the headquarters for seventy-five or so stocks. Along the sides of the floor are large open-sided phone booths, each phone connected by direct wire to some brokerage house.

On a busy day a couple of thousand men crowd into the floor. About half of them are members who own seats (often financed by their firms). The other half are messengers, pages, and clerks. There are many other men visible but they are not strictly speaking on "the floor," being required to stay inside the trading posts or behind a painted line that runs along the edge of the floor in front of the phone booths. Observed from the visitors' gallery above the floor, these two thousand men, shouting and writing hurriedly on scraps of paper, appear to be milling about aimlessly. But pick out one man and watch him for a while and you will see that his behavior is far from aimless. He may start out from a phone booth along the wall and begin threading his way across the floor. He eventually ends up at a particular trading post where he exchanges a few brief shouts with one or two men standing there, writes on a pad, then threads his way back to the same phone booth from whence he came.

Now let's trace an order from a man who lives, say, in Houston, Texas, who wants to buy one hundred shares of a stock, for example the XYZ Oil Company (name fictitious). He need only phone his order to an account executive or customer's man in a Houston brokerage house, who in turn sends a message over a teletype to the firm's New York office. There the order is immediately phoned to a clerk on duty at a booth along the side of the exchange. The clerk pushes a button which causes a number to turn up on a big annunciator board high up on the wall. Each member keeps an eye on the part of the board where his number is located. When he sees that "his number is up" he hurries from wherever he is to the booth to pick up the order which in this case is "Buy one hundred XYZ at the market." The member threads his way to the spot where he knows that XYZ is traded. The outside rim of each post is divided into sections labeled A, B, C, D, etc. Ten or fifteen different stocks may be traded at each section. In particular, practically all trading in XYZ stock—five or ten million shares a year—takes place at one of these sections, no matter in what part of the world the buyers and sellers happen to be. In similar spots around the exchange are traded millions of shares of other stocks. This is the secret of the ready and continuous market available to investors.

As the member with the buy order from Houston approaches the post, he sees several other members standing there, so he calls out, "How's XYZ?" Note that he gives no hint as to whether he wants to buy or sell. Someone answers with a price spread, for example, "52—a quarter," meaning that $52 a share is the highest price that anyone is willing to pay for XYZ at the moment and that $52.25 a share is the lowest price at which anyone is willing to sell. Now if the member had a big block of XYZ to sell or buy, that is, quite a few hundred shares, he might ask for the size of the market, that is how many shares were for sale at 52¼ and how many were wanted at 52. But since his order is only for a hundred shares, the minimum amount traded at the post, he likely begins to bargain, saying "52⅛ for a hundred." Note that if he could buy 100 for that price he would better the market by an eighth of a point and save the purchaser $12.50. At that point a quotation page at the post, hearing a new bid an eighth above previous bids, pencils the bid and asked quotations on an IBM card which is placed in a card reader. The reader, in turn, scans the pencil marks and transmits the information up to the quotation room computer, where current bids and offers on all stocks are instantly made available by telephone to inquiring member firms.

If nobody takes the member up on his offer to buy one hundred shares at 52⅛, he may wait around for a while in hopes of buying at this price. Suppose in the meantime another member does arrive asking, "How's XYZ?" He has an order from one of his firm's clients in Jacksonville, Fla., to sell one hundred at the market, although he does not reveal this detail. He is told, "52⅛—a quarter." The newcomer says, "Sold a hundred at 52⅛." A stock exchange employee called a reporter at once jots this information down and inserts it into the reader which scans it and sends it to the ticker room computer so that in a few seconds the transaction will appear on the high-speed tape, which is duplicated almost immediately in member-firm offices all over the country. Each member then makes a written notation to send back to his own firm, showing the name of the stock, the number of shares bought or sold, and the name of the firm on the other end of the deal. No written communication is exchanged between the members. They have made a verbal contract, and in all the history of the exchange, while there may have been honest misunderstandings, no member has ever reneged. Following the transaction, each member makes his way back to his firm's phone booth on the side of the floor. The clerks phone the results of the deal to their offices where the information is put on wires to Houston and Jacksonville. Within a matter of minutes, the man in Houston learns that he has bought one hundred XYZ at 52⅛, plus commission, while the man in Jacksonville learns that he has sold one hundred at the same price minus commission and a small transfer tax. On the fourth business day following the transaction, actual shares of stock will be delivered by the selling firm to the buying firm and the certificate will be sent to Houston via XYZ Company's transfer agent.

From that example you can see that the stock exchange is an auction market. The highest bidder, the member representing the buyer, bought from the lowest offerer, the member representing the seller. The deal was arrived at openly and audibly so that all members in the vicinity had an equal chance to interpose by making better bids or offers. Had two bid the same price simultaneously, the matter would have been decided by matching coins. Not all transactions on the exchange, however, are quite as simple as the one outlined above. Suppose that a member wanting to buy 100 shares of XYZ arrives at the post and finds the lowest offer is 52¼. He offers to pay 52⅛, but no one steps up with 100 shares to sell. What does the member do? Since he has an order to buy at the market, the best he can do, obviously, is to buy at the offered price of 52¼. If he does so, from whom does he buy? Chances are in this case that he buys from the person who originally informed him that the market was "52—a quarter." This person is "the specialist," a member whose main job it is to maintain a fair and orderly market in certain stocks assigned to him by the Board of Governors. He stands at his post all day, furnishing current quotations and holding himself ready to buy and sell as required.

The specialist   Each section of each trading post has its own specialist. Sometimes there are several who specialize in the same stocks. From time to time the specialist writes out current quotations on a slip so that a reporter may send them up to the stock exchange quotation room.

One reason for the specialist is that most large orders from professional money managers are not put in at the market but at a particular price. Thus a trust fund officer, instead of ordering his broker to buy at the market might have ordered him to buy a block of XYZ at 51½. He would have realized that this was three-quarters of a point below the lowest offer, but he would have hoped to get his shares during a dip in the price. He could make his offer good for just one day, or good for one week, a month, or until canceled. Similarly, another investor, instead of ordering his broker to sell at the market, could have instructed him to sell at 53. Such orders at a particular price are known as limit orders.

Now when a member comes to the post with a limit order, say an order to buy XYZ at 51½, he can't stand around waiting for the market to dip to that level. That might take a day, a week, or a month. And in the meantime he has other orders to fill at other posts. But the specialist, who is always standing at his post, will take the order for him and agree to execute it if and when XYZ dips to 51½. In return for this service the specialist receives part of the member's brokerage commission. In this type of transaction he is a broker's broker. Thus the specialist may have various orders to buy XYZ from 52 all the way down through 51, 50, 49, and even down to 40 if some investor is optimistic enough to think that someday he can get it for that price. On the other side of the specialist's book might be orders to sell starting at 52¼ and going up through 53, 54, 55, and so on, perhaps to 60.

The specialist's book also may contain limit sell orders *below* the market and buy orders *above* the market. This happens in the following way. Suppose an investor had bought XYZ at 40 and it has risen to 52. He had a twelve-point profit but did not want to sell because he hoped it might go higher. However, to protect his gain, he might put in a "stop-loss" order instructing his broker to sell him out automatically if the stock went down and hit 50. This order would end up on the specialist's book. Conversely, a man who had sold short at 52, that is, sold the stock without actually owning any in the hopes that he could buy it back at a lower price, might put in a buy-stop order at 54. Thus if he had guessed wrong and the stock began to rise instead of fall, his losses would be cut because his broker would have arranged for an automatic purchase at 54 to cover his short sale. The member handling this limit buy order would also give it to the specialist, who would enter it in his book.

As it turns out, then, the specialist has a book full of all kinds of orders "away from the market," that is, either higher or lower than the current trading level. Remember that limit orders are actually the majority of all orders placed. This may be hard to realize if you are a person who buys or sells stocks only occasionally because you probably do so "at the market." But professional investors and traders prefer orders at a specific price.

Ordinarily, then, even if there is no great activity in a stock, there are still plenty of actual bids and offers on the specialist's book, and even though there may be no other members around, the specialist is ready to give a bid and offer. The bid will be the highest bid he has in his book, which in the case of XYZ might be 52, and the offer might be the lowest offer, which might be 52¼. But what if there were so little interest in XYZ and so few limit orders in the book that the highest bid was only 51 and the lowest offer 54? That would seldom happen in a widely traded stock, but it might in an issue that was less active. Such a three-point spread would be undesirable in the view of the Board of Governors of the exchange. The board prides itself on "close markets" and "continuity" in price movements. Thus under ideal conditions there should be small fluctuations between successive trades. An investor hates to think that a stock he has just bought for $54 a share would, if sold back a few minutes later, bring only $51. So if it happens that the highest bid on the specialist's book is 51 and the lowest offer 54, the specialist is expected to do something about it. Specifically, he is supposed to "improve" the market by certain judicious buying and selling for his own account. Thus he can arbitrarily narrow the 51–54 gap by offering to buy for his own account at 52 or sell at 53.

Any customer will thereby be saved a point, or $100 per round lot (100 shares).

This combined role of the specialist as broker for others and dealer for himself caused considerable criticism in the years following the stock market crash of 1929. In the heyday of the boom, specialists had participated in pools and helped rig markets. Today, however, the specialist works under stringent rules and the strict scrutiny of the Board of Governors of the stock exchange. He is supposed to trade "against the trend" most of the time. In other words, he is supposed to slow rapidly declining markets by buying stock for his own account even if he doesn't particularly want it. He also is supposed to slow rapidly rising markets by supplying stock, selling short if necessary. That means selling stock he does not own but which he borrows to deliver to the buyer. Later he must buy an equivalent amount to return to the lender. If the price goes up in the meantime, he is in the position of having to pay more for the stock than he originally sold it for.

Where, you might ask, does a specialist borrow as much as ten thousand shares of stock when he has to sell that much short? Officers, directors, and large stockholders of a given company usually make large blocks of stock available for lending to specialists and other members.

Here are a few of the rules that a specialist must observe.

He may not, under pain of expulsion, buy or sell stock for his own account at a price at which he holds an order to buy or sell for a customer. He must pay an eighth of a point more or sell for an eighth less.

A specialist must be able to buy and hold at least four hundred shares of each of the stocks in which he is a specialist. In actual practice he has capital to buy or sell a good deal more than four hundred shares. This is a precaution to enable him to slow down runaway markets should they occur.

When a specialist wants to fill a limit order entrusted to his care by buying from or selling to himself, he must first send for and get the approval of the floor member from whom he got the order. Thus if the broker doesn't think the price fair, no trade is consummated.

A specialist may not show his book to other members.

A specialist makes money on commissions for executing limit orders and by trading for his own account. But he constantly runs the risk of losing back a slug of his profits in a very short time. One of the specialist's jobs is to "open" the market. That is, in the few minutes before ten o'clock in the morning of each trading day he studies his book and determines from the buy and sell orders the fair bid and offer prices to be announced at the opening. Sometimes overnight news will have caused either a flood of buy or a flood of sell orders with no balancing sellers or buyers. It then becomes the specialist's duty to step in and make a market. This may require heavy buying or selling for his own account until bids and offers reach a balance.

As you can see, the role of the specialist is vital. What makes it so is the size of the exchange's business. Years ago specialists were not needed. The members originally sat around a table at their designated "seats" (a term still used to describe a membership) while the president read off the names of the stocks, one by one. If a member wanted to buy or sell, he shouted out his bid or offer. Gradually, this formal method broke down into a general auction at which brokers shouted their bids and offers at any time. Then, as volume grew, it became customary for members interested in particular stocks to congregate at certain definite points on the floor. The first specialist is said to have been a member who broke his leg and who therefore had to sit in one place. He offered to hold and execute orders for other brokers.

Odd lots Now suppose that you order not 100 shares but only a small amount such as 10, in other words, an odd lot. This order would come in the same way to a phone booth at the side of the floor, but then instead of being handed to the firm's floor trader, it would be placed in a pneumatic tube that would carry it directly to the inside of the proper trading post. There the order would be time-stamped and placed on a hook. At each post several odd-lot dealers are constantly on duty. They fill all buy and sell orders themselves, occasionally running around to the outside of the post to obtain or get rid of round lots (100 shares) to balance their position. Odd-lot prices are not determined by the auction method directly. Rather they are tied to the prices of round lots. Thus when you buy an odd lot, you pay an eighth or a quarter of a point more than the next succeeding round-lot sale after your order is in possession of the odd-lot dealer. When you sell, you get an eighth or a quarter less. The differential is an eighth on stocks selling at 54% a share and under, a quarter on stocks selling at $55 or over. There is a slight compensation to the odd-lot investor in that his brokerage commission is $2 less than it would be on a round lot.

In the case of a 10-share order for XYZ, assume that the next round-lot sale after your order arrived was at 52½. At that moment you would be credited with a purchase of 10 shares at 52⅝. But your brokerage commission would be $2 less than if you had bought a round lot. Specifically, it would be 1% plus $7, or $12.26 minus $2, or $10.26.

There are two odd-lot houses on the New York Stock Exchange. Carlisle & Jacquelin and De Coppet & Doremus. Each workday evening they plunge into the mountainous problem of sorting out thousands of transactions of various sizes. To arrange for delivery of odd lots sold to customers, these firms must send round lots to the transfer agents of hundreds of companies and obtain stock certificates in various smaller sizes, including fractions. On the other side of the picture, they must assemble all the odd lots bought from other customers, arrange them in round-lot sizes, and get the little certificates transferred into big ones. If you don't think this keeps the clerks busy, remember that on an average day nearly a half million shares are bought in odd lots and an additional half million different shares are sold.

Incidentally, the question is sometimes asked, can you buy one share of stock on the stock exchange? The answer is yes. The brokerage commission is figured on the dollar value of the purchase. So the commission on one share of a stock costing $250 a share is the same as that on five shares of a stock costing $50 a share. Of course, if you buy one share each of five different stocks, that means five transactions with all the incidental paper work. Even so, if that is your considered decision as to how to invest, you should go ahead and do it. Many of today's fortunes were founded years ago on the purchase of a few shares of good stock here, others there. It's not the quantity you buy each time so much as what you pick.

AMEX—The American Stock Exchange This exchange, a little brother to the New York Stock Exchange, has a colorful history. The first organized market in securities in New York sprang up well over one hundred years ago under a buttonwood tree on lower Wall Street. In the street and on the sidewalks, robust traders sold stocks to each other and to the public, rain or shine, by shouting their bids and offers and making hand signals. There are people alive today who can remember when the American Stock Exchange, then called the Curb, operated outdoors. It was a colorful sight, the brokers wearing different colored hats for identification, and buying and selling by sheer lung power, all the while sending secret wigwagging, head-scratching, or hat tipping signals to their clerks leaning out of office windows above. Eventually in 1920, long after the more dignified New York Stock Exchange members had begun meeting around a table and making their bids and offers in orderly and quiet fashion, the Curb also moved indoors. Today, however, the AMEX still retains some of its early speculative flavor. The stocks it lists and trades are generally those of newer and less seasoned companies than those listed on the NYSE. In 1961 and 1962, the U.S. Securities and Exchange Commission, charged with regulation of the securities markets, made some telling criticisms of the way in which the Board of Governors, the standing committees, and the specialists of AMEX operated their exchange. As a result, numerous reforms and organizational changes were made and the self-policing policies of the American Exchange were brought closer into line with those of the NYSE.

Other exchanges   The New York Stock Exchange handles 80% of the dollar trading volume in "listed" securities; that is, stock listed on any exchange. The American Stock Exchange, also located in New York City, handles another 11.5%. The balance of transactions in listed stocks is handled by some fourteen regional exchanges scattered across the country. The chief ones are the Boston, Midwest, Philadelphia-Baltimore-Washington, Pacific Coast, Cincinnati, Detroit, and Pittsburgh Stock exchanges. In addition there are mining exchanges, specializing in shares of gold and other mines, in Salt Lake City and Spokane, and very small exchanges in Colorado Springs, Honolulu, and Richmond, Va. There is one other exchange in New York City, the National Stock Exchange, founded in 1962, which lists the stocks of only a handful of companies. Most of these regional exchanges have a long history. Those in the East were started in the early days of the republic. Those in the Midwest and the West sprang up to promote development of industry and commerce as civilization spread west. San Francisco's first exchange, for example, was opened in 1862 to help finance mining ventures. A Los Angeles stock exchange was organized in 1900 with expansion of California's oil fields. The growing supply of local capital for Midwestern enterprises led to the organization of Chicago's first exchange in 1882. After World War II many of the local exchanges began to consolidate. The present Midwest Stock Exchange represents the merger in 1949 of the Chicago, Cleveland, Minneapolis-St. Paul, and St. Louis exchanges. The Pacific Coast Exchange was formed in 1957 by combining the San Francisco and Los Angeles exchanges. Today trading floors are maintained in both cities, and a modern communications system permits them to act as a single unit.

At first regional exchanges traded only local issues. But as time passed, many local companies grew bigger and eventually listed their stock on the New York exchanges in order to acquire nationwide distribution of their shares and to attract investment funds nationally. Other companies switched from regional exchanges to the over-the-counter market for similar reasons. To compensate for loss of local issues, regional exchanges began to handle securities that also were traded on the New York and American exchanges. Now over 90% of the dollar volume of trading on the regionals is in stock also traded on the NYSE and AMEX. The regional exchanges manage to stay in business because smaller brokerage firms that cannot afford seats on the NYSE can afford seats on the regional exchanges. And their memberships in the regionals permit them to buy and sell NYSE and AMEX securities, which they otherwise could handle only by turning transactions over to larger brokers and paying out part of the commission. Also the regional exchanges provide a means of splitting up large stock transactions when the very size of the deal might distort the price per share. If, for example, an investor were to try to buy three thousand shares of XYZ Company on the New York Stock Exchange, by the time he had purchased his first one thousand shares, the price might have begun to rise. Thus he might obtain a better price on the remaining shares by ordering them through a regional exchange. Prices on the regional exchanges generally parallel those on the NYSE.

Additional possible advantages to trading on regional exchanges include the following: because of the difference in time zones, the Pacific Coast Exchange is open two hours after the New York Markets close; some investors prefer to buy or sell national securities on regional exchanges because they can deal with local brokers whom they know and who offer special personal services; trading on regional exchanges can save transfer taxes especially when a large number of low-priced shares is involved, since the New York Stock

Exchange transfer tax, generally levied on the seller, amounts to from 1¼ to 5 cents a share; regional exchanges still provide a market for the securities of companies too small to qualify for listing on the big New York exchanges.

Over-the-counter markets   There are roughly fifty thousand companies whose stocks are bought and sold by investors. Of these, only some 2500 companies have their shares listed on any stock exchange. Of the remaining issues, many, of course, are inactive but some thirty thousand are traded outside the exchanges in what is known as the over-the-counter market. The basic differences between the two markets are these.

Trading on an exchange is concentrated in one place—the floor. There buying and selling is done by the auction method, bids and offers shouted out for all to hear. In the over-the-counter market, trading is done by negotiation over telephone and teletype wires by individual dealers who may be thousands of miles apart. If you put in an order for an over-the-counter stock, the order does not go to any central place, but is handled by the dealer you call. It may be that he has the shares you want in his own inventory, in which case he will sell them to you at his offered price. If he does not have them, he will shop by phone or teletype until he finds a dealer who does have the shares. In this case, he will buy them for you and resell them to you, perhaps at a small mark-up over the price he has paid. Or, he may simply charge you the price he paid plus a commission that usually matches the New York Stock Exchange rate.

The stocks traded on the New York Stock Exchange, and to a lesser degree on the other exchanges, tend to be only those of large and well-established companies that appeal to large numbers of investors and therefore are heavily traded every day. In the over-the-counter market you find almost all kinds of securities but they tend to be those that, for one reason or another, are less heavily traded. Over-the-counter dealers, in fact, will handle almost any kind of stock or bond for which there is any public demand. Thus in the over-the-counter market you can buy a good many stocks that actually are listed on the stock exchanges, plus issues of thousands of small, medium-sized, and fairly large companies that are traded locally or are not well known enough or seasoned enough to be admitted to trading on the exchanges. Specifically, the following kinds of securities are traded over the counter: practically all government, state, and municipal bonds; most corporate bonds; a large number of preferred stocks, many of them high grade; almost all stocks of banks and insurance companies; shares of mutual investment companies; and, of course, the aforementioned common stocks of companies of almost every size and description from American Express Company to Hialeah Race Course, Inc.

Prices of over-the-counter stocks are quoted in a different way from the prices of stocks listed and traded on exchanges. The ticker tapes of the exchanges tell the public the prices at which stocks actually are being bought and sold almost at the very moment. In the over-the-counter market, prices quoted are those at which dealers were prepared to buy or sell on the previous business day. Actual prices at which over-the-counter trades are made are not published, only bids and offers. And generally speaking these bid and offer quotations are not as "up to the minute" as the prices that appear on stock exchange ticker tapes. Thus when you buy in the over-the-counter market, you negotiate a deal based on much less definitive quotations.

At the present time there are some 1200 "member firms" who hold seats on the various exchanges. Most of these firms also maintain over-the-counter departments. In addition, there are several thousand broker-dealers who do not belong to any exchange but who concentrate on over-the-counter trading. These broker-dealers are representatives of the oldest form of securities market we have. Over-the-counter trading began during the earliest days of the republic when the Continental Congress and canal and turnpike companies raised capital by offering their stock and bonds to the public. The actual offerings were made through banks. Thus a bank generally kept a supply of securities on hand and when a customer wanted to buy a particular stock or bond, he would pay the bank by check or cash and the banker, in turn, would hand the security over the counter. The price would be a matter of negotiation between the bank and the buyer. In those early days, too, certain issues became very much in demand. It was natural that what the English called "stock jobbers" would begin buying and selling these popular issues as a full-time business. The first organized market sprang up under the famous buttonwood tree on lower Wall Street. Two groups, which eventually became the New York Stock Exchange and the American Exchange, moved indoors and developed the formal auction method of trading. But the negotiated trading, engaged in first by banks and later by dealers, continued to flourish and the two markets grew up side by side. Their early differences persist even to this day.

THE STOCK MARKET AS A MEASURE OF PRICES

A good deal of the machinery of the stock market is devoted to keeping track of prices. In fact, the common meaning of the term "stock market" simply is the general level of stock prices and the direction these prices seem to be moving. If the price trend is up, the market is strong, if the price trend is down, the market is weak; if not many shares are changing hands, the market is dull.

At all times, of course, some stocks are rising while others are falling. Nevertheless, the buyers and sellers are somewhat like sheep and tend to surge in one direction or another. Thus, if one large auto company comes out with a report that sales and earnings are off, owners of stock in all auto companies will begin to worry. They fear there may be something wrong with auto sales. So they may decide to sell their stocks, or at least not buy any more. If enough people decide to sell leading stocks, they may set off a trend which may cause many other stock prices to soften. This explains why millions of people are interested in the general price trend. But discerning and measuring the over-all trend of thousands of stocks is not easy. Here is how it is done.

The Dow-Jones Industrial Average   On a certain day the stock market, as measured by the Dow-Jones Industrial Average, rose 6.40 points. But oddly enough, out of the 1600-odd issues listed on the exchange only five actually matched this 6-point rise. And no well-known stock rose anything like 6 points. General Motors was up 1⅜, General Electric up 2, DuPont up 1, while Standard Oil of New Jersey was up only a half and A T & T only a quarter.

No wonder that the movement of the averages brings confusion to investors. And no wonder stockholders sometimes complain, "why can't my stock ever go up like the averages?"

Actually, the Dow-Jones and the other "averages" aren't true averages at all. The Dow-Jones Industrial Average, for example, is based on the prices of thirty leading stocks, beginning alphabetically with Allied Chemical and ending with Woolworth. Theoretically, if you add up the prices of these thirty stocks at any given time and then divide by thirty, you ought to get the Dow-Jones Industrial Average. But in practice you won't. To get the Dow-Jones Average as it is published every day, you divide not by thirty but by two and a fraction. Thus, actually, this makes the published average about 14 to 15 times higher than it would be if it were an ordinary arithmetical average.

Here is how this comes about. When the Dow-Jones Industrial Average was first compiled back in 1896, it was composed of twelve stocks and was computed by adding the prices of the stocks and dividing by twelve. Later there were twenty stocks and the sum of their prices was divided by twenty.

But then a problem arose. Companies began splitting their stock or issuing stock dividends. Thus, for example, if a stock selling at one hundred were split two-for-one, the company would issue stockholders two shares in place of every original share. Naturally, since ownership of the company would be represented by twice as many shares, and since the value of the company as a whole would not have changed, the market value of each share would be only half as much as it was originally, or around $50 a share.

You can see that this kind of thing would raise hob with an average. Suppose an average were composed of three stocks, Company A worth $30 a share, B worth $50, and C worth $70. The average would be 150 divided by 3, or 50. Then suppose that Company C split its shares two-for-one. Overnight its stock would drop from 70 to 35. The split would cause no loss to anyone since each stockholder would have twice as many shares, each one worth half as much as before. Yet the average, unless adjusted, would fall from 50 to 38⅓ (115 divided by 3), giving a false picture of what had happened to the stocks.

One way to correct this false impression would be to adjust the divisor. In this case, you could add the new prices of the three stocks —30 plus 50 plus 35—and still get an average of 50 if you divided the result by 2.3 instead of by 3. The adjusted divisor would compensate for the changes in the shares and give an average that more truly reflected the movement of the prices.

Over the years, then, the divisor has been adjusted in this way, shrinking each time. As a result, if the 30 stocks composing the Dow-Jones Average today rise an average of one point, the average itself will rise 14 to 15 points. To try to avoid this type of confusion, the *Wall Street Journal* and other publications show the change in percentages as well as in points. Thus if the average were 900 and dropped 9 points, the drop would be recorded also as 1%.

The Standard & Poor's Average   Standard & Poor's, which publishes a number of averages including a 425-stock industrial average, has tried to solve the problem of stock splits in another way. In compiling its average, it uses not the prices alone but the price of each stock multiplied by the number of shares outstanding. This avoids the use of an ever-shrinking divisor. The sum of all these amounts is related to a base period, 1941–43. This percentage is then divided by 10. The original idea of dividing by 10 was to keep the final index close to the average price of New York Stock Exchange stocks.

Nevertheless, Standard & Poor's Industrial Average already has moved away from the true, or flat, average of NYSE stocks. The true, or flat, average price of all stocks listed on the NYSE has for years run between $40 and $60 a share. In 1957, when Standard & Poor's started its new method of computing its Industrial Average, it stood at 47, while the flat average price of New York Stock Exchange stocks was about 49. Some ten years later the flat average price of NYSE stocks still stood at about $49 a share while the S & P Average had risen to nearly 100.

The heart of the matter can be put very simply. Over the years, a sum of money invested in stocks has tended to rise in value and will continue to do so. The popular stock market averages are designed to measure this rise and to provide the investor with a valid comparison with the past. Therefore, these averages also will continue to rise over the long run.

The NYSE and AMEX averages   The actual average per share price of all stocks listed on the New York Stock Exchange, however, probably will stay in the $40, $50, $60 range. The same is true of the American Exchange, although here the actual average price is in the $15 to $20 range. In 1966 both exchanges began publishing indexes of their own listed stocks. The NYSE Index is a "value" index reflecting both the price of a stock and the number of its shares outstanding. The AMEX Index runs along closer to the actual average price of all stocks on the exchange. Both indexes are less volatile than the Dow-Jones Average. Whenever the NYSE Index, which initially was between 50 and 60, reaches 100, it will be split two-for-one.

Usefulness of the averages   Now how can the Dow-Jones Industrials (thirty stocks) or the New York Times Industrials (twenty-five stocks) measure the movement of stocks numbering in the thousands?

Actually, an average composed of a relatively few stocks of large, widely owned companies in important industries seems to give about the same picture as one composed of several hundred. The Dow-Jones, New York *Times,* and Standard & Poor's Industrial Averages, along with the over-the-counter stock average, published by the National Quotation Bureau, run fairly parallel courses. For special purposes, of course, there are special averages. If you own railroad or utility stocks and want to compare their performance with that of similar stocks, there are Railroad and Utility Averages. Standard & Poor's compiles indexes of low-priced common stocks and high-grade common stocks, along with averages of representative stocks in dozens of industries. For example, there is an average of the prices of aerospace companies, air transport companies, aluminum companies, and so on.

Barron's Weekly carries similar group stock averages. The National Quotation Bureau, publisher of the "pink sheets" which show bids and offers in the over-the-counter market, compiles the average of Over-the-Counter Industrial Stocks.

The thing to remember about all these averages is that they are useful only in comparisons: today's market level with that of some period in the past; the performance of one group of stocks with another. The fact that the Dow-Jones Industrial Average rose six points yesterday or dropped five the day before in itself has little real significance. What is important is the average's long-term upward tilt. It proves that money invested in the past in a list of good quality industrial stocks, such as those included in the Dow-Jones, Standard & Poor's, or New York *Times* averages, would have grown substantially. And it indicates that money similarly invested in the future should do as well.

Other stock market measures Other statistics besides the averages are used to measure and classify each session of the stock market. Every day, of course, some stocks rise in price, while others fall. The ratio between the number that went up and the number that went down is significant. Sometimes you may find a disparity here. The Dow-Jones Average can go up while a majority of the 1600 stocks listed on the New York Stock Exchange can go down. If this seems baffling to you, don't worry. It baffles everyone. Another measure is the ratio between new highs and new lows. The price action of every listed stock is plotted day by day. As its price moves erratically up and down, it establishes a temporary range. Starting in January, a stock might move up and down in a range from 25 to 30. Then one day it might go to 30¼. That would be a new high for the year and would be so listed by the analysts. At some other point it might drop to 24¾, which would be a new low. Every day some stocks are making new highs, while others are making new lows. *The Wall Street Journal* and other newspapers publish the list. On a bad day there might be a hundred new lows and only a dozen new highs. On an exceptionally good day the ratio might be reversed.

Note two other measures, the daily volume and the list of most active stocks. The volume on the New York Stock Exchange generally ranges from six million to ten million shares. This range sometimes is violated either on the low or high side. If the volume dries up when the market is declining, that is an optimistic, or "bullish," sign. But if the volume increases as stock prices fall, that is bad or "bearish." Conversely, a rise on expanding volume is good, while a rise on a smaller volume is not. Each day the newspapers also list the ten or fifteen stocks most actively traded at the latest session. The list indicates the current fads among traders. And some traders make serious use of the list. If the most active list is largely made up of low-priced, speculative issues, the market is said to have poor leadership. But if the stocks of big, strong companies, known as "blue chips," are prominent in the most active list, the market's leadership is thought to be strong.

All in all, as you can see, the stock market is a complicated, volatile place, not easy to understand or keep track of. Fortunately, its daily gyrations are useful mostly as a conversation piece. The real problem in investing is to select the right stocks for your own purposes. And this is a problem that is not quite so hard to get your arms around.

CHAPTER 7

The Mechanics of Investing

Not many years ago a person with $500 or $1000 to invest would hardly have dared walk into a broker's office. Rightly or wrongly, he was afraid of being called a cheap skate. But times change. Today a good many brokers have put out the carpet for the small investor. They have decided that, to stay in business, they must broaden out and attract customers from further down the income pyramid. So even with a relatively small amount of capital an investor can walk into most brokerage houses as unconcernedly as he walks into his bank. No reason why he shouldn't! There is no longer anything particularly mysterious or exclusive about a brokerage house. A broker, like a banker, sells a financial service. Also like the banker, the broker will often give advice if asked. But that is not his real business, which is simply to provide the machinery for converting cash into securities and vice versa.

Your broker   What can you expect a broker to do for you? Even if you have a relatively small amount to invest, you can expect the average broker to:

❡ Treat you courteously.

❡ Spend a certain amount of his time helping you clarify your thinking on what kind of stocks you want to buy.

❡ Offer the use of advisory services or manuals.

❡ Give you current quotations on stocks you are interested in.

❡ Make for you whatever purchase or sale you decide on at the standard commission rate.

You should *not* expect *any* broker to:

❡ Spend an hour of his time discussing a small investment on which the commission will amount to only a few dollars.

❡ Help you decide whether or not you should invest at all. You should make that decision before you go in.

¶ Tell you whether the market is going to go up or down. No one knows that, not even your broker.

It is interesting to understand how this business works and who are the people you deal with, directly, or at the far end of the transaction.

The particular brokerage firm you deal with is strictly a matter of personal choice. If you were seeking one, you might do well to ask your bank or a businessman whose judgment you trust for a recommendation. In most towns there is a choice among several. There may be one or more branches of large New York houses as well as local firms who may, or may not, have membership in the New York Stock Exchange. Even if a local firm does not belong to the exchange it is likely to have a New York correspondent that handles its stock exchange business.

Unless you know your way among the local firms, you may want to choose one belonging to the New York Stock Exchange. The salesmen or customers' men employed by NYSE member firms must be registered representatives of the exchange, which means that they have served an apprenticeship and passed an examination given by the exchange. Also the NYSE does a tough policing job on its member firms, requiring them to maintain certain minimum liquid capital and restricting the trading and borrowing that the firm's partners may do. Each member firm receives one examination a year from the exchange's accountants and also one surprise audit from an independent accountant. In addition to the NYSE member firms in your town, there may, of course, be old, established houses with fine reputations who are nonmembers. When in doubt, however, choose a member firm, at least for a starter.

The man you deal with in the firm you choose will be a salesman. His title used to be customer's man. Today it is the more dignified "account executive." After you have dealt with him awhile, you simply refer to him as your "broker." But regardless of these titles, remember that his main job is to sell the services of his firm. And these services consist largely of handling buy and sell orders. Like any other salesman, a broker will give advice, if requested to, or often whether requested to or not. But that is not his real business. His real business is simply to provide the machinery for converting cash into securities and vice versa. And his income is pretty closely tied to the amount of this business he does.

No matter how fancy or simple it looks, a broker's office consists

essentially of salesmen, a ticker tape usually blown up and projected onto a screen so that anyone may see prices at which transactions on the New York and American exchanges are occurring, and
a teletype for sending orders rapidly to the floor of the exchange for
execution.

The older brokerage houses generally have a board, like the score-
board at a ball park, where prices of leading stocks are posted and
kept current and also the hourly level of the Dow-Jones Averages.
Opposite the board may be chairs for the professional traders and
speculators, or the professional "watchers" who like to follow the
continual fluctuations of the market.

Anyone can walk into a brokerage house and check the prices or
sit for a while and watch. In many offices an electronic gadget is available on which are lettered buttons. Punch in a symbol of a listed stock
and you will immediately get the latest quotation.

Opening an account   Opening an account with a brokerage house
is the simplest part of investing. (The hardest part, of course, is to
make money at it.) If you walk into a brokerage house absolutely
cold, the receptionist will introduce you to a salesman or "account
executive." When he learns which stock you are interested in, he will
get you a quotation, or current price. At the same time he will give
you a "new account" form to fill out, plus a signature card. The account form calls for your name, address, occupation, employer, and
bank reference, roughly the same information you would give in opening a charge account anywhere.

Several decisions are required at this point. Do you want a joint
account with right of survivorship, similar to the joint account you
and your spouse might have at your bank? Also, do you want the
stock certificate put in your name, or names, and delivered to you,
or do you want to leave it with the broker in what is called "street
name"? If you plan to hold your stock as a long-term investment, it
will save the brokerage house a lot of bookkeeping if you have certificates put in your own name. But if you plan to do quite a bit of buying
and selling, it will be more convenient to leave your stocks in street
name.

If you open a margin account, you will automatically leave your
stock in street name. Under present rules, you can buy stock only
by putting up a sizable hunk of the purchase price. The rest you
borrow from the broker, usually at interest of 6% or more. After you

once own your stock, theoretically, under NYSE rules, it can decline until your loan is three-quarters of the price before you have to put up more margin. Many brokers, however, have house rules that permit a decline only until the loan is two-thirds of the price. To open a margin account with most brokers requires at least $2000, which is applied to your initial purchase.

When you give your order to buy, you must decide whether you want to buy "at the market," in other words, pay the going price, or put in a "limit order" specifying that you will pay a certain price and no more. Such an order may be "open"; in other words, you can leave it with the broker indefinitely so that if the stock ever comes down to your price, you'll get it. Most orders by individual investors, however, are put in at the market. If you give such an order, you will, if you request it, receive confirmation of your purchase, along with the exact price paid and the commission, within a matter of minutes. A written confirmation will come along later.

COMMISSION RATES

Listed stocks Here is a table showing how the commission is figured on a round lot by the New York, American, and other major stock exchanges. A round lot is almost always one hundred shares. The commission is the same whether the order be a purchase or a sale.

COMMISSION ON EACH ROUND LOT

Money Value	Commission
Under $100	As mutually agreed, usually 6%
$100 to $399	2% plus $3.00
$400 to $2399	1% plus $7.00
$2400 to $4999	½% plus $19.00
$5000 and over	⅒% plus $39.00

In the case of an odd lot; that is, an order for less than one hundred shares, the commission rates are the same as above, less $2, but in any event not less than $6 per single transaction. Remember, too, that when you buy or sell an odd lot, you must pay the "odd-lot differential." This is, in effect, an extra charge for breaking up a round lot into smaller units. On the New York Stock Exchange the odd-lot difference is ¼ of a point for stocks selling at 55 or above, and ⅛ of a point for stocks selling at 54⅞ or below. On the American Stock Exchange the odd-lot charge is ¼ of a point for stocks selling at $40 a share or over, and ⅛ of a point for stocks selling below $40 a share. Note that on the NYSE there are a very few stocks where a round lot is 10 shares. On the AMEX some stocks are traded in round lots of 10, 25, or 50 shares. There are special odd-lot differentials involving these stocks which are best determined by inquiring of a broker.

It is important to keep in mind that when you buy or sell in multiples of 100 shares, the commission is figured separately on each round lot, then all commissions are added together. Thus the commission on 200, 300, 400, etc., shares, would be the applicable 100-share commission multiplied by 2, 3, 4, etc., respectively. In a case where you bought or sold, say 120 shares, the commission would be figured separately on a round lot (100 shares) and an odd lot (in this case, 20 shares). The two commissions then would be added to give the total charge. The odd-lot differential, of course, would be charged only against the 20 shares.

Once you get your confirmation, payment is not legally due until the fourth business day after the purchase. A few brokerage houses make it a practice to suggest immediate payment of all or perhaps half the amount. But you can be sure that when you sell they will wait until the fourth business day before giving you your money.

Over-the-counter stocks The way in which customers are charged for purchases or sales in the over-the-counter market is much less uniform than it is on the exchanges. Buyers and sellers for listed stocks are always available. The specialist sees to this. Thus commissions can be, and are, standardized. Over-the-counter dealers, however, undertake to handle a wide variety of securities, many of which are sparsely held and thinly traded. The problems of finding a buyer or seller often are unpredictable.

As an example, assume an investor wants to buy an over-the-counter stock known as First Consolidated (name fictitious). He asks for a quote from his broker. The broker looks up the stock in the quotation sheets and finds that half a dozen over-the-counter dealers make a market in this particular stock; in other words, they stand ready to buy or sell it at any time. The broker may then call two or three of these dealers to get a quote. He does not reveal whether his customer is a buyer or seller. Let us say that the quote is, in one case, 25½ bid,

26⅜ offered, in another, 25½ bid, 26¼ offered. The stock, then, can be bought by the broker for 26¼. But in order to pay his overhead and make a profit on the deal, he will have to charge the investor somewhat more. Perhaps he will quote his customer a price of 27. If this is agreeable, the broker will buy the stock at 26¼, resell it to the investor for 27, and make a mark-up of ¾ of a point or roughly 2¾% of the purchase price.

However, instead of marking up the stock, the broker in the above example could have resold it to his customer at the 26¼ price, and charged a commission. Some brokers who are members of the New York Stock Exchange, and who do most of their business in listed stocks, do charge the NYSE commission rate no matter whether a stock is listed or over-the-counter.

In the case of a sale, the seller most often receives the bid price and is charged a commission, usually equivalent to the NYSE rate. The reason why there may be a mark-up in the case of a purchase, and a commission in the case of a sale, is this. When the dealer sells a stock to a customer, he may go, or have gone, to considerable expense to make the deal. For example, he may have done a lot of research in order to be able to recommend certain issues that he thinks are desirable. Thus he may feel that a mark-up, which may be more than the NYSE commission rate, is justified. On a sale by a customer, however, no such merchandising is required. The customer simply has the stock and wants to sell. Thus the transaction is more or less cut and dried and the dealer generally will not mark the stock down but will charge a commission instead.

When you purchase or sell stock in the over-the-counter market, the mark-up or commission will depend on a number of factors: the kind of broker you are dealing with (big house, small house); the kind of security; how widely it is traded; the size of the transaction in dollars (the smaller the transaction the larger the mark-up or commission will be percentagewise), and so on.

Over-the-counter quotations The way the over-the-counter dealers keep track of the prices of the thousands of securities they deal in is rather intricate. Unlike New York Stock Exchange prices, which are prices at which transactions actually take place, over-the-counter quoted prices are bids and offers. The bid is what you might expect to receive, minus a commission charge, if you sold the security, while the offer is what the dealer will have to pay to get the stock for you (assuming he doesn't make a market in it himself). Thus the offer prices you see in the paper are not the prices you can expect to be charged. The dealer will either mark these prices up by, say 2% or 3%, or else will charge you the offer price plus a commission.

Here is how these bids and offers are ascertained and published. There is a central organization known as the National Quotation Bureau. Traditionally, between two o'clock and four o'clock each afternoon, each over-the-counter dealer who makes a market in any given security sends in the bid and offered prices at which he is willing to buy or sell. The information is then tabulated on what are known as the "pink sheets." These are simply legal-sized sheets of pink paper on which are printed alphabetically the names of the most widely traded over-the-counter stocks. After each stock appear the names of the dealers who make a market in it, along with their current bid and offer. These pink sheets are available in every brokerage house and may be inspected. Selected over-the-counter quotations are listed in the daily papers. Widely held stocks are listed on what is known as the "National List." In addition, most papers carry a separate list of stocks of local companies.

HOW TO BE A STOCKHOLDER

Your own name or street name   Once you have decided to be a stockholder, one of the first decisions you have to make is whether to have the certificate delivered to you or whether to leave it with the broker "in street name." Each course has its advantages and disadvantages. When you leave your certificate with the broker, he doesn't actually register the stock in your name. Instead, he carries the stock in his firm's name, along with hundreds or thousands of other shares in the same company, and makes a bookkeeping entry showing how many of those shares belong to you.

There are some advantages in this arrangement. The broker does a certain amount of bookkeeping for you. He receives dividends and credits them to your account, sending you a monthly statement. He also keeps the certificates in his vault and insures them against loss, fire, and theft. And even though the shares are in the broker's name, as long as you have paid for them and not borrowed against them, they are segregated; that is, the broker cannot lend them or put them up as collateral for loans.

Also, when your stock is in street name it is somewhat easier to sell. There is no problem about hunting up the certificate, endorsing it and taking it or mailing it to the broker. A simple telephone call will complete the job.

Last but not least, most brokers provide these services free. They do it, of course, to accommodate the big investors who own hundreds of shares of stock and who buy and sell frequently. Because of this, if your account is fairly small and if you don't intend to do much trading (which you probably shouldn't unless you are quite sophisticated) your broker may be reluctant to hold your stock in street name. He may even quote you a small service charge. This is because the commissions he will get from you probably won't pay for the cost of the safekeeping and the bookkeeping. So while theoretically the service is available to all customers, large or small, in actual practice whether you can use it or not depends on the house policy of the individual broker.

Now note that carrying stock in street name may have some disadvantages. As your dividends accumulate, they will be put into your account and may lie idle for a while and won't be drawing interest. There is a way to overcome this, however. Most brokers maintain a dividend watch list. If your name is on it, your dividends will be mailed to you as soon as the broker receives them.

Another point: Although fully paid shares held in street name are segregated, the cash in your account is not. It is mingled with the funds of other customers and the broker can use it in his business. So what happens when a brokerage house gets into trouble and goes through liquidation? Several years ago, when a NYSE house went bankrupt, the exchange stepped in with seven million dollars raised from other member firms. The customers with fully paid securities (that is, securities not in a margin account) received their stock and their cash within a couple of weeks. A longer delay was experienced by customers who held margin accounts, but in the end they also got their money out. This action by the NYSE was a precedent-setting case. Just what would happen to customers of a non-NYSE member firm, in case of bankruptcy, is not predictable.

There is also this to be said for having your stock registered in your own name: Company reports, proxy material, and dividends will come directly to you. When stock is held in street name, this material is forwarded to you by the broker and there can be some delay. Offsetting this, perhaps, might be the possibility that, as long as the broker holds your stock in street name, he'll remember you own it and may be expected to call you when he hears good or bad news about the company. Beware of the broker, however, who is always calling you up with good or bad news designed to persuade you to keep buying and selling.

Actually there is another arrangement in which you can have the stock registered in your name, but leave it with the broker along with a "stock power" which authorizes him to sell it on your order. One advantage to this is that dividends, annual reports, and notices come direct to you. Yet the broker provides safekeeping of your securities. Here again, most brokers are reluctant to make this arrangement where the account is small or inactive. The cost of safekeeping and taking inventory is too great. However, if you were going on a trip and wanted to leave your securities with the broker under this arrangement, he probably would accommodate you.

Single or joint ownership The next question to answer after buying stock might be whether to register it in a single name or in the joint names of husband and wife, mother and daughter, and so on. Registering in "joint name or the survivor" has three advantages. First, under the 1964 tax law revision, husband and wife can get a dividend exclusion of $200—as against $100 if the shares are in one name only. Second, if one person dies, the stock will pass directly to the other without going through probate. And since the executor's fees are generally based only on the assets in the probated estate, this will save on administration costs. Third, if the stock is in joint name, the survivor can get immediate possession. On the other hand, if the stock is in one name only, the survivor would have to wait for weeks or months to get the stock or the proceeds from its sale.

Of course, even when a stock is in joint name and one owner dies, the broker may be reluctant to accept a sell order from the other party without a good bit of identification and explanation. Nevertheless, if, for example, a husband and wife own stock jointly and the husband dies, the wife has the right to sell it and receive the proceeds.

If you want to have stock registered in the name of yourself and another person, or the survivor, it would be sensible to introduce the other person to your broker at the time of purchase and make sure that he understands that the other owner is the one that has the right to sell the stock.

What records? Where?   The best place to keep stock certificates, assuming they are not in street name, is in a bank safe-deposit box. And note that the box rental is deductible for income tax purposes. Before putting the certificate away, write down its number, the number of shares, the cost or value when acquired, and the name and address of the transfer agent. Put this information in a different place from the certificate itself. If you lose the certificate or it is destroyed, write at once to the transfer agent. You can get a new certificate, but you may have to buy an indemnity bond from a surety company to guarantee against some unauthorized person turning up with the original certificate and selling it by forging your name.

For tax purposes you should keep the confirmation slip you receive from your broker when you purchase or sell a stock. When you receive a dividend check, keep the attached explanation of the payment, if there is one, or the notification from the company. In addition, it is well to keep a stock and dividend record showing the name of company, number of shares owned, serial numbers of certificates, date purchased, commission and tax charged, net cost, amount of each dividend paid and when, date sold, price, commissions and charges, and net profit or loss. You can make up a form or buy one ready-made at a stationer's.

Can you borrow? How much?   Once you own stock you can put it up as collateral for a loan. One advantage is that such a secured loan almost always carries a lower interest rate than an unsecured note or an installment loan. Your bank will make what it calls a "nonpurpose" loan of from 50% to 75% of the market value of the stock, assuming it's of average or better quality. The percentage will depend on (1) the policy of the bank, (2) whether the stock is listed on an exchange, (3) the stock's quality, (4) how good a customer you are of the bank. In addition, many do not like to make a loan on just one stock but prefer to lend on a diversified portfolio.

One bank, for example, will lend 60% of the value of listed stocks and will go to 70% for its best customers, but will lend only 50% on unlisted stocks and then only to good customers. Another bank says it will lend 75% on good listed stocks and 66% on good unlisted stocks. These are called "nonpurpose" loans because, in the case of listed stocks, the proceeds may not be used to purchase or carry securities and the customer usually must sign a statement stating that the loan is not for this purpose. The interest charged on non-purpose loans is subject to negotiation between the bank and its customer. It might be 6% simple interest or less.

If you want to borrow money on your stock either to help pay for it or to pay for additional stock, you are making a margin loan. A margin account must initially have in it at least two thousand dollars of cash and/or securities. The Federal Reserve Board's margin regulations require you to put up a substantial amount of cash. The amount varies depending on the economic climate of the times. In recent years the regulations have required the buyer on margin to put up 70% in cash, which means that you could borrow only 30% of the stock's value. The easiest way to make such a loan is to do it through your broker. He will credit the money to your account and charge you the going rate of interest.

If you have borrowed against your stock and it goes down, you don't necessarily have to put up money right away. But if it continues to go down, at some point the lender will want part of the loan repaid. Brokerage houses generally insist that the loan be no more than two-thirds of the current value of the stock. Thus if you bought $1000 of stock on margin, putting up $700 in cash and borrowing $300, the value of your stock could then decline to $450. At this point the loan of $300 would be two-thirds of the value and any further decline would result in a margin call.

Bank policies vary. Some banks insist that the loan be no more than 75% of the value; others no more than 60%. Here's an example of the 75% rule. If $700 were borrowed against $1000 of stock and the value dropped to around $935, the bank might call for more collateral.

Keeping informed   To keep up on the affairs of a company, watch the financial pages of the newspaper and read the financial reports that are sent to stockholders. The financial reports in particular are valuable. They are audited, you can trust their accuracy, all right, but even so you can't be sure they'll tell you exactly what you want to know unless you can read between the lines a bit. Here's how.

Most annual reports look like magazines and are filled with pictures of the company's products and optimistic predictions for the future, but the heart consists of:

1. The balance sheet, which matches the firm's assets against its liabilities and shows the fundamental soundness of the company.

2. The income statement, sometimes called the statement of profit and loss, which shows how much the company made over the last year and, if you have the statements for the past several years, what the trend seems to be.

3. The footnotes, which might change the whole picture.

Probably the most commonly used stock-buying touchstones are the earnings per share and the price-to-earnings ratio.

Earnings per share—or rather the potential earnings per share— do most to determine the market price of the stock. To find the earnings available for common stock, start with the net income, subtract any dividend requirements on preferred stock, and divide what's left by the number of common shares outstanding.

To see how it works, look at the income statement of For Example, Inc. below. Net income is $505,000. Divide this by the number of common shares, 400,000 (from the balance sheet), and you get $1.26—earnings per common share. If the report had shown any preferred stock dividend requirements (say, $700,000 at 5%, or $35,000), you would have subtracted that from the net income and then divided by the number of common shares to get earnings per share.

CHART 21: FOR EXAMPLE, INC. INCOME STATEMENT*

Net sales		$7,000,000
Cost of sales and operating expenses		
Cost of goods sold	$4,500,000	
Depreciation	900,000	
Selling and administrative		
expenses	600,000	6,000,000
Operating income		$1,000,000
Other income		
Dividends and interest		100,000
Total income		$1,100,000
Other deductions:		
Interest on bonds		140,000
Income before taxes		$ 960,000
Provision for taxes		455,000
Net income for the year		$ 505,000

* Copyright by *Changing Times.*

CHART 22: FOR EXAMPLE, INC. BALANCE SHEET, December 31

ASSETS

Current assets			
Cash		$ 2,050,000	
Accounts receivable			$ 1,900,000
less: provision for bad debts		150,000	
Inventories			1,900,000
Total current assets			2,700,000
			$ 6,500,000
Property, plant, and equipment			
Land	200,000		
Buildings	4,000,000		
Machinery	1,000,000		
Office equipment	150,000		
	$5,350,000		
Less: accumulated depreciation	2,100,000		
Net property, plant and equipment			3,250,000
Deferred charges			150,000
Goodwill, patents, trademarks			610,000
Total assets			$10,510,000

LIABILITIES

Current liabilities		
Accounts payable	$1,500,000	
Notes payable	910,000	
Accrued expenses payable	200,000	
Income taxes payable	455,000	
Total current liabilities		$ 3,065,000
Long-term liabilities		
First mortgage bonds, 5% interest due 1970		2,800,000
Total liabilities		$ 5,865,000
STOCKHOLDERS' EQUITY		
Common stock, $5 par value authorized, issued, and outstanding 400,000 shares	$2,000,000	
Retained earnings	2,645,000	
Total stockholders' equity		4,645,000
Total liabilities and stockholders' equity		$10,510,000

In a healthy company, both net sales and earnings per share should increase yearly.

The price-to-earnings ratio is simply the ratio between the price of the stock and the earnings per share. To find it, divide the market price by the earnings per share. Say For Example sells for $18. Divide that by $1.26 and you get 14, which means that For Example's common stock is selling at 14 times earnings. This can be compared to the Dow-Jones Average price-to-earnings ratio. A high price-to-earnings ratio might indicate the stock is overpriced, but a high ratio might be justified if the earnings have been increasing steadily and the trend can be expected to continue.

The current ratio tells you whether the company has enough working capital. Find it by dividing the total current assets by total current liabilities. In the illustration:

$$\frac{\$6,500,000}{\$3,065,000} = 2.1$$

Thus, For Example, Inc., has 2.1 times as many current assets as current liabilities. The ratio ought to be at least 2 for industrial companies; less, maybe, for industries that have no need to carry large inventories, like electric utilities.

It's not essential, but you can go one step further and check the quick assets—assets that can be turned into cash in a hurry, which leaves out inventories. To find quick assets, subtract the inventories from the current assets, which in For Example's case leaves $3,800,-000. To find the quick assets ratio, divide this by the current liabilities:

$$\frac{\$3,800,000}{\$3,065,000} = 1.24$$

Thus For Example has $1.24 in quick assets available to meet each $1 of current liabilities. This ratio, in most industries, should be over 1.

You find the operating margin of profit by dividing the operating income (the net sales minus cost of sales and operating expenses) by the net sales. Using For Example's report, that would be:

$$\frac{\$1,000,000}{\$7,000,000} = 14.3\%$$

A good company to buy into is one that is increasing its sales year after year and at the same time is converting 15% to 30% of these sales into operating profits.

The equity to debt ratio (sometimes called capitalization ratio) is the proportion of the company's long-term debt (represented by bonds it has sold) to the stockholders' equity. You find the ratio by dividing the value of the common stock (the current market value —$18 in this case—times the number of shares) by the face value of the outstanding bonds:

$$\frac{\$7,200,000}{\$2,800,000} = 2.57$$

Thus the value of For Example's common is 2.57 times as much as its bond debt. For industrial companies, a ratio of 5 to 1 is desirable, but utilities and railroads may safely run as low as 1½ to 1.

Take note that in figuring the value of common stocks for this purpose, you have to multiply the number of shares by the current market value of the stock. Do not use the par value given under "stockholders' equity" on the balance sheet, as the par value generally has no relation to actual value.

A company can be made to look good or bad simply by the accounting method used. For example, there are several ways of figuring depreciation, none of them particularly easy to understand. If a company switches from one method to another, it can make quite a change in financial results. A big vending machine corporation switched a few years ago, and the effect was to make a 4-cent increase in its earnings per share look like a 13-cent increase. If there has been a changeover, the footnote should tell you and alert you to check the significance.

Again, there are two basic methods of valuing inventories. One is called last-in-first-out (LIFO) and the other first-in-first-out (FIFO). While prices are advancing, the FIFO company will tend to look better; when prices are in a slump, the LIFO company will. Neither method is good or bad in itself, but you've got to know who's using which when comparing companies. And you should be aware of a change from one to the other. The footnotes should tip you off.

Occasionally, annual reports can be blatantly misleading. Until 1962, for example, one aerospace company issued "consolidated" reports—ones incorporating the performance of both the parent company and its subsidiaries—to the Securities and Exchange Commission, but not to the public. The subsidiaries were taking a licking and knocking total company profits out of the window, a detail you couldn't see in the glowing annual reports. Only the footnotes gave a hint that subsidiaries might be influencing the picture. The company eventually made peace with the Securities and Exchange Commission by making its reports to the SEC and to the public uniform.

Most companies give stock options to key executives. Too large a percentage of options in relation to the number of shares outstanding can dilute the value of the rest of the stock. A high percentage would be 10%. And the footnotes should tell the story.

Studying all of this may sound like a lot of work, but the money at stake should be worth the trouble. And sometimes you won't have to do all the arithmetic: the ratios and earnings per share may be figured out for you already—especially if it's been a good year.

HOW TO LOOK UP A STOCK

The most convenient place to find reference material is a broker's office. Many offices are run on an informal basis, and the reference books are out where anyone can use them. Or, if not, a customer's man usually will be glad to make the reference books available for limited use by anyone who looks like a potential customer.

The two most widely used reference services are published by Moody's and Standard & Poor's. Each offers the basic material in several forms ranging from very abbreviated to very complete. For a quick rundown on a company, for example, you can try Standard & Poor's *Stock Guide*. This is a little booklet, measuring 5 by 8½ inches, that is crammed with information about nearly five thousand stocks. (A similar booklet covers bonds.) On each company it gives the following information: ticker symbol, company name, where traded, quality rating, number of institutions holding the security, company's principal business, price range of previous years, trading volume and high, low, and last price for most recent month, dividend record, abbreviated balance sheet, capitalization, and past and current earnings. If you wanted a personal reference book to carry around in your pocket, this little guide would fill the bill. It is published monthly. Moody's publishes a similar one, *Handbook of Widely Held Common Stocks,* quarterly.

Going up the line to a more detailed compilation, you come to Standard & Poor's *Stock Reports*. These are loose-leaf volumes kept up to date by quarterly substitution of new pages. The *Listed Stock Reports* cover stocks traded on the New York Stock Exchange and the *American Stock Reports* cover stocks listed on the American Stock Exchange. The *Over-the-Counter Reports* cover a wide variety of unlisted stocks and the larger mutual funds. In each series the companies are listed alphabetically, and each company gets two sides of a sheet.

The typical *Listed Stock Report* begins with a recommendation as to whether the stock should be held or not. Then comes a graph showing prices for five or so years back compared with prices of similar stocks and with the Standard & Poor's 500 Stock Average. Next come discussions of the company's recent sales or revenues, its near-term and long-term prospects, recent developments, and recent earnings and dividend payments. On the back of the sheet appears a table showing sales, profit margins, earnings, dividends, and price ranges going back ten or more years. Balance sheet items, assets, liabilities, ratio of current assets to current liabilities and book value are covered for the same period. In addition, there is a description of the company and its position within its industry. The *American Stock Reports* and the *Over-the-Counter Reports* contain similar information.

For most purposes, Standard & Poor's *Stock Reports* are adequate. But for a really complete set of facts and figures about a company, you can refer to either of two voluminous references: Standard & Poor's *Corporation Records* and Moody's *Industrial, Transportation and Public Utility Manuals.* These are huge volumes covering thousands of companies in great detail. Information is kept up to date by the addition of new pages. To get a complete report on a company, you have to look up the basic material, then make considerable use of the index to find the various new items that are sprinkled through the most recently added pages.

For a quick picture of the past course of a stock's price, you can refer to a chart book available in most brokerage offices called *The Stock Picture,* published by M. C. Horsey & Co. It contains complete charts of 1600 stocks plus abbreviated information on earnings, dividends, and so on.

To keep current If you live in a large city, you can get some news about stocks from the financial pages of your daily newspaper. Such papers as the Baltimore *Morning Sun,* the Boston *Globe,* the

Chicago *Tribune,* the Los Angeles *Times,* and the Dallas *Morning News* give quite complete data on daily transactions on the New York and American stock exchanges. They also furnish selected quotations for investment companies and over-the-counter securities.

However, while it is interesting to know the price at which a stock changed hands the previous day, it is much more important to keep track of the company's sales, new orders, earnings, and other measures of progress. And newspapers generally can provide such information only on the largest and most widely held companies. There are thousands of publicly owned companies that never get into the general financial news. *The Wall Street Journal* publishes the earnings statements of thousands of companies as they become available.

Weekly financial newspapers and magazines give similar but less complete coverage. *Barron's Financial Weekly* includes in its table of stock quotations both dividend rate and most recent earnings. Other publications to consider are *Forbes Magazine,* published twice a month, and *Financial World,* published weekly.

TAX TIPS

Knowing the ins and outs of income tax regulations regarding stock ownership can save you many dollars. Here are some hints on how to handle your dividends and capital gains and losses.

Cash dividends   You don't have to pay tax on all cash dividends you get. The first $100 of dividends on your stock is excluded from taxable income. If your wife (or husband) owns stock in her (or his) name, up to $100 of dividends she (or he) receives is also tax-free. If all your stock is jointly owned, you pay no tax on the first $200 of dividends.

Suppose stock in your name earns $130 in dividends and stock in your spouse's name earns $60. You must declare $30 of your dividends as income. You would avoid paying any tax if the stock were in joint ownership. (But other considerations enter into joint ownership. Check it out with your professional adviser first.)

What if stock yielding $140 in dividends was owned jointly, while stock paying $50 was owned in your name alone? Half the dividends on the shares jointly held, or $70, are credited to you, half to your spouse. For tax purposes, you have $120 in dividends, of which $20 is taxable. Your spouse has $70 tax free.

Dividends in stock   If a company pays a dividend in the form of its own stock rather than cash, you pay no tax on the extra shares. But if you have the right to choose between cash or stock, then you must pay even if you take the stock. You list the stock's equivalent cash value as income. The same rules apply to stock rights (certificates issued by the company entitling you to buy your pro-rata share of a new stock issue.)

A stock split is different. A two-for-one split, for example, means you get another share of stock for each one you own. You pay no tax on the extra shares.

If you have sold some stock   Profits you make by selling stock are known as capital gains. The tax on such gains may be less than you would pay on ordinary income. If you hold the stock for more than six months, you've got a long-term capital gain (or a long-term loss if you sell for less than you paid). You've got a short-term gain or loss if you sell before six months. Net short-term gains are taxed just as your other income is—that is, at your regular tax rate. But long-term gains get favorable treatment. You are taxed, in effect, at only half your regular rate—and never more than 25% of the gain in any case. The gain is the difference between the actual cost of the stock (including buying commission and fees) and your selling price (reduced by sales commission, transfer taxes, and similar expenses).

How do you treat capital losses? If you have no capital gains, then capital losses, whether long-term or short, can be deducted dollar for dollar, within certain limits, from your income. You can deduct no more than $1000 in capital losses in any one year, though you can carry the excess over to following years.

If you have a mixture of gains and losses, the tax is figured on a net basis. Divide your dealings into two sets: long-term and short-term. Subtract all your long-term gains from long-term losses, or vice versa. Do the same for short-term transactions.

Do you have a long-term gain and a short-term loss? If the gain is larger, the difference is a long-term gain. If the loss is bigger, the difference up to $1000 can be deducted from your income.

Do you have a short-term gain and long-term loss? If the profit is greater, the difference is a short-term gain. If the loss is bigger, the difference is deductible.

If you are thinking about unloading stock, here are a few pointers. Look at deals you've already made. Do you have:

❨ A short-term gain? It may pay to sell a loser to offset the gain, which would otherwise be taxed as ordinary income.

❨ A long-term gain? Even if you're bent on selling a loser, consider waiting till next year. That way, you pay only half your regular tax rate on the gain this year, but deduct the full loss next year.

❨ A long- or short-term loss? You might simply hold onto your other stock and deduct the loss from your regular income. If you've got a short-term gainer you're sure won't go higher, you can sell it now and take the profits tax-free—for these profits will be offset by your loss. But hold off selling long-term gainers for another year. In other words, let the losses reduce regular income one year, pay a long-term capital gains tax on profits the next.

If you haven't sold stock this year, check your "paper" gains and losses. Do you have:

❨ A potential long-term gain? Don't worry about the tax angle if your investment goal is to hold stocks for the long haul. But if you think you will be in a higher tax bracket next year, you might consider realizing part of your gains now. If your income will go down or hold steady, delay taking gains.

❨ A potential short-term gain? Hold onto the securities until you've had them for more than six months. The gain then is long-term.

❨ A short-term or long-term loss? You might consider selling now if your tax rate will be lower next year.

❨ Long-term gains and either short- or long-term losses? Avoid taking both gains and losses in the same year. The losses would offset your long-term gains, and only the net gain is taxed at the capital gains rate.

Mutual fund shares Mutual funds generally pay two kinds of dividends:

❨ Ordinary dividends, that is, income from dividends and interest on stock or bonds the fund owns. These are taxed just as other dividends on stock you own.

❨ Capital gains dividends. These are your share of the profits the fund makes by selling securities. They are taxed as long-term capital gains, even if you actually held the mutual fund shares for less than six months.

A small number of mutual funds retain capital gains instead of distributing them. They will then pay a capital gains tax directly to Uncle Sam on your behalf, at the maximum 25% rate. What if your capital gains rate is lower? You can recover the difference. Say the fund told you your share of the gains was $100 and it paid a capital gains tax of $25 for you. Report the $100 as a long-term capital gain. If your capital gains bracket is, say, 10%, you'd pay $10 on this amount. Then list the $25 under "income tax withheld" on page 1 of the tax form. Thus you get a net credit of $15. One final step: Add $75 to the original cost of your investment for computing any future gain or loss when you sell the stock. (The law assumes you received the $100, paid $25 in tax, then reinvested the rest.)

When figuring the profit or loss on the sale of stock, special situations can sometimes complicate matters.

Stock dividends when sold You sell some common stock that includes shares you had previously received as a tax-free corporate dividend. Generally, you'd first divide the total number of shares held after the stock dividend into the cost of the original stock. Say you bought 25 shares of American Box at $21 each, for a total of $525, then received five more shares as a dividend. The cost of each share, for tax purposes, then becomes $525 divided by 30, or $17.50. (You would pay the long-term capital gains tax rate on any profit from sale of the extra shares so long as the original shares were held at least six months.)

Stock splits You'd apply the same sort of arithmetic to figure profit or loss when you sell stock that's been involved in a split. A two-for-one split, for instance, would cut the cost of all the shares you then hold to half the cost of the original shares.

Stock rights Many stockholders are able to buy extra shares in a company at cut-rate prices by exercising rights issued by the firm. In most cases, the simplest way to figure the cost of these new shares, for tax purposes, is to use the price you paid for them. You would not then have to average out the cost of the old and new shares.

Stock bought in blocks   Say you buy 30 shares of stock in a company in 3 installments of 10 each, and each lot had a different price. How would you figure the gain or loss on one lot of 10 you sell? If you can identify the particular lot, the gain is the difference between the original cost and your selling price. If, for strategic reasons, you want the least gain or the biggest loss, you would sell the lot that cost you most. To get the biggest gain or tiniest loss, unload the cheapest shares. What if you can't identify the particular lot you sell? Your gain or loss is the difference between the cost of the first lot you bought and the price at which you sell.

Gifts   Perhaps your father gave you stock that originally cost him $1000. If you sell it for more than $1000, you pay capital gains tax on the difference—no matter how much the stock was worth when you got it. Suppose you sell the stock for less than $1000. Then you take a capital loss for the difference between the selling price and the original cost, or the market value at the time of the gift, whichever is smaller. Say the stock was worth $1500 when you got it, then fell to $500 when you sold it. Your loss is only $500—the original cost of $1000 less $500. Was it worth only $750 when you received it before dropping to $500? Your loss is $250—that is, the market value of $750 less $500.

Inheritance   You inherit some stock when a parent dies, then sell it later on. You figure the profit or loss, as a rule, on the value of the stock on the date of death. Exception: An executor may choose to value your parent's estate (for estate tax purposes) as of one year after death. In that case, your stock cost is the value at that date.

Deductions   If you itemize on your return, you can deduct certain costs of buying or maintaining stock:
(State stamp taxes, usually imposed on the purchaser of stock. Note, however, that if you deduct this expense you can't add the tax to your cost in computing profits or losses when you sell the stock.
(Safe-deposit rental if the box contains stock—or other income-producing property, such as savings bonds.
(The cost of stock market newsletters, investment services, and other professional advice.

❡ The value of stock donated to charity. Giving away stock that has appreciated in value can make sense. You don't pay any tax on the profit. And you can deduct the full market value as a contribution.

CHAPTER 8

Investment Advice

Most investors cannot devote full time to the study of economic trends and the statistics of industries and companies. They feel the need of a certain amount of professional advice. This need will vary from person to person. At one extreme is the man or woman who will want to assimilate facts and figures and make his or her own decisions with a minimum of outside help. At the other extreme is the investor who prefers to hand over all decisions to professionals. In between are those who want to make their own judgments but who welcome sound ideas and analyses. For all such investors, the baffling questions are— Who is really competent? How can you tell the sound advice from the worthless?

The difficulty here is that there is more advice floating around on the subject of investing than on almost any other. The board rooms of brokerage houses abound in tips, rumors, and hearsay which are best disregarded completely. Brokers themselves, in order to acquire new customers and keep up the interest of old ones, feel obliged to furnish free market advice. In addition, there are advisory services that advertise their wares in financial publications often by means of introductory offers that appear to be quite reasonable. Lastly, there are investment counselors who make their services available to clients much as do doctors and lawyers. But the fees are such that as a practical matter, only those with investment capital of $200,000 or in some cases even $400,000 can afford them.

Your broker He (or she) is the person with whom you'll be in closest touch. The broker's main function is to execute your orders promptly and correctly. He also will give advice if you want it— sometimes whether you want it or not. If you have no idea of what kind of stocks you want to own, then your broker will be happy to suggest some. But you probably are better off deciding on your investment philosophy in advance, then telling your broker what you have in mind and checking your ideas of good stocks against his. Thus, in choosing a broker, it is well to try to find one whose investment philosophy is not too different from your own. Remember that one broker can keep thoroughly up to date on, say, half a dozen industries and only a certain number of stocks in each industry. Maybe, then, he will be familiar in detail with the doings and prospects of perhaps fifty companies. He will have only superficial or hearsay knowledge of the thousands of other companies whose stocks are available. So if you are interested in owning top quality growth stocks, you want a broker whose interests also lie that way, who instinctively, on his own hook, digs into the kind of information you need. If, on the other hand, your interests are more speculative, you want a broker who has a good feel for the faster-moving, riskier issues that often go up and down like a Yo-Yo on a string. What you don't want, if you are interested in long-term growth, is a broker who grabs the phone and calls you whenever he thinks a high flyer is about to move. Also, you don't want one who will be calling you and suggesting that you sell every time one of your stocks shows a paper profit. Remember that brokers make their money on the commissions from purchases and sales. This tends to give their advice a bias toward trading in and out. Beware of any broker who, in the jargon of Wall Street, is "hungry" for commissions.

Settling on the right broker probably is easier than finding a doctor or lawyer. You can move your account from one brokerage firm to another without feeling at all guilty. Some investors maintain accounts at several brokerage houses at the same time. So it's not a bad idea to shop around for a while, trying out this broker and that one, until you make a connection that is satisfactory. But always keep in mind that your broker is not infallible. If his advice were perfect, he would not be in the brokerage business at all. He would be a big, wealthy investor taking life easy and making calls to *his* broker.

Advisory services   As mentioned in the previous chapter, there is a wealth of published advice available to investors. You should try to make a judgment as to that which is realistic and useful and that which falls into the miracle or crystal ball category. Although there probably are exceptions, generally speaking the advice that is most flamboyantly advertised in financial newspapers and magazines is the kind of advice to be most wary of. For example, how would you like to have the names of seven stocks likely to triple in value? Or a list of low-priced blue chips? Or thirty-seven candidates for stock splits? Or a set of charts to tell you which way the market will go? All of this enticing information and more is offered for a few dollars—some of it even for free—in the ads that appear on the financial pages of newspapers. Probably you've wondered, though, just how good this information is. If the people who peddle the advice know so much, how come they aren't lolling on their yachts off the Riviera?

A realistic answer might be that no one can foretell the actions of the market as a whole, or of an individual stock. About the best you can expect from any investment advisory service is a conscientious job of research, good factual material, and sober recommendations. As to the services that offer tips for quick profits or charts that are supposed to foretell price actions—be wary. If that sort of information were reliable, it would be worth much more than a few dollars or even a few hundred. In fact, it would not be for sale. So if you do feel the need for some kind of investment advice, don't grab the service with the most exciting ad. First take a look at the whole field. It may save you money and disillusionment.

The big financial services Moody's, Standard & Poor's, United Business Service, Babson's, Value Line, Argus and Investment Counsel, Inc., of Detroit, are examples of the experienced organizations that have been in business for many years. Each provides a periodic report or survey covering business conditions in general and according to industry. Facts, figures, and recommendations are presented on the stocks of selected companies. One issue of such a report may present a group of growth stocks thought to be attractive, another a list of stocks yielding good income, and so on. From time to time reviews are made of stocks previously recommended. Some of these services also provide personalized consultation by mail. In some cases this privilege is included in the subscription price. In others it is not. Annual subscriptions range from $50 to $160.

If you are basically self-reliant and have the time to study, perhaps you can utilize the material that's available from market letters, investment services, and the like and be your own adviser. For many people this method is satisfying, but it could be expensive for someone who didn't have the knack.

Trust departments of banks About 26% of the banks in the United States have trust departments. These offer several possibilities. Depending on the policy of the bank, an investor with, say, $50,000, can either open an investment advisory account or set up an individual living trust. Banks that offer an investment advisory service will do the selecting of stocks subject to the customer's approval, furnish statements, collect dividends for him, and so on. Fees generally match those charged by investment counselors, typically ½ of 1% of the market value of the fund and with a minimum annual fee of $500. In the case of a living trust, the customer turns the money over to the bank for investment and specifies how the principal and income are to be handled. A favorite arrangement is for the bank to pay the investor the income and to permit him to draw upon principal in emergencies.

Bookkeeping and handling charges are proportionately too great for a bank to accept small trust accounts. Many banks, however, have an arrangement for pooling small trusts and investing them as a whole in what is called a common trust fund. By this device, amounts ranging from $15,000 upward can be put in trust and the principal and income be paid out in the same way as they would be under an individual trust. A large bank may maintain several common funds to fit the different objectives of the individual trusts: a diversified fund of stocks and bonds for general use; an equity fund of stocks, and a fixed income fund of bonds, notes, and a relatively small amount of stocks. It may also have a tax-exempt bond fund.

In considering trusts of this kind, remember that a trust is not primarily an investment medium. People most often set up trusts to achieve some special objective—providing for the care of a dependent, minimizing taxes, assuring sound financial management for those who cannot or should not manage for themselves, letting someone have income from property without controlling the property itself, and so on. Investing money is simply one of the duties that a trustee may be called on to perform in carrying out the purpose of the trust. And since a trustee is required by law to be particularly careful with the capital he has been given to manage, he must be prudent. Some states restrict trustees to a "legal list" of prescribed investments. Thus trust funds may earn less than capital invested through other channels. Today the income of bank trust funds probably averages about 4%. The principal may be expected to grow during periods of rising stock prices. The more aggressively managed fund probably has increased in value 50% over a ten-year period. Thus a person who put $50,000 in trust ten years ago might have $75,000 in his account today; assuming no withdrawals of principal he might be receiving 4% on $75,000, or $3000 a year, which would be 6% on the original capital.

There are no standard fees for trustees. In some cases, however, the state sets maximums. Fees usually are expressed as a percentage of the trust's income or capital, or both. In one state the annual commission is limited to ½ of 1% on the first $50,000 of capital, ¼ of 1% on the next $450,000, and ⅕ of 1% on all over $500,000. There's an additional commission of 1% on any principal paid out of the trust fund. The trust also would be charged for legal fees, brokerage commissions, and certain other expenses incurred by the trustee. Smaller trusts are subject to minimum annual fees. The bank might charge, say, $125 to $250 if the trust is invested in one of its common funds, and about double those rates if it is invested as a separate unit. (See Chapter 14 for more detailed information on trust funds.)

Investment counselors These professionals, like doctors and lawyers, are in the business of diagnosing and advising for a fee. Generally speaking, however, you do not consult an investment counselor on a one-time basis. The relationship is a continuing one, it rather resembles the fabled relation between a Chinese patient and his Chinese doctor, in which the doctor is paid, not to cure a specific ill or disease, but to keep the patient healthy. The investment counselor treats each client individually. He determines the client's circumstances, needs, and desires and selects a special bundle of securities to fit. This portfolio then must be continually reviewed and kept up to date. The investor may be consulted on all changes, or he may give the counselor carte blanche. Such constant supervision, plus research and overhead, costs money. Thus investment counselors commonly charge a fee of ½ of 1% annually based on the capital at stake. This percentage often is lower on assets valued at over $500,000. Since it involves as much work, and perhaps more, to supervise a small amount of capital than a large one, counseling firms generally set a minimum fee, in some cases $500 but in others $1000 or even $2000 a year. Obviously, a person with only a few thousand dollars to invest cannot afford this expense.

A very few counseling firms have made an effort to cater to the smaller investor; that is one with capital of $25,000 or $50,000. Such firms, however, may simply have certain supervised lists of stocks into which they put clients' money rather arbitrarily without too much investigation of the individual's needs and his other assets. Also, the fee, as a percentage of the money being managed, is considerably above the ½ of 1% ordinarily charged on larger funds.

Selection of an investment counselor is difficult because it is hard to make a judgment on the firm's performance. One of the best ways, of course, is by personal recommendation of another investor who has been a client of one or more firms. Thus, if you were seriously considering opening an account with a firm of investment counselors, you would be perfectly justified in asking them for the names of one or two old clients whom you could consult. Many investment counseling firms publish advisory or market letters. A subscription to such a letter can give an idea of the soundness of the firm's recommendations. Also many investment counseling firms manage investment trusts. The record of these trusts is readily available in many publications. And it might reasonably be assumed that a firm that can manage an investment trust competently can also manage an individual investment account at least as well. There also is a professional society, the Investment Counsel Association of America, located in New York City. It has high ethical standards but a rather small membership. By letter addressed to the association you can ascertain the members in your area.

Investment counseling services Some organizations that are not primarily in the investment counseling business will give investment management for a fee, or, if the recipient is a good enough customer, without charge. Thus an investor with substantial capital could open an advisory account with a large bank. Or, if he were already a substantial customer of the bank, he might obtain free investment counseling without having to establish a formal arrangement. Similarly, a big investor can hire a brokerage firm to manage his portfolio. Or, if he is a big enough customer of the firm, he can obtain a great deal of counseling without charge. It is assumed that the firm will be reimbursed by the commissions on the customer's purchases and sales.

Investment trusts   For the person who does not have a substantial amount of money to invest; that is, less than $100,000,
one of the most convenient and satisfactory ways to get professional management is to buy shares in a well-managed investment
company or investment trust (two names for the same thing). This
amounts to buying investment advice, not on an individual but on
a mass basis. The idea is that instead of owning stocks direct, you
might prefer to own an interest in a bundle of securities selected by
someone else—in this case the managers of the investment company.
One advantage is that you spread a relatively small number of dollars over a number of different stocks or bonds and thus diversify
your risk. Another is that if the trust is well managed these stocks
or bonds are selected on the basis of careful research by professional
analysts. Quite possibly the professionals can do a better job of
selecting than you could yourself. That is the investment trust theory, but the practice of it is not so simple. There are several hundred
trusts available so that the task of selecting the right one for any
given investor, or even the one with the best record, is comparable
to the job of combing through the stock market to find a good
stock. Some advice on choosing a well-managed investment trust
will be given in the next chapter.

CHAPTER 9

Mutual Funds and Other
Investment Companies

You turn your car over to the auto mechanic for repairs, your health problems to a doctor. Why shouldn't you turn your investment problems over to professionals and let them put your money to work? Maybe you should, especially if your capital is not large enough to warrant opening an individual account with an investment counseling firm. One way to achieve somewhat the same result is to buy shares in what is variously known as an investment company, investment trust, or investment fund. You may be more familiar with the term "mutual fund." A mutual fund, howevever, is only one kind of investment company. There are others that do the same job.

When you make this kind of investment, you buy an interest in a bundle of securities selected by the managers of the fund. Instead of owning stock in one or two operating companies, such as Eastman Kodak or Standard Oil of New Jersey, you own a tiny cross-section slice of dozens of companies. You have automatic diversification, and all the while the managers of the fund are weeding out stocks they feel are doing poorly and substituting stocks they believe have more promise.

VARIOUS TYPES AVAILABLE

Fine and good. But shopping for an investment company is like shopping for anything else. There are many types and brand names on the market. Some are sold aggressively by energetic salesmen knocking on doors. Others are available only if you learn about them and seek them out. Some are available at a discount; others are sold strictly at the pro-rata value of their assets. Still others are obtainable only by paying a premium.

Some try for growth; others for income. Some invest in blue chips; others in lesser known companies. Some are cautiously managed; others tend to shoot the works for big gains. Some have a splendid record of competent management going back over the years. And unfortunately, others seem to have been thrown together to give would-be managers something to manage and hungry salesmen something to sell. So it's well to be familiar with the field before you begin to narrow down your choice. Start with a few definitions and characteristics.

Net asset value per share   This is the net dollar value of the securities the fund owns divided by the number of its shares outstanding in the hands of the public. Thus on a given day a certain fund might own securities having a market value of $10,000,000. If it had outstanding in the hands of the public one million of its own shares, then the net asset value per share would be $10.

Capital structure   The two types here are the closed-end fund, which is the older and less publicized, and the open-end, or "mutual," fund, which is newer, more aggressively sold, and the kind you are more likely to hear about. Actually, both types are mutual funds in the sense that those whose money is being managed are also the stockholders. But in practice, the term mutual fund is applied only to the open-end type.

Closed-end funds   Closed-end means that at some time in the past the fund has sold a block of shares to the public but makes no continuous offering of additional shares. Thus the number of shares outstanding is constant. Most closed-end shares are traded on the New York Stock Exchange or over-the-counter just as are shares of manufacturing companies, railroads, utilities, or banks. Examples are Lehman Corporation, Tri-Continental Corporation, and Niagara Share traded on the New York Stock Exchange.

If you want to buy into a closed-end fund, you get in touch with a broker and through him buy shares from another investor who already owns shares and wants to sell. The price the buyer pays, or the seller receives, depends to some extent on supply and demand. It may be above or below the net asset value. If the price is above the net asset value, the stock is said to be selling at a premium; if below, at a discount. The commission is almost always at the New York Stock Exchange rate.

Mutual funds   Open-end, or mutual, funds, which in recent years have become very popular, are based on a different idea. Open-end means that the fund stands ready at all times to sell new shares or redeem old ones. Thus the number of outstanding shares of an open-end fund is always changing. While these transactions are usually done through a broker, there is no public trading. Thus the law of supply and demand does not affect the price. Open-end funds almost never sell at a premium or discount. When you buy, you pay net asset value plus commission commonly 8½% or 9%. When you sell, you receive net asset value, usually without payment of a commission. Examples of open-end funds are Massachusetts Investors Trust, Chemical Fund, and Dreyfus Fund.

As you can see, in one major respect closed-end and open-end funds are the same. They are in the business of investing money entrusted to them by the shareholders. In most other ways, however, they differ.

Discounts and premiums on closed-end funds   In recent years many closed-end funds have been available in the market place at a discount from net asset value. This enables you to buy part ownership in a list of stocks, for example, DuPont, Union Carbide, Honeywell, and IBM, at, say, 10% or 15% or even 25% less than their market value. There's no particular gimmick about this except that, if you later sold your shares, you might have to sell at a similar discount. In the meantime, however, for every 75, 85, or 90 cents you had invested, you would have a dollar's worth of capital working for you. Also, the discount could narrow, which would be an advantage. Discounts generally do narrow during booms and widen during declines.

There are several explanations for this discount. The main one, perhaps, is that there are no salesmen aggressively pushing the shares and creating a demand. The broker to whom you would go to buy closed-end shares can just as well sell you shares in any one of a thousand or more companies listed on the New York Stock Exchange. The commission would be the same either way. In fact, brokers have very little interest in selling you closed-end shares, since money put into such a fund is likely to stay there rather than to move into and out of various stocks, thereby providing additional commissions.

Some closed-end funds at times sell at a premium over net asset value. The reason is that investors become enamored of particular funds, either because of their outstanding management record or because of favorable publicity or for some other reason. As a matter of fact, however, there is often no discernible reason why one fund will sell at a premium while another, which appears equally well managed, will sell at a discount. As in all free markets, investor psychology plays an important and mysterious role.

Mutual fund sales commissions   Closed-end funds, having a fixed number of shares outstanding, can grow in terms of net asset value only. Mutual funds, on the other hand, can grow both in net asset value and in the number of shares in the hands of the public. Thus mutual funds make up a very fast-growing type of security. One reason is that the salesmen have a greater incentive to sell open-end funds than almost any other form of investment. The sales commission generally runs around 9% of the net asset value. It is not, however, usually stated as a percentage of the net asset value but as a percentage of the offering price, which is the net asset value plus the commission or "loading." If you wanted to buy one share of a mutual fund having a net asset value of $10 and the load was 8½%, you would pay $10.93. (The 93 cents is the sales commission and is 8½% of $10.93, which is the sales, or offering, price.) Actually, of course, the 93 cents, in relation to the net asset value of $10, represents a commission of 9.3%. Therefore, it is considerably larger than the 1%, 2%, or 3% of the market price you pay when you buy closed-end shares or other listed stocks. And the salesman who sells you open-end shares receives about a third of the total sales commission—a return that makes it worth his while to seek out prospective buyers at office or home. It should be noted that on purchases of over $10,000 the typical sales commission begins to decrease until on a $100,000 purchase it may be only 3%.

Thus there has grown up a new type of security salesman who resembles the life insurance salesman and who is trained to sell open-end funds exclusively. This differs from the usual concept of a broker as being one who stands ready to sell you stocks, bonds, listed or unlisted, traded anywhere in the world, you name it.

Most open-end funds make no charge for redeeming shares. This is in contrast to closed-end shares, where you do pay a selling commission of 1%, 2%, 3%, or some other amount, depending on the size of the transaction.

No-load mutual funds   These are a strange breed of cat because they are not sold by salesmen at all. In fact, a no-load fund is one of the few things in this world that you can buy without paying a sales commission, directly or indirectly. The reason that you don't hear much about no-load funds is that no salesman knocks at your door trying to persuade you to buy one. Why should he? He wouldn't get any commission. Yet, except for the lack of a sales charge, these no-load mutual funds are run just the way the others are.

You might wonder, then, what's up? Why should a mutual fund be willing to offer its shares at cost? And if it does, why doesn't everyone buy the no-load funds and save the commission?

For the answer, note that all funds, open-end as well as closed-end, whether a sales commission is involved or not, charge a management fee for handling the shareholders' money. In most cases, this fee is ⅓ to ½ of 1% per year of the capital under the fund's management, although it can be higher or lower. Thus the managers of a fund having assets of $100,000,000 might receive an annual management fee of $333,000 to $500,000.

Now while the managers of a no-load mutual fund receive no part of any sales commission, they still receive the management fee and thus are compensated for investing the stockholders' money. In addition, most managers of no-load mutual funds are investment counseling firms who handle large sums for private investors. For such firms the mutual fund may just be a side line, although it can be a useful one, as the following example will show.

An investment counseling firm ordinarily accepts only wealthy clients, charging a management fee, usually ½ of 1% of the money at risk. The smallness of the fee makes it uneconomical for such a firm to accept amounts of less than, say, $100,000, and it avoids the problem by charging a minimum fee of $500 or more a year. Such a firm still, however, may want to accommodate the son of a good client or perhaps a young executive who promises to be a customer in the future. In many cases, too, wealthy clients want to establish small accounts for minor children or grandchildren.

One way to take care of the younger and nonwealthy investor

is to set up a mutual fund. To such potential clients the firm can say, "Our mutual fund is managed in the same way as our big accounts. Put your money into the fund and you'll get the same treatment. There is no sales charge." Once such a fund gets started and begins to grow, it generally is offered publicly so that anyone may buy in.

This sounds like a good deal, but remember that you have a larger choice among the funds with loads because there are more of them. And the important thing is performance. One fund with a load might perform so much better over the years than one without a load that you would be foolish to buy the no-load fund merely to save the commission.

OBJECTIVES

Because the investment company field is such a desirable place for the man with, say, $500 to $25,000 to put his money (and even professional investors such as pension fund managers are increasingly using this medium), the investment community has developed many types of funds to provide an appeal to the large mass market.

There are, for example, balanced funds, which generally keep a quarter or more of their capital in cash, bonds, or preferred stocks. There are funds that invest only in bonds, and others that try to provide the largest possible income to their shareholders and so on. Here are the several types.

Common stock funds   These make up the greatest proportion of all funds. They can be either open-end or closed-end or no-load. In most cases the emphasis is on long-term growth. Generally known as diversified common stock growth funds, these generally keep more than 80% of their assets in common stocks, though in a declining market they may switch temporarily to greater holdings of cash or bonds. One type of growth stock fund puts more emphasis on income. While such a fund generally follows a policy of long-term growth, it aims for a greater income return from dividends than do the pure growth funds. Either type of growth fund is eminently suitable for most investors. Usually such investors already have enough fixed assets in the form of life insurance, a stake in social security and a pension plan, and perhaps savings accounts or savings bonds.

What's needed is an investment in equities that will grow fast enough to outrun inflation, heavy taxes and the other burdens that beset the ordinary family. Another point, why hire someone to invest your money in fixed assets such as bonds when you can do it so easily yourself?

Balanced funds These are useful to a person who wants complete management of all his assets, including fixed-income investments. Examples might be wealthier persons or those in retirement. But the investor who already has life insurance and savings or bonds may not need a balanced fund. Other disadvantages: The management fee takes a considerable slice of the income from the bonds and preferreds. This fee would be saved if the investor bought his own bonds or preferreds, which, generally speaking, are more easily selected than common stocks. Also, the balanced fund does not provide as big an opportunity for growth as does the stock fund.

Bond and preferred stock funds Income, rather than growth, is the objective and, again, the management charge can be a substantial part of the income.

Income funds These strive for a high yield and thus invest in companies that pay out a major part of their earnings in dividends. Such companies show little growth, and the risks in a free economy being what they are, a company that is not growing is in danger of declining.

Industry funds These spread their money over many companies in one industry. By buying into several such funds you could obtain tremendous diversification. But diversification simply for diversification's sake is not always advisable. It is probably better to buy into a common stock fund that attempts to pick out a few of the most desirable companies in numerous industries.

Geographical funds These concentrate on one state, such as Florida, or one area, such as the Southwest. Since the managers are confined to one area, and yet must obtain diversification, they may be forced to buy stocks not as promising as others they could be buying if they were operating nationally.

Special situation funds These seek out companies in trouble financially or whose stock is available cheap for some unusual reason. Results of this type of investment can be very good or very bad. Since these funds are so speculative, they would not seem to be desirable for the average investor.

Foreign securities funds In recent years, European, Japanese, and Australian stocks have risen and also fallen, sometimes spectacularly. Thus there is more risk in foreign securities than in those of American companies. One risk is political instability; another is unpredictable taxing policies. The investor who wants a stake in foreign operations can obtain it by purchasing shares in leading United States corporations that have interests abroad, such as Goodyear, Pfizer, or IBM.

Performance funds In these funds the managers aggressively try for the maximum gain in the shortest possible time. The idea is to move nimbly into the market to catch a rise in a particular company or industry, then move nimbly out again and into something else. Performance funds are sometimes referred to on Wall Street as "go-go" funds because they put the emphasis on fast action and are likely to go up and down faster than other funds. In some cases the portfolio turnover of a performance fund is five times that of run-of-the-mill mutual funds. The long-term growth, however, may be no greater than that of a well-managed growth fund.

Dual-purpose funds These have appeared in the United States in recent years, having originated in Europe. Such a fund offers two classes of stock to investors—preferred and common. The holders of the preferred receive all the income from the fund's portfolio, while the holders of the common receive all the capital gains. One problem faced by the managers of such a fund, of course, is how to select stocks which have equally attractive prospects of growth in asset value and income. To favor one type of investment over the other would be to favor one class of the fund's investors.

Leverage funds This is a rather rare type of closed-end fund that has several types of security outstanding in the hands of the public. Suppose a company is organized with assets of $15,000,000, one-third represented by preferred stock and bonds and two-thirds by common stock. The holders of the preferred stock and bonds would have a $5,000,000 fixed interest in the fund, and the remainder would belong to the holders of the common stock. If the stock market dropped and the fund's holdings declined in value by 20%—to $12,000,000—the loss would be magnified on the common stock. The owners of the bonds and preferred stocks still would have claim to $5,000,000, so there would be only $7,000,000 as equity for the common stock—a 30% drop from $10,000,000. On the other hand, if the market value of the holdings increased by 20%—to $18,000,000—the gain to the common stock holders would be magnified: owners of the "senior securities" would still have a claim on only $5,000,000, so common stock equity would jump 30% to $13,000,000.

Most closed-end funds, such as Lehman Corp., have just one kind of stock—common. But a few also have issued senior securities, and these are said to be leverage funds. Many years ago, this feature made the common stock of such funds a venture strictly for the speculator. Today, though, the leverage factor usually is looked on as insignificant.

PRICE QUOTATIONS AND MANAGEMENT FEES

Price quotations   Prices of the larger mutual funds are quoted on newspaper financial pages under two headings, "bid" and "asked." The asked price is the offering price; i.e., net asset value plus sales commission. The bid price is simply net asset value. If the fund has no load, bid and asked prices are the same. Closed-end funds are quoted in the New York Stock Exchange and over-the-counter quotations. In addition, each Monday *The Wall Street Journal* and the New York *Times* list the prices of closed-end shares and the discounts or premiums as a percentage of net asset value.

Management fees and other matters   How much do you pay to have your money managed by an investment company? The cost to the company of obtaining investment advice usually runs around ⅓ to ½ of 1% of the total net assets. Other expenses such as commissions, auditing, legal and custodian fees, and overhead are added to this percentage and may bring it up to ¾ of 1%. Expressed in terms of the gross income of the investment trust, expenses usually amount to 7% to 15%, sometimes to 25% or even higher. Since the largest item of expense in management is the advisory fee, it is important to know whether the percentage drops with the increase in the size of assets. In many cases the level does not decline, no matter how big the fund's assets get. This is contrary to the usual practice in the investment advisory field. Some funds do pay on a sliding scale; for example, a fee of ½ of 1% on the first $50,000,000 of net assets, ⅜ of 1% on the next $50,000,000, and ¼ of 1% on the portion over $100,000,000. Note also that in some cases the investment company provides its own management and when it does so, the expense ratio is likely to be very low. It can, in fact, be as low as ¼ of 1% a year, or ⅓ of the expense ratios of similar funds that pay advisory fees to outsiders.

Mutual funds do a tremendous amount of buying and selling in the stock market and thus can channel a great deal of brokerage business to favored firms. How do the funds determine who shall get these plums? About 40% of mutual funds have some connection with a brokerage house. Either the fund's advisers are brokers themselves, or they own an interest in a brokerage firm or they have interlocking personnel with such a firm. In such cases much business is channeled to the affiliated broker.

This still leaves a great deal of brokerage business that must go to someone. And such brokerage business may be regarded as a valuable resource owned by shareholders of mutual funds which can be exchanged for some service such as investment research or statistical information. One brokerage house may have a widely respected expert on oil stocks, for example, whose knowledge and judgment would be available to mutual fund clients.

The obtaining of such services, however, is of secondary consideration to many funds in allocating business to a given broker. The primary consideration may be how good the broker is at selling the mutual fund's own shares to the public. In other words, when a broker sells a sizable volume of shares in a particular mutual fund, he not only receives most of the sales commission of 8½% or 9%, but he also may stand to get a bonus in the form of brokerage business from the fund itself.

Who runs the funds?   Suppose the management of a mutual fund is indifferent and the advisory fee above average? What will the shareholders do about it? Probably nothing. Theoretically, they can vote out the directors and fire the advisers. But as a practical matter, such action would be most unlikely. Since mutual funds appeal to the small investor, ownership is widely diffused among many small holders. At many a mutual fund annual meeting no shareholders show up at all, or at most a handful. Shareholders vote almost exclusively by proxy and under these conditions management control often is a virtually automatic consequence of possession of the corporate proxy machinery by the promoting management group.

This promoting management group often has several sources of income stemming from the mutual fund. It may collect a fee for advising the fund, part of the commission on sales of the fund's shares to the public, and part of the brokerage commissions on the fund's purchases and sales of portfolio stock. In some cases managing groups have increased their earnings to a point where they have been able to sell their own shares to the public at large capital gains to the founders.

There are certain provisions of the law, of course, designed to protect the shareholders' interest in this welter of overlapping activities by management groups. Under the law, at least 60% of a mutual fund's board of directors must not be affiliated with the fund's regular broker. And at least 40% must not be affiliated with the fund's investment adviser. However, as it turns out, these "outside" directors generally are selected and nominated by members of the advisory-management group. Therefore the so-called independent directors often are close personal friends, relatives, or business associates of the investment adviser. This tends to consolidate the advisory group's control over the fund. The end result is that, even though the advisory contract must be approved each year by either a majority of the shareholders of the fund or a majority of the independent directors, so influential are the advisers that there is hardly an instance of a mutual fund refusing to renew a contract.

In many cases, of course, there are no ill effects from this. Many mutual fund shareholders buy a particular fund in order to get the services of a particular advisory group. A person might buy One William Street Fund chiefly because its adviser is Lehman Brothers, or Dividend Shares because its adviser is Calvin Bullock, Ltd. And it could be that lack of shareholder attendance at annual meetings indicates approval of management's record.

Some mutual funds also have independent advisers who do not spend their energies selling the funds, shares or handling its brokerage business. No-load funds charge no sales commission, so there is no underwriting profit to be had. A substantial number of mutual funds do not have any external adviser but manage their own portfolios. These include Massachusetts Investors Trust, Massachusetts Investors Growth Stock Fund, Broad Street Investing Corp., and National Investors Corp.

It should be noted, also, that the best funds make a fetish of selecting outstanding men to serve as outside directors. Such men usually are meticulous observers of the fund's activities and guardians of the shareholders' interests.

MAKING A CHOICE

There are a number of criteria in selecting an investment trust. The two main ones are these. First, are the managers of the trust trying to invest the money entrusted to them the way you would invest it yourself? For most investors this means putting the money into common stocks of good quality and aggressive companies. Second, are the managers of the trust doing a bang-up job? In other words, is their investment record better than the average record of trusts with similar objectives?

Once these tests are met, there are other measures to apply. Is the sales charge reasonable? Is the annual management fee a modest one? Can shares be purchased in convenient amounts, assuming you do not wish to make a large lump-sum investment? In the case of closed-end funds, you can usually buy them a few shares at a time through the Monthly Investment Plan of the New York Stock Exchange, as will be explained in the next chapter. In the case of open-end funds, there usually are minimum amounts that may be invested. For example, a fund may require a minimum initial investment of $250 or $500 and subsequent investments of, say, $50 at a time. Does the trust permit reinvestment of dividends and capital gains distributions conveniently and inexpensively? In many cases, funds permit reinvestment of capital gains distributions at net asset value, but charge the usual sales commission for reinvestment of dividends paid out of income. Other funds permit the reinvestment of both capital gains distributions and dividends at net asset value.

Here are other points to watch for.

Size   The biggest and most widely known trusts are not necessarily the best. The managers of the very largest open-end funds with the hardest hitting salesmen cannot confine their investments to a relatively few outstanding stocks. They have so much money coming in from shareholders that it must, perforce, be spread over many stocks. The largest open-end funds get so heavily invested in so many companies that they become, as it were, muscle-bound and cannot buy and sell with any freedom. Too often the diversification is so broad that the results are mediocre. This underscores the fact that only the best companies can equal, or beat, the stock market averages.

Acquisition costs   While not as important as performance, they do enter into the selection.

Sponsorship   Who manages the trust and why? Selling shares in mutual funds has been a good business over the past few years. The principle of investing through trusts has been sound, but unfortunately there is reason to feel that a few managers are more interested in the sales commissions and management fees than in providing the best possible results for the shareholders. Several such trusts have reduced management fees as a result of stockholder suits.

Performance   An outstanding long-term performance record is important. In addition, the investor may feel better about putting in his money if he knows that the managers have thought enough of the trust to put their own money in also. Of course, no one person could own a substantial interest in an investment trust with assets of hundreds of millions of dollars. However, a few could be mentioned, such as Lehman Corporation, Chemical Fund, State Street Investment Corporation, and Tri-Continental Corporation, in which the managers and their families do have substantial holdings.

Which companies have done the best? This is the most important question and one on which many investors go astray. It is important because when you buy shares in an investment trust you are paying someone to manage your money. If you don't get good management, you get nothing.

Some investors go wrong because they buy the first trust they hear of. Or they may fall for some salesman's spiel without realizing that alternative, and perhaps better, investments are available. Other investors buy a poorly managed trust because they see that it has made money during the past few years. As a matter of fact, nearly all trusts have made some money during this period because the stock market itself has gone up. It is advisable to check on what management did over longer periods.

There are, in fact, several tests that should be applied to the management record of an investment trust. Ideally, the net asset value per share should go up with, or faster than, the stock market as a whole and decline more slowly. So one measure is to compare changes in net asset value per share with stock market averages during periods of rising prices and also during periods of declining prices. In addition to the rise and decline in the value of the shares, you naturally must take account of the amount of capital gains paid out. Most investors should reinvest these capital gains, but in some compilations of investment trust records, these gains are listed separately. Dividends should be considered of less importance by most investors.

Below are the names and descriptions of several books that will help you investigate various funds.

Investment Companies, by Arthur Wiesenberger Services, 61 Broadway, New York, New York 10006, published annually, is crammed with information on the theory of investment trusts in general as well as detailed information on all open-end and closed-end trusts. The book may be examined in almost every brokerage house in the country and in almost every library.

Investment Trusts and Funds From the Investor's Point of View is another valuable publication put out each year by the American Institute for Economic Research, Great Barrington, Mass. The authors, using certain criteria, select a small number of funds, some open-end and some closed-end. These funds are then compared with their composite average.

Johnson's Investment Company Charts is perhaps the most intriguing gadget for judging the largest open-end funds (but not the closed-end type). It is published annually by Hugh A. Johnson, Rand Bldg., Buffalo, New York. Each fund gets a page. Its management record is measured by a line on a chart showing how much your shares would be worth today (including all capital gains distributions) if you had invested $10,000 in the fund ten years ago. You can look at this book in the offices of most investment dealers or in a library.

EXAMPLES OF INVESTMENT COMPANIES

Remember, there are some 350 investment trusts offering shares. You should look over many funds before making your selection. And generally speaking, this selection should be based on two considerations: First, do the fund's investment objectives correspond to your own? Second, is the management the best you can find?

The common stock funds listed below are not recommendations but ·examples of some that have done well over a long period of time. Their selection has been based on performance records, management costs, and other factors. There are many other funds that have done as well, and some that have done even better if you consider only the record of the past year or two. So consider these funds as examples selected to show, among other things, the variety available. And keep in mind that the fact that a certain fund is not included in this list does not mean that it isn't a good investment.

Affiliated Fund   63 Wall St., New York, New York 10005. An open-end fund started in 1934. Investment objective long-term growth of capital and of income, without excessive fluctuations in market value. Distributor: Lord, Abbett & Co. Investment adviser: Lord, Abbett & Co. Sales charge 7½%. Minimum initial purchase $250.

Carriers & General Corp.   1 Wall St., New York, New York 10005. A nonleverage, closed-end fund organized in 1929. Shares traded on New York Stock Exchange. Policy is to concentrate investment in a relatively few attractive-appearing common stocks representing large and well-managed corporate enterprises. Investment adviser: Calvin Bullock, Ltd.

Chemical Fund   65 Broadway, New York, New York 10006. An open-end fund organized in 1938. Investment objective is growth of capital and income. The name implies that the trust specializes in chemical company stocks, but actually it has interpreted the field so broadly that it offers considerable diversification among industries as well as companies. Included are producers of drugs, glass, rubber, paint, etc. Distributor: F. Eberstadt & Co. Investment adviser F. Eberstadt & Co., which employs Arthur D. Little, Inc., and the Stanford Research Institute as scientific advisers and consultants. Sales charge 8½%.

De Vegh Mutual Fund   20 Exchange Place, New York, New York 10005. An open-end no-load fund started in 1950. Investment objective: long-term capital appreciation. Distributor: none. Shares sold direct by fund. Investment adviser: Wood, Struthers & Winthrop. Sales charge, none. Minimum initial purchase, $300.

Dreyfus Fund   2 Broadway, New York, New York 10004. An open-end fund incorporated in 1947 and now aggressively managed and known as a "performance" fund. Investment objective growth of capital. Distributor: the Dreyfus Corporation. Investment adviser: the Dreyfus Corporation. Sales charge, 8⅜%. Minimum initial subscription, 10 shares.

Energy Fund   2 Broadway, New York, New York 10004. An open-end, no-load fund founded in 1954, specializing in stocks of companies operating in the field of energy and its sources. Investment objective: growth of capital. Distributor: Ralph E. Samuel & Co., Investment adviser: Ralph E. Samuel & Co. Sales charge, none. Minimum subscription, 10 shares.

Fidelity Capital Fund   35 Congress Street, Boston, Mass. 02109. An open-end performance fund organized in 1957. Investment objective is long-term growth of capital. Distributor: the Crosby Corp., 225 Franklin St., Boston, Mass. 02110 and 134 S. La Salle St., Chicago, Ill. 60603. Investment adviser: Fidelity Management & Research Co. Sales charge 8%. Minimum initial purchase $500.

Investment Company of America   900 Wilshire Blvd., Los Angeles, Calif. 90017. An open-end fund incorporated in 1933. Investment objective: long-term growth of capital and income. Distributor: American Funds Distributors, Inc., Investment adviser: Capital Research and Management Company. Sales charge 8½%. Minimum purchase, 1 share.

Keystone Custodian Fund–S 4   50 Congress St., Boston, Mass. 02109. This is one of several funds managed by Keystone Custodian Funds, Inc., a company organized in 1932. The S-4 Fund is an open-end "performance" fund. Investment objective is to achieve capital appreciation by concentrating on newer and smaller companies specializing in the development of new products, processes, or services. Distributor: the Keystone Co. of Boston. Investment adviser: Keystone Custodian Funds, Inc. Sales charge, 8.3%.

Lehman Corporation   1 South William St., New York, New York 10004. A nonleverage, closed-end fund founded in 1929. Shares traded on the New York Stock Exchange. Investment objective: conservation and growth of capital along with reasonable rate of income. Investment adviser: Lehman Brothers.

Madison Fund   1400 Delaware Trust Bldg., Wilmington, Del. 19801. A closed-end company with a small degree of leverage due to existence of an issue of convertible preferred stock. Founded in 1929. Shares traded on the New York Stock Exchange. Investment objective: long-term growth of capital. Investment adviser: none. Company is managed by its directors and officers.

Massachusetts Investors Growth Stock Fund   200 Berkeley St., Boston, Mass. 02116. An open-end fund started in 1932. Investment objective: long-term growth of principal and future income. Distributor: Vance, Sanders & Co. Investment adviser: none. Company is managed by its directors and officers. Sales charge, 8½%.

National Investors Corp.   65 Broadway, New York, New York 10006. An open-end fund founded in 1937. Investment objective: long-term appreciation and an increase in future dividends. Distributor: Broad Street Sales Corp. Investment adviser: company's directors and officers. Sales charge 7½%.

Niagara Share Corp.   70 Niagara St., Buffalo, New York 14202. A closed-end nonleverage company founded in 1929. Shares are traded on the New York Stock Exchange. Investment objective: long-term growth. Investment adviser: none. Company is managed by its directors and officers.

T. Rowe Price Growth Stock Fund   1 Charles Center, Baltimore, Md. 21201. An open-end no-load fund organized in 1950. Investment objective: long-term appreciation of capital and income. Distributor: none. Shares sold directly by fund. Investment adviser: T. Rowe Price and Associates. Sales charge, none. Minimum initial purchase, $500.

State Street Investment Corp. 225 Franklin Street, Boston, Mass. 02110. This is a hybrid kind of fund. Shares are purchasable only in the over-the-counter market, but will be redeemed by the fund at net asset value less 1%. It was organized in 1924. Investment objective: conservation and growth of principal. Investment adviser: State Street Research and Management Company.

Tri-Continental Corp. 65 Broadway, New York, New York 10006. A closed-end leverage company founded in 1929. Shares traded on the New York Stock Exchange. Investment objective: conservation of capital and growth of both capital and income. Investment adviser: none. Fund is managed by directors and officers.

CHAPTER 10

Dollar Cost Averaging

Here is one of the most foolproof ways of investing in the stock market.

First. Pick out one or more sound common stocks or an investment trust. Do the best job of selection you can. That is all-important.

Second. Pick a sum of money that you can conveniently invest once a month, once a quarter, twice a year or once a year. Don't be too ambitious. Choose a sum small enough to be spared even in bad times.

Third. Buy monthly, quarterly, semiannually, or annually as many shares of the stock or investment trust as your chosen sum will cover. As you go along, reinvest all dividends and capital gains.

Fourth. Once you have started your program, keep it up, not for months but for years.

This method of investment is known as "dollar cost averaging." It is theoretically not as good as buying low and selling high. Unfortunately, however, the buy-low, sell-high method doesn't work. It is impossible to tell positively when the market is low and when it is high, or when it is about to go up or down. Even the so-called experts have been proven woefully inadequate in their efforts to forecast price movements. So dollar cost averaging is a substitute for guessing. And it works because it guarantees that the eventual cost of your investment will be reasonable.

HOW AVERAGING WORKS

Dollar cost averaging does even more than this. Note that when you invest a fixed number of dollars each time this amount buys more shares when the price is low and fewer when it is high. Thus if you keep up your purchases over a long period of time, you will end up with a lower cost per share than if you had bought each time a fixed number of shares. If that sounds impossible, note this simplified example. Say you buy $100 worth of stock on the first of each month. The price, originally $100 a share, declines and then recovers to the original price. The following table shows that after seven months the stock you bought cost you $85.89 a share, or $1.25 per share less than the average price during the period.

CHART 23

Date of purchase	Price per share	Amount invested	Number of shares bought	Cumulative cost per share
Jan. 1	$100	$100	1.00	$100.00
Feb. 1	90	100	1.11	94.79
Mar. 1	80	100	1.25	89.29
Apr. 1	70	100	1.43	83.51
May 1	80	100	1.25	82.78
June 1	90	100	1.11	83.92
July 1	100	100	1.00	85.89
	$ 87.14	$700	8.15	$ 85.89
	Average price per share	Total amount invested	Number of shares bought	Cost per share

No matter whether the price of the stock rises, falls, or just fluctuates, the use of this system ensures that you will pay less than the average price. And over a long period of time the saving in cost will mount up to worth-while proportions. In fact, if you follow the dollar cost averaging method and the securities you pick turn out to be of average quality or better, your investment will grow over the long run at an average rate of 6% to 12% or perhaps more. Moreover, this kind of program can easily be started and maintained. Machinery for making such a bit-by-bit investment is available. Many brokers welcome the kind of customers who plan to make small regular purchases. Investment clubs are flourishing. They are groups of ten to twenty-five investors who pool their money and knowledge. Almost all investment trusts also offer plans whereby shares can conveniently be bought at regular intervals.

Before starting such a program, however, you should note the reasoning behind the four precepts listed at the beginning of this chapter.

First, make sure your investment is of good quality. Obviously, if you buy into a company that is going slowly downhill, the longer you keep up your purchases, the worse off you are going to be. Choice of a poorly managed investment trust would be almost as bad. Your investment would not be growing as it should, and, in addition, the money you paid for professional management would be going down the drain. So long as prices go up and down, dollar cost averaging turns the fluctuations to your benefit and keeps your cost reasonable. But to profit in the long run, your stock should be of such quality that its value will rise. If the long-term trend is down, nothing will help you except a switch to another stock.

Second, don't be overly optimistic as to the amount you can afford to invest. One of the surest ways to lose money in the stock market is to commit money that will have to be used for something else. If you do this, you may find that you will have to suspend your program or even sell your stock at the worst time—when prices are depressed.

Third, don't cash in your dividends or capital gains, plow them back. These small amounts are easily frittered away. But if reinvested they give you the advantage of compounding and over the years they will make your investment snowball.

Fourth, keep buying rain or shine. It won't do to stop when the price of your investment goes down. In fact that is the time to keep going because when the price is low your fixed sum will get you more shares. On the other hand, don't stop either when the price seems high. While it may seem high in relation to past prices, it may actually be low in terms of what prices will be in the future. So don't try to second-guess the market. Just plug along with the averaging. It will guarantee you a reasonable cost.

A PLAN OF YOUR OWN

Save up first. The mechanics of buying stocks in regular installments are not difficult. Perhaps the cheapest way is to make one or two purchases a year. For example, you could deposit in the bank each week or month a sum that would amount to $500 on June 30 and $500 on December 31 of each year. Then on those dates you could order through a broker the number of shares of your chosen stock that $500 would cover. The New York Stock Exchange commission on a purchase of $500 would be around $12. If the purchase were an odd lot, you would pay only about $10 commission, but you would be charged the odd-lot price, which would be an eighth of a point above the last round-lot sale price on stocks selling below $55 a share, and a quarter of a point more on stocks selling above $55.

Note the smallness of the commission—not much over 2%. It shows how you can keep costs down by accumulating the money yourself and buying direct through a broker. If, instead, you had joined an accumulation plan and put a small amount into a stock each month, the commission might have been nearly three times as much. If you had bought the most common type of mutual fund, the commission might have been four times as great.

FORMAL PLANS

There are some advantages, however, to joining a formal accumulation plan.

(You usually make a cancellable agreement to invest so much a month or a quarter, and each time you invest, you receive a statement of account and often a reminder of the next payment due. For many people the agreement and reminders help keep the program going.

(In many plans the amount of each purchase, minus commission, is fully invested down to the fourth decimal place. This purchase of fractional shares is not possible in ordinary purchases of stock made through a broker.

(You may specify that your dividends automatically be reinvested in stock. In this way you never see the dividend checks and are not tempted to spend them.

MIP The most widely available plan for regular purchases of stocks is the Monthly Investment Plan of the New York Stock Exchange, offered by its broker members. Here is how it works. Go to a broker who is a member of the New York Stock Exchange with the name of your stock picked from among the more than 1600 listed on the exchange. Decide how much you can afford to invest per month or per quarter. It can be as little as $40 or as much as $999. If you want more than one stock, you can split or alternate your payments.

When you decide what you want to do, you sign a cancellable

agreement whereby you undertake to make the payments regularly. There is no penalty, financial or otherwise, if you miss a couple of payments, although the broker reserves the right to terminate the plan if you miss four payments in a row. The commission you pay will be 6% on amounts under $100; 2% plus $1 on amounts from $100 to $399 (with a minimum of $6) and 1% plus $5 on amounts above. Remember, also, the odd-lot differential. Each payment you make, minus the commission, will be invested in full and fractional shares of your stock to the fourth decimal place. Thus if your payment is $50 and the odd-lot price of the stock is $18, the commission will be $3 and your account will be credited with $47 worth of stock or 2.6111 shares.

You probably will want to leave your stock in the broker's custody until you complete your plan or purchase the desired number of shares. Or you can get free delivery after you have acquired 50 shares. If you want delivery beforehand, there will be a $1 mailing fee per delivery. If you decide to quit the plan, you will receive the number of full shares in your account without delivery charge. Any fractional shares will be sold and a check sent to you for the proceeds.

If you work in a company that will make payroll deductions for this type of investment, you can have as little as $4 a week deducted from your paycheck and sent in to buy stock.

For more information on this plan see the nearest broker who is a member of the New York Stock Exchange or write to the Exchange at 11 Wall Street, New York, New York 10005, for a free copy of *The Story of MIP*.

Mutual funds Over 200 open-end mutual funds offer some kind of plan whereby their shares may be acquired by small, regular purchases. Of the funds offering accumulation plans, most require that the initial purchase be at least $100 or $250 and that subsequent purchases be $25 or $50. Some plans, however, have no minimums and investors may put in any amount.

Front-end or level load One important detail about an accumulation plan is whether it is of the level-charge or the prepaid-charge type. In the level-charge type the sales commission is a fixed percentage, say 8½% on every purchase. If you make 100 payments, the commission is the same on the first as on the last. In the prepaid-charge type, also known as the contractual or penalty plan, you agree to make to the firm sponsoring the plan a specified number of monthly payments. The sponsor will deduct sales commissions and other fees and invest the remainder. But a good portion of the sales commissions and other fees for the whole series of payments will be lumped together and loaded onto the first few payments. Hence the prepaid-charge plan has what is known as a "front-end load."

In many cases of the front-end load, less than half of your first year's payment actually is invested. The rest goes to the sponsor. If you continue the plan to its completion, the commissions and fees will average down. But if you stop in the early months, you get back less than half of what you paid in because the sales commissions and sponsor's fees are not refundable. You are thus "penalized." There is nothing new about the principle. Life insurance traditionally is sold with a front-end load, half or more of the total sales commission usually coming out of the first year's premium. In life insurance, however, there seldom is an alternative available, while in the case of mutual funds, you have the choice of starting either a front-end load plan or a level-load plan.

In the frantic Twenties, many investment companies were sold with a front-end load, but the practice fell into disuse. In the late Fifties and early Sixties, however, it was revived with tremendous vigor. A growing number of open-end funds discovered that if a salesman could count on a big chunk of commission right at the start, he would push the plan much harder than if he got his money in little bites over a period of years.

Open-end funds that took up the contractual plan claimed that it was also good for the investor on the grounds that he needed to be "sold" on investing, and the harder the sell, the better. Another reason given was that the penalty feature forces the investor to keep investing regularly.

Opponents of the front-end load including the U. S. Securities and Exchange Commission have pointed out that almost all open-end funds offer voluntary, or level-load, plans in which the sales commission is the same percentage of every purchase no matter when it is made. Member firms of the New York Stock Exchange also offer their Monthly Investment Plan, which permits level-load purchases of stocks, including shares of closed-end investment companies. Why, these critics have asked, should an investor choose a plan that could cost him over half his investment if he discontinued in the first year or so, when he could adopt a plan in which an early dropout would cost only the regular sales commission of 6%, 8% or 8½%?

Although most contractual plans involve purchase of open-end funds, you can use this method to buy certain common stocks. In 1938, H. Dean Quinby, of Rochester, New York, worked out an investment contract plan with Lincoln Rochester Trust Co., whereby investors could purchase stock in Eastman Kodak. Later he added a plan for acquiring General Motors, A T & T, DuPont, Standard Oil of New Jersey, and General Electric.

Whatever the outcome of the battle between proponents and opponents of the front-end load, make sure you understand the ins and outs of this method of investing before you sign up.

Reinvestment of income Another point to keep in mind when starting an accumulation plan. Most open-end funds will reinvest your capital gains distributions without charging a sales commission. But in many cases, a sales commission is charged for automatic reinvestment of dividends. The U. S. Securities and Exchange Commission also has criticized this practice. Some funds will reinvest both kinds of distribution at net asset value; that is, without charging a commission.

INVESTMENT CLUBS

Have you ever thought that it might be fun for you and a few good friends to get together, pool your money, and use your combined knowledge and experience to select and buy some good stocks? You probably have thought of this and so have thousands of others. The result is there are over forty thousand investment clubs spread all around the country and more are starting all the time.

An investment club, of course, is much smaller and more informal than an investment trust. Furthermore, club members do their own portfolio managing. Only occasionally do they ask for outside help. This can be all to the good because the members learn about investing by actual experience. And that is usually the best way.

Here are some other reasons why investment clubs are popular: An investment club provides an inexpensive way to invest. In most clubs each member contributes $10 a month. (It could be more.) Ten dollars, of course, is not a lot, but over the years it does mount up. The first modern investment club on record was started in Detroit around 1940. Using the $10-a-month formula, each of the original members deposited $3000 in sixteen years. But at the end of the period the securities this money bought were worth $17,360.

If, during a period when stocks appear to be attractively priced, you want to invest more than $10 a month, you can take advantage of the club's research program and buy extra shares for your own account. But if you do this and happen to buy when the market is high, don't blame your losses on the investment club idea.

One primary investment club rule is to stick to dollar cost averaging, that is, investing a fixed number of dollars each month regardless of the level of the market. So if you have extra money to invest, consider using a similar dollar cost averaging plan and investing a fixed amount each month over a period of years. Otherwise you may buy high and suffer a loss.

An investment club is educational. A new research committee is appointed each month. Thus, in the course of a year or so, everybody participates in digging up facts and figures and deciding which stocks look most attractive.

Starting a club is not hard. Procedures are standardized, and model bylaws are available. Brokers generally are happy to accept a club account and give some organizational help, although after that a club ought to do its own stock selecting to gain the experience. It is probably easier to start a club, incidentally, than to try to get into an established one. Most existing clubs want to stay small and will take in a new member only when there is a vacancy.

If all this makes you think you might like to start a club, fine. But before you go ahead with the idea, consider also the possible disadvantages.

Looking at it from an investment standpoint, buying shares of a well-managed investment trust might be safer and more profitable than joining a club. The managers of the trust are professionals; those of the club, amateurs.

A club started when the market is relatively high could lose money if it disbanded within a few months or even a few years because the market might then be lower.

Unless members are congenial, a club could be wrecked by disagreement and wrangling.

Starting a club Now, if you still want to go ahead, that's all right too. Here is how it is usually done. One person with imagination gets the idea and puts it up to two or three friends. All then sit down and suggest names of four or five others who might be interested. When the group reaches six or eight, it meets again to round out the membership to about fifteen. In this rounding-out process, it is advantageous, although not necessary, to add a lawyer and an accountant. The more different interests and professions represented, the better.

Next step usually is to join the National Association of Investment Clubs and get an investment club manual. Annual dues are $10 per club. The cost of the manual is $3, which may be applied to the first year's dues. The manual covers the following ground: articles of agreement or bylaws, with an explanation of how to operate the club; investment policy; record keeping; reporting for income tax; stock study aids with a blank form; model agent agreement to be made with the broker handling the club's account.

Here is the address to write to: National Association of Investment Clubs, 1300 Washington Boulevard Building, Detroit, Michigan 48231.

When the club holds its first organizational meeting, it may invite a competent investment man to discuss the mechanics of investing and methods of selecting growth stocks. Two members generally are appointed as agents. They open a two-name account with a brokerage house, put in the actual buy and sell orders, and handle the money. The club's broker provides a safekeeping account, holds the club's securities, collects dividends, and provides a monthly statement.

Guides for investing Now comes the most important part, the investing. At this point you will be interested to know that there is a set of tested investment principles that have worked out well for clubs over the years. The pattern was set by a pioneer club in 1940. Two Detroiters, Fred C. Russell, a purchasing clerk with the Federal Mogul Corp., and John Biscomb, a clerk with the Ford Motor Co., decided they wanted to accumulate enough money to go into business for themselves. They discussed the idea with a friend, George A. Nicholson, Jr., of Watling, Lerchen & Co., a Detroit brokerage firm. Nicholson suggested the club idea and laid down three guiding principles, which have now become famous.

The first is to invest each month all the money collected from members regardless of the level of the stock market or the business outlook. This gives the advantages of dollar cost averaging, as noted previously.

The second principle is to reinvest all dividends. This gives the snowballing effect of compound interest.

The third principle is to invest for the long pull and stick to common stocks of sound growth companies. Speculating is frowned on. Most clubs that have tried it have failed.

Acting on this good advice, Russell and Biscomb recruited six more young Detroiters—two clerks, an army officer, a salesman, a repairman, and a foreman—and the club got under way. It succeeded from the start. As word got around about the new method of investing, club members began to get letters from people who wanted to start clubs of their own.

By 1951 the idea had spread so far that the Detroit club could hardly handle the mail. There definitely seemed to be a need for an organization to help would-be clubs get started and give them guidance. So one of the charter members of the original club in Detroit, Thomas O'Hara, organized the National Association of Investment Clubs.

Since selecting good stocks is probably the hardest, and also the most important, job that a club has, the NAIC has done considerable work on growth-stock selection methods. It recommends, first, that a club take up an industry each month. Ideally, an industry should be selected from among those that are growing faster than the economy as a whole. A two- or three-man investment committee is appointed to build up a list of the leading companies in the industry, along with pertinent facts and figures on prices, earnings, etc. The committee reports to the full membership at the next meeting, and one stock is selected for purchase.

There are several ways in which the investment committee can get its information. The brokerage house where the club has its account will make available statistical market services. Often it will allow club members to take out pertinent material overnight. The investment committee may also write directly to the president of any company in which it is interested and ask for the annual report and whatever other material is available. Such letters will usually bring in a raft of information, sometimes direct from the president of the company himself.

The ideal stock for an investment club has the following characteristics: a history of increasing sales and earnings; good prospects that sales and earnings will continue to increase; reasonable yield; a price that is also reasonable, considering quality, and that is likely to rise in the future.

To select the stock that comes closest to this idea requires that all stocks under consideration be broken down and rated uniformly as to sales, earnings, dividend, price, etc. When a club is new, a simplified table may be about all the members want to tackle.

Later, they can graduate to the more complicated *Investment Club Stock Selection Guide,* recommended by the NAIC. Filling out this form is somewhat like computing your income tax, but once a club gets the hang of it, it is really not so bad.

The first problem in using the selection guide is to pick out those companies whose sales and earnings have grown by at least 10% a year for the past five years. A form is used for each company. Columns are provided for recording past years' sales and earnings. Figures are plotted on a ratio chart, and the lines projected to give an idea of how fast sales and earnings may be expected to increase over the next five years. A projected increase of 10% a year should be the club's overall goal. And 15% is more desirable. The NAIC also recommends that 25% of the portfolio be in major companies in major industries where the growth may be more like 5% to 7%, and that another 25% be in smaller, faster-growing companies.

Growth stocks are not likely to pay as high dividends as stocks of more stable companies. Nevertheless, a prospective dividend rate of at least 4% within five years is desirable so as to enhance the effects of compounding.

Next problem is to answer the question, Is the stock a good buy at today's price? By use of the basic figures, a judgment can be made on the chances of the stock's going up in price compared with the chances of its going down. The NAIC's ideal ratio is three to one; that is, the price should theoretically be as likely to go up three points as it is to go down one point. Obviously, there is nothing hard and fast about such calculations. Their basis necessarily lies in estimates. But estimates based on known facts are better than guesses.

When a member resigns What happens if a member of a club wants to resign? Usually he need only give thirty days' notice, and he will receive his pro-rata share of the market value of the club's securities. The liquidation value of each $10 share is calculated each month by dividing the total value of the club's holdings by the number of shares outstanding. The withdrawing member gets the liquidation value of his shares minus a 1% penalty and minus, also, any commissions the club incurs to sell securities and raise cash.

The club's broker All kinds of people have formed investment clubs: policemen, stenographers, bridge players, church groups. There are likely to be a few clubs in almost any given city, but in some places, Detroit, Michigan, Albany, N.Y., and Indianapolis, Ind., for example, there are many more than you might expect. In those places live-wire brokers have contributed a good bit of their time and energy to encourage new clubs. This relationship between the members of an investment club and the broker who "sponsors" it, that is, who helps it to get organized, should be clearly understood.

A broker gets very little direct benefit from handling the account of the typical investment club. Assume that the club buys $200 worth of stocks each month. The broker's commission is around $6. Certainly that would not pay him for meeting with the club once during its organizational period and later making available his firm's market services, answering questions on specific stocks, etc.

There are certain benefits, however, that a young broker in particular gets from an association with one or more clubs. Club members will give him word-of-mouth advertising and help him widen his acquaintance. Also there are usually some members who buy stocks for their own account, basing their selection on the monthly choice of the club. Young men and women in business who don't have much to invest today may turn into good customers in ten or fifteen years.

There is another reason why some brokers want to lend a helping hand in the investment club movement. They believe that the more people that understand the free enterprise system and have a stake in it the more support it will get and the better it will work. So if you are starting a club, don't be oversuspicious of the broker's motives. He stands to get something out of it, sure. But chances are he will make a net contribution of his time and energy.

One more point about a broker: Get one with experience and a reputation for good judgment. A young one is okay, but not a dumb one.

Whether you do your dollar cost averaging through an investment club, through MIP, through mutual fund accumulation plans, or just by saving up dollars and making periodic purchases directly in the market, you will benefit from certain built-in advantages. You won't have to worry about the ups and downs in the market. Your costs will be averaged out for you. Then, if you have selected securities of good quality, you will begin to see your money snowball. If you started out putting $25 a month, or $300 a year, into good growth stocks and kept it up for 25 years, you should acquire an investment worth many thousands of dollars. Invest $1000 a year and you should end up with a small fortune.

CHAPTER 11

New Issues—Should You Buy Them?

How about freshly issued stock? Should you consider buying it? It depends a lot on your investment objectives and what kind of company is issuing the stock. There are three general types of new issue. First is stock issued by an established company that needs additional capital. From time to time even the biggest companies issue new stock to finance expansion, retire debt, or for some other purpose. Buying such stock would be about the same as buying the company's stock in the open market. In other words, the risk of owning newly issued stock of a company like General Motors or General Electric would be no greater or less than owning GM or GE stock that had been on the market for some time.

Two other kinds of new issue, however, are in a different class. Stock often is issued by a brand new company with only a short history of operations. There is considerable risk here, of course, because of the difficulties new companies always face. Then there is the case of stock issued by a company that has been operating for some years but that heretofore has been privately owned or perhaps even family owned, but which has decided, for some reason, to "go public." While such a company may be well established and profitable, buying a new issue of its stock may be quite risky because of the uncertainty as to where the stock's price eventually will settle. When underwriters offer a company's stock for the first time, they have to put a price on it, but they have no way of knowing whether their price will turn out to be higher or lower than the price that eventually will be put on it by the public.

In a sense all money raised from the sale of stock is "risk capital." But for the purposes of this chapter, risk capital will be considered to be the stock issued by new companies or companies that have only just decided to go public.

THE NEED FOR CAPITAL

Note that business can get money for expansion and development of new products in three ways: one, by borrowing; two, by plowing back earnings; three, by selling stock.

Borrowing is all right, but a company has to be pretty sound and substantial to borrow big sums of money. A new, young company with a bright new idea can't do it. Also when a company does contract a big debt and feels the weight of it hanging over its head, it is apt to be very cautious about using the money for any new venture, experiment, or research that could, but won't positively, return the money intact.

Stockholders' money, on the other hand, whether it comes from plowed back earnings or from the sale of new stock, doesn't have to be paid out, or back, on any particular date, or ever, for that matter. So a company financed by its earnings or sales of its own stock is likely to feel freer to put that money to work in a way that may be somewhat risky but that also may bring in substantial profits. Remember, however, that a new company probably has few earnings to plow back. So it may have to depend on the sale of stock for its capital needs. Also a family-owned company, even though it may have good earnings, may also have good reasons for offering a block of stock to the public. Large stockholders may want to diversify their holdings or raise money for estate tax purposes.

Here is an example to show why risk capital is needed and how it often is raised. Say there are a couple of young men who have learned a lot at college about the atom and who have designed a measuring device based on nuclear principles that they think will help industry make very accurate and rapid measurements. The young men naturally want to sell this at a profit. But in order to get into production they need a building, machinery, workers, salesmen, and working capital to meet payrolls and various other expenses. Where are they going to get the money?

You can be pretty sure of one thing. They are not going to get it from a bank. The banker might be the first person to approve of their plans and wish them success. He might even put some of his own money into the project. But he won't put in any of the bank's money. The bank uses its depositors' money very cautiously, for loans that are safe and fairly liquid. These might be short-term loans to well-established and successful businesses or conservative loans to individuals backed up by improved real estate, sound stocks, or the cash value of life insurance policies. So the bank is out.

How about the stock market? Can the young men incorporate and sell stock on the New York Stock Exchange? Positively no. Before a company's stock will be admitted to trading on the exchange, the company must have been in business a good many years, be large and prosperous, and have its stock widely distributed throughout the country. So the stock exchange is out.

So where will the young men, with their bright idea and their knowledge, turn for help? In the old days they would either work hard and save up enough capital to buy the machinery and equipment themselves, or they would go to one or two or more wealthy men in their home town and offer them an interest in the business in return for the capital to get started.

The original backers That is still the way it is today. If the nuclear measuring device sounds plausible, if the young men appear to have knowledge, skill, and energy, then they may be able to arouse enthusiasm among the local banker, lawyer, or undertaker. Perhaps the banker, lawyer, and undertaker will decide to "risk" $10,000 apiece. In return they will get shares of stock in the new venture. Note well that word "risk." The banker, lawyer, and undertaker are not making the young men a loan. They are putting money into a business and getting a part ownership. If all fails, their money is lost. If the business prospers, they own a part of it and can share in the profits.

Assume, now, that the young men's idea is good, that the $30,000 capital put up by their financial backers is enough to buy the equipment and lease the building, that within a few months production gets under way and there is a real demand for the new measuring device produced and sold by Nuclear Measuring Devices, Inc. The young men and the banker, lawyer, and undertaker then each own one-fifth of what promises to be a successful business. Assuming the contribution of the young men in ideas and knowledge is worth $20,-000, the total capitalization is now $50,000.

Soon, however, a problem arises. Business improves so much that the young men can't meet the demand with the small building and few machines they have. Customers, waiting impatiently for delivery, turn to other suppliers. The business needs more room, more machinery, a better location with a rail siding, and more working capital to expand their sales force. Where will the money come from?

The banker, the lawyer, and the undertaker, although they are pleased with their original investment and want to keep their stock, don't feel like putting up any more money just now. But on the other hand, the druggist has heard how well the young men are doing and he would like to put up a little money himself. But who will sell him stock?

The banker and the lawyer can solve this easily. They recommend that the company create some new stock. Instead of five shares there will be ten. The company will sell the five new shares, not at the same price as the old shares sold for, but for $15,000 a share. The increase is justified because the business is established now and no longer as risky as it first was, although, of course, there is still some risk. Each owner of an old share will get a chance to buy a new share at the new price. Any new shares not taken up by the original stockholders will be sold to anyone who cares to buy them.

So the druggist gets a chance to buy in. He realizes that even though the company is prospering it could still lose out to a competitor with a better measuring device, or the plant could burn down or any one of a number of things could happen to jeopardize his investment. But still, he feels that chances are pretty good that the business will keep growing and make a lot of money later, so he is willing to pay $15,000 a share for stock and will buy two shares. Furthermore, his brother-in-law will buy another share, and the newspaper publisher will come in for two.

So now the young men have taken in new backers and have thereby brought in $75,000 of new money for a bigger building, more machines, and more salesmen. Note that the original investors, who once owned the whole company, now only own half of it. But whereas they originally owned a company worth $50,000, they now own half a company worth $125,000, so they have already made a paper profit of $12,500.

So far so good. The company goes along selling its nuclear measuring devices until one day the newspaper publisher comes up with the news that in the next town there is an old, established company that makes fine calipers. The elderly man who owns the company wants to sell it so there will be enough cash to pay estate taxes when he dies. Naturally he wants to sell to someone that will keep the company going. If he finds the right party he will sell at a reasonable price.

The directors of Nuclear Measuring Devices, Inc., are interested. Here is a chance for them to add a new line and diversify their products. But they have no cash to offer. The banker suggests giving some stock to the owner of the caliper company in return for his building, machinery, patents, and inventory. In case of his death, some of the stock could be sold to raise money for taxes.

Preferred vs. common stock   When the proposal is put up to the elderly manufacturer, he demurs. Nuclear measuring devices are brand-new to him. He wonders whether they are here to stay. But the banker persists. What if he got "preferred" stock? That would give the old man or his heirs prior claim over the assets of Nuclear Measuring Devices, Inc., if the company had to dissolve. And it would give prior claim to any money paid out in dividends. In other words, the preferred dividends would have to be paid in full before any dividends could be paid on the common.

That satisfies the owner of the caliper company, so the deal goes through. Nuclear Measuring Devices, Inc., acquires the assets of the caliper company in return for one hundred shares of Nuclear Measuring Devices 5% preferred stock.

Stock splits   When this news gets around, many townspeople begin to get interested in this prosperous new company run by the young physicists. A demand grows up for its stock. But there are so few common shares, only ten, that there seldom comes a chance for anyone to buy. In the meantime, the lawyer dies and leaves his stock to his two sons. Since it is only one share it is hard to divide. The stockholders of the company, taking thought of all this, decide to split the stock 100 for 1. That means that the owner of every share of the original common stock will exchange it for one hundred shares of the new common stock. Each new share will then be worth $\frac{1}{100}$ as much as each old share. But each stockholder will have one hundred times as many shares.

After the stock split, Nuclear Measuring Devices has one thousand common shares outstanding. The original founders each own one hundred shares except that the lawyer's one hundred shares are now divided equally between his sons. One decides to sell his fifty shares, so he drops in on the local broker. The broker has had inquiries about the stock and feels sure that he can sell fifty shares without any trouble. He figures it is now worth around $135 a share and that is what the lawyer's son gets for it, minus the commission.

Making a market   Pretty soon other shares come on the market and the broker is doing quite a business in it. The stock of Nuclear Measuring Devices is then said to be traded "over-the-counter" as described in Chapter 6 of this book. Once trading is large enough to cross state lines, the company will be required to register its stock with the U. S. Securities and Exchange Commission.

The case history of Nuclear Measuring Devices is a fictitious one, but there are many real companies that got their start in the same way. The Ford Motor Company had similar humble beginnings. When a company's stock is finally listed on a major stock exchange, there is always a ready market for any new stock that it might wish to issue for the purpose of raising risk capital.

Profit and risk   Look back for a minute at the beginnings of the Nuclear Measuring Devices, Inc. Who made money on it? The early stockholders made the most. But remember, they took the most risk. They bet their money on two college graduates with an idea. The rest of the people in the town had their money safely stashed away in the bank or savings and loan association where they knew they could lay their hands on it, intact, any time they pleased. But they were getting 4% or 5%, while the investors in Nuclear Measuring Devices were getting many times that.

As the company became established and better known, others bought its stock and they also prospered. But by that time the investment carried less risk. So the later investors made less. As the stock was traded more widely, it no doubt fluctuated in price, like all stocks. Some people probably bought it with money they really couldn't spare, had to sell later at a bad time, and thereby lost. But even the latecomers, those who bought after the company had become big and strong, could make 6% to 10% or more by buying and holding over the years. That assumes, of course, that the company kept its vigor, brains, and wise management.

UNDERWRITING

Suppose, now, that at some point in its history, Nuclear Measuring Devices wants to raise additional capital by the sale of a block of new stock. The company probably would go to an underwriter. When a company sells its own stock to the public, the underwriter acts as a middleman. The underwriter buys the securities from the issuing company, holds them for the account of his own firm, at least temporarily, then offers them to the public. A broker, on the other hand, merely acts as agent for the buyer and seller. Many firms that do a day-to-day brokerage business also frequently underwrite new issues.

Established companies The biggest part of the underwriting business consists of the selling of new securities of established companies that need additional capital for modernization or expansion, so consider these first. Such issues are often so large that no single investment banker can handle the whole job. Syndicates are formed in which a dozen houses may join together, each buying a portion of the securities and reselling its share to its customers at a mark-up. This mark-up pays the overhead and provides the profit to the underwriter. The average mark-up in the case of shares sold by companies listed on the New York Stock Exchange is less than 4%. The financial pages of the newspapers carry ads every day for such newly issued securities—bonds, debentures, preferred stock, common stock, convertible debentures or preferred, and so on. An expanding utility company, for example, may offer a large issue of bonds to finance new power lines or generators. A large finance company may sell debentures to raise money to relend to auto buyers.

Rights Almost always in the case of common stock of established companies existing stockholders are given the opportunity to buy these additional shares. This opportunity is given via the issuance of "rights." As an example, suppose you own 25 shares of the ABC Co. and you get a letter from the president saying the company is issuing additional stock and enclosed are 25 rights entitling you to buy 2½ more shares.

Here is how such rights come to be issued. Say the ABC Co. wants to expand and needs more capital. It decides to sell additional stock, increasing its outstanding shares from 100,000 to 110,000. This decision affects you and every other stockholder because it threatens to decrease slightly your share of ownership and profits unless—and here is the crux of the matter—unless you buy your pro-rata share of the new stock. In that case you will maintain your original position.

For this reason many states require companies to offer new stock to their stockholders before they offer it to the public. Go back to your 25 shares of ABC. You have received 25 rights, one right for every share you own. Since the company is increasing its capitalization by 10%, you now have the privilege of increasing your holdings by the same amount, or of buying 2½ more shares. Your 25 rights will come in the form of two certificates. One will be a full certificate representing 20 rights and entitling you to buy 2 shares of new stock. The other will be a fractional certificate representing 5 rights and theoretically entitling you to buy half a share. As a matter of practice, you generally can't buy half a share. Your fractional certificate must be combined with others to make up a full certificate. Either you buy enough additional fractional certificates from someone else to make up a full share, or you sell your fractional certificates for cash.

On each certificate there are instructions. If you want to sell the certificate for cash, you sign in one place. If you want to subscribe to new shares, you sign in another and make out a check based on the subscription price. If you have a fractional certificate and want to buy additional fractions to make up a full certificate, you can do that, too. You will be billed later for the cost. In all cases you send your certificates back to the ABC Co.'s transfer agent, which may well be a New York bank.

How much are stock rights worth? In actual practice they are worth what other investors are willing to pay for them on the open market. But there is a formula by which their theoretical value can be judged. Assume the ABC is currently traded at $25 a share. The rights entitle you to buy 2½ new shares at $22 a share. The company has set this low price to encourage you to buy. But if you don't care to buy, what can you get for your rights?

To get the theoretical answer, write down the market price of the old stock, $25; subtract the subscription price of the new stock, $22; then divide by 1 plus the number of shares you must own to buy one new share, which in the example is 10 shares.

The theoretical value of ABC rights, then, would be—

$$\frac{\$25 - \$22}{1 + 10} = 27\frac{1}{3} \text{ cents}$$

Since you have 25 such rights, their total theoretical value is $6.83. If you decide to sell them, you may get a bit more or less, depending on how brisk the demand is and what is happening to the price of ABC stock on the market.

Whatever you do about your rights must be done promptly. When the ABC Co. offers to sell new stock at $22 a share, or $3 under the market price, it is highly vulnerable. Suppose the stock market dropped suddenly, carrying the price of ABC down to $20. The right to buy new shares at $22 would be worthless, and the new issue would not get sold. Naturally, the ABC Co. wants its stockholders to make up their minds in a hurry. Still, they must have time to read and understand the proposal, fill out the forms, and mail them. The New York Stock Exchange therefore requires listed companies to give stockholders 16 days to use or sell their rights. Companies not listed on the exchange generally allow a comparable period. The stock exchange also sets a date at which the stock will sell "ex-rights." This ex-rights date is the date after which the stock no longer carries the right with it.

Whether you should exercise rights or sell them depends on how you feel about the stock in question and whether or not you should be buying more of the same or diversifying into other stocks. Don't be swayed too much by the appearance of a bargain. The price of the stock will be automatically reduced, as of the ex-right date, by the value of one right. So in the end you are about even with the board if you sell the right and take the money instead of subscribing to the new stock offering.

Warrants These are long-lived rights. Some have expiration dates; others are perpetual. They generally come into being as a "sweetener" to make an issue of stock or bonds more attractive. Usually the price at which a warrant entitles the holder to buy a specified number of shares of common stock is considerably above the market price of the stock at the time. But there is always a chance that the market will rise to a point where exercise of the warrant will be profitable. This gives it a speculative appeal.

Small or new companies   Another part of the underwriting business is offering for sale the securities of new or privately owned companies that have decided to "go public." Such new issues, being smaller than offerings by established companies, require fewer underwriters and the underwriting mark-up is likely to be higher, 6% or 7%. As noted previously, when a small company offers securities to the public for the first time, it generally issues common stock. Its future, in all likelihood, is too uncertain for it to attract the type of investor likely to buy bonds. However, capital can be raised by making a bond convertible into common, which gives the bondholders the first claim against the company's assets and a chance to buy the common stock if the company does well.

In the case of a very small, new, speculative company, one underwriter alone may handle the whole issue. And the underwriter may do it on what is known as a "best efforts" basis. In other words, instead of buying the whole issue and taking the responsibility for reselling it to investors, the underwriter may undertake only to sell as much of the issue as he can. If he fails to sell it all, the balance is left in the hands of the issuing company. When stock is offered on a "best efforts" basis, it often indicates that the underwriter is not too confident that he can place the whole issue, or that he does not have enough capital to swing the deal on the usual basis.

Underwriter's obligations   Now what are the obligations of the underwriting house when it offers securities to the public? It has a certain obligation to the issuing company. The job there is first to advise the issuer as to timing, price, terms, etc., of the issue, then to get the issue sold and the proceeds into the hands of the issuer at the least cost. The underwriting firm also has obligations to its customers, for it is to them, largely, that it expects to sell the securities. A reputable broker or investment banker doesn't want to recommend purchase of securities and then have them go sour and decline in price. That would be an excellent way to lose customers and go out of business. Finally, of course, the underwriting firm has a responsibility to its own partners, and this simply is to meet expenses and make a profit so that the business can prosper.

An underwriting firm with years of experience and a reputation to maintain will make every effort to offer its customers only sound securities reasonably priced with respect to the issuer's underlying assets and prospective earnings. Large issues of the securities of nationally known companies generally are offered by syndicates headed by large New York underwriters. Even so, there can be no guarantee that the securities so offered will turn out to be good investments.

When it comes to local issues, the prospective investor must be even more careful. In most cities there are local firms that have been in business for years and that exercise the greatest care in choosing which issues they will underwrite. However, in addition to outstanding and reputable local underwriters, there are also those who are less choosy about what they will do. The worst of these are simply looking for stock that they can unload on the public at as high a profit as the traffic will bear. Unfortunately, the space age has provided a label that apparently can be stuck on to almost any small company to give it glamour. The most prosaic small companies have gone public and at the same time have changed their names to include such words as missiles, electronics, and the like, whether or not they were actually in the missile or electronic business.

Gimmicks to beware of   Here are a couple of notorious gimmicks designed to take your money. One is known in the trade as a bail-out. The following is an actual case with names omitted. A group of mining promoters organized a company having 6,000,000 shares of common stock. They put in $10,000 in cash and 115 claims covering 2,260,-000 acres in Utah which had cost them $30,000. In return for their investment of $40,000 in the company they received 3,000,000 shares of stock and offered the other 3,000,000 shares for sale to the public at 10 cents a share.

Right there you can see that if all went as planned and the public paid 10 cents a share for the stock, the promoters' own stock would have a market value of 10 cents a share or $300,000. Not only that, but they would be in control of a company having a quarter of a million dollars of capital (the $300,000 from the public sale of stock minus selling expenses). This is known as a bail-out because the public would have "bailed out" the promoters and acquired assets of dubious value.

Now how about the underwriters? In this case they agreed to sell the stock on a best-efforts basis. For this they received between 25% and 33% of the selling price. All they had to do was to ballyhoo the stock and every time they sold 1000 shares they raked in $25 to $30. They owned no stock themselves, nor did they agree to buy any.

Therefore they took no risk. The big risk, of course, was taken by those who paid 10 cents a share for stock that had a true worth of a good deal less than that.

The other notorious gimmick used by small and unscrupulous underwriters is known as a "lock-up." In this case the underwriters bring out a new issue of a glamorous-sounding stock and give it a big advance ballyhoo. They let it be known that this is going to be a "hot issue" and that the demand for it will be so great that the stock will have to be "allocated." In other words, eager customers who want 100 shares will be lucky if they get 10 or 25. To guarantee that the issue will be hot, the underwriters let their friends and relatives (although this is against the rules) sign up for large blocks of the issue in advance. This does, in fact, create an apparent scarcity. A would-be purchaser, finding that he cannot get any stock allocated to him on the day of the offering, starts bidding for the stock in the open market. This runs the price up. During the height of this price run-up, the insiders quietly begin leaking out their "locked-up" stock at perhaps double or triple the price they paid at the offering.

It is a well-known fact that many small underwriters have this reputation: If you are a good friend or customer and buy their new issues, they will get you in at the offering price and get you out at the top of the run-up. It's not hard to guess who is left holding the bag. It's the uninformed investor who buys at inflated prices and fails to get out in time.

Why is this sort of thing allowed to go on, you might ask. Actually, a great deal is being done to prevent it by both the Securities and Exchange Commission and the National Association of Securities Dealers. But it's a difficult job to police the 100,000 securities salesmen scattered over the country. And while the SEC requires the issuers of securities to make the most detailed advance disclosure of their assets, prospects, how the money is to be used, and the risks involved, the unfortunate truth is that a great many investors simply won't bother to read registration statements but prefer to base their decisions on what they hear from a salesman or someone else supposedly in the know.

HOW THE SEC PROTECTS INVESTORS

In regard to new issues, the basic SEC law is the Securities Act of 1933, sometimes known as the "truth in securities" act. When securities are first offered to the public, a summary of the company's business operations and its financial condition must be furnished to prospective buyers free. In the case of large issues of stock this summary is known as a prospectus. When the amount of stock is less than $300,000, an abbreviated summary known as an offering circular may be used.

In either case, whether a salesman solicits an investor in person, by mail, or by phone, a copy of the prospectus or offering circular must be furnished. If it is not, the nearest regional office of the SEC would like to hear about it. Sometimes the first written communication a prospect receives is the confirmation of an order he has given by telephone. Even at this late date, he may be able to cancel his purchase if the offering circular reveals information he was not given over the phone.

But the truth is, few purchasers of small new issues really study the offering circular or prospectus. In this case it's pretty hard to protect them from their own folly. However, the SEC and the NASD do have other rules designed to prevent the other form of skulduggery mentioned earlier in this chapter.

When a new issue comes out, the underwriter and members of his firm and his immediate family are not allowed to purchase any stock at the offering price unless such purchases are disclosed in the prospectus and conform to their past pattern of investing. And even if such persons have a history of investing in every new issue underwritten, they are supposed to receive only a reasonably small percentage of the issue and to buy it to hold for investment, not to sell for "a quick turn."

What is a reasonably small percentage and what is a pattern of investing? These are terms, of course, that are susceptible of different interpretations. In almost every large offering of a hot issue, the NASD or the SEC, or both, has required the underwriter to fill in exhaustive questionnaires showing the disposition of every share of stock. Fines have been levied against culprits who violate the spirit or the letter of the rules.

The same rules apply to broker-dealers who may not be members of the original underwriting group but who have received expressions of interest in the stock from their own customers. If they receive an allocation of stock from the underwriter as an "accommodation," they must accept it at the offering price, less a selling group concession, and sell it to their customers at the same price.

Should you buy new issues?   Despite all the pitfalls in the new issue market, there are bound to be attractive opportunities for investment. In recent years the breakthrough in research has peppered the land with new, exciting ventures. Engineers, chemists, physicists, advanced mathematicians, and young men with energy and big ideas have splintered off from established companies and started up new businesses with glamorous names and space-age products that mystify, and yet intrigue, the layman. One company turns out quartz high-vibration frequency systems while another uses the latest electronic computers to solve complicated problems for business and government. A third develops atomic isotope application, radioactive analyses, and nuclear power technology, while a fourth offers a revolutionary electronic teaching machine. A fifth has developed a ceramic coating for missile nose cones, while a sixth sells a heat-resistant paint to protect missile launching pads.

Many of these young companies have sold stock to the public and have achieved success so rapidly that their stock has skyrocketed. Naturally, the question arises in the mind of the investor, should he not try to participate in this space-age business and acquire shares in young companies that seem to be growing like Jack's beanstalk and outstripping even the old-established leaders in electronics and chemistry?

This is a hard question to advise on. Undeniably, many of these little companies will grow and prosper and pay off handsomely for those who get in on the ground floor. Many more, however, because of lack of capital, lack of management know-how, or inability to compete with the larger groups, will eventually fall by the wayside. The most difficult problem is selection.

The information is available to evaluate the prospects of a new enterprise. The U. S. Securities and Exchange Commission sees to that. But the average person hardly has time to read and compare the prospectuses of dozens of companies. And he probably should consider a good many before selecting even one. The large, reliable statistical services cannot evaluate the thousands of small new issues constantly appearing on the market. In the end, the investor is almost forced to ask for help. And chances are the person he will consult about a particular new issue will be the very underwriter who is trying to peddle it.

Unless you are prepared to take a rather high risk, you should leave small new issues strictly alone. Yet the business of raising public money for small, enterprising companies is a legitimate one. Every company from General Motors on down had its humble beginnings. If it had not been for courageous investors willing to finance promising new ventures, we would not be a great industrial nation with a high standard of living. Think what a service the backers of Henry Ford performed, both for themselves and for the public. They made themselves millionaires but also enabled Ford to begin mass production of automobiles.

If you are interested in trying to get in on the ground floor of small new companies, you should do everything possible to avoid the pitfalls and realize also that these are more numerous than in any other kind of investing.

Guides to use   Here are some ideas for investing in small new companies.

Deal with a reputable underwriter. You can get names of good ones from your banker. Those houses that are members of the New York Stock Exchange generally fall into this category.

Learn everything you can about the company before you buy. Read the prospectus if the stock is already out. If it isn't, get what is called the "red herring." This is a preliminary prospectus containing what the company considers to be information required by the SEC. If the SEC does not raise any questions as to the adequacy or accuracy of the red herring, it becomes an effective prospectus. Otherwise, the underwriter revises it and resubmits it. All the facts about the company, and particularly all unfavourable facts and contingencies, are clearly set forth in the final prospectus. It would cost a potential investor thousands of dollars to buy such a complete and unbiased picture of a company's operations. The SEC makes the issuer and underwriter provide it to you free. So use it.

SBIC'S

There is another way to buy stock in new, small companies. That is to buy stock in a "small-business investment company," which invests its capital in selected small growth companies.

These small-business investment companies, or SBIC's, are a fairly new phenomenon. They are privately organized but can borrow money at nominal rates from the government and also receive certain tax advantages. In return, SBIC's must agree to lend to or invest in businesses having limited assets and net profits. Such small businesses historically have had difficulty raising capital or obtaining long-term financing.

After 1958, when Congress passed legislation fostering SBIC's, hundreds were organized. Many are closely held and difficult to buy into, but many others have "gone public." Their stock is traded over-the-counter or on exchanges. So by buying into one of these, you indirectly invest your money in the small companies that the SBIC itself selects, finances, and, in some cases, advises. If these small companies prosper and grow, so will your investment. If they do not, chances are you'll lose money. The risk is there, and in some cases it may be more than if you invested in some small company yourself.

Here are the most pertinent facts about this kind of investment.

Professional management This probably is the most important single consideration. An SBIC may be organized by any group of people with capital. Many have been set up by banks. Others have been established by investment counselors or management men well versed in making large-scale investments. Many SBIC's, on the other hand, have been set up by obscure businessmen who operate on the local level. In such cases the ability of the management is unknown.

Management policy If you are interested in small growth companies that may be on the verge of a large expansion, there are SBIC's that concentrate on this type of investment. Others buy into run-of-the-mill concerns. One SBIC, for example, invested in a chain of bowling alleys, a small iron and steel rolling mill, a clay-products company, a traprock company, a printing company, and a string of motels.

Price When SBIC's first began selling stock to the public in volume, there was not much investor interest, and many SBIC shares were selling below net asset value. Later, the public became enthusiastic about SBIC's, and in some cases their stock soared. Later still, after the glamour wore off, prices fell until many SBIC's were selling at a discount from net asset value.

Any investor contemplating purchase of stock in an SBIC should ascertain the relation between the market price and the net asset value per share. All other things being equal, of course, it is better to buy at a discount or at least not pay a very high premium.

Leverage This is a characteristic of investment companies that use borrowed money. Suppose an SBIC has X dollars of invested capital, and borrows twice as much at a nominal rate of interest from the federal government. If it then makes a large profit on its total capital, this profit (after interest is paid) accrues to those who put up the original money.

Tax advantages An SBIC and its stockholders receive preferential tax treatment. Dividends the company receives from investments are completely exempt from corporate income taxes. By comparison, ordinary corporations receive only an 85% exemption. Then, if the SBIC suffers losses on its stock investments, these losses may be deducted either from ordinary income or from capital gains. Also, if stockholders in an SBIC sell their shares at a loss, this loss, too, may be deducted from ordinary income.

SBIC's resemble ordinary investment trusts, but there is one difference. An investment trust generally puts its money into well-established companies with a record of earnings extending back at least ten years. By contrast, an SBIC must confine its investments to small companies. And many companies that SBIC's invest in have never had any earnings at all and, at most, have what might be considered good prospects. As a matter of fact, there are on the market shares of investment trusts and mutual funds that also invest in glamorous growth companies. So if you want glamour, consider these trusts as well. And don't forget that a good many old, established companies are developing new products and new methods all the time. Sometimes the underwriters can make a brand new little company sound pretty glamorous. But companies like IBM or Minnesota Mining and Manufacturing are pretty glamorous too, and still they have been in business a good long time.

CHAPTER 12

Invest in Real Estate?

For thousands of years real estate has represented a good portion of the world's wealth. One reason is that, when you own land or a building, you own something solid. It may be a vacant lot at the edge of town, a gas station leased back to an oil company, or a share of an apartment house. On some of those investments the yield can be as high as 15%. The value of others can double over the years. But even smaller rates of return are not to be sneezed at.

Against these advantages, of course, there are a few drawbacks. A venture into real estate usually takes a bigger chunk of capital than other investments. And since the market is slow and ponderous, buying and selling real estate must be a long-range proposition. Real estate is not as liquid as stocks and bonds. If you own a security listed on a stock exchange, you can sell it in five minutes. But to get your money out of a building or a vacant lot may take weeks or months.

Real estate as an investment, then, is not something you can jump into and out of. To be successful, you need time and the patience to investigate every proposition. Also, you should have the common sense to seek out good advice and take it. Then, once you have put your money in, you should be able to leave it alone, usually for a period of years. You should have resources enough so that some emergency won't force you to dump your property on the market, sell to the first buyer that comes along, and take a loss.

SYNDICATES

If you and half a dozen friends pooled your savings and bought a small apartment house or office building, you would have formed a real-estate syndicate. This kind of operation can be very profitable provided the syndicate has an able manager. Such a syndicate is usually started when a real-estate broker finds a likely piece of property that he believes can be bought cheaply and operated profitably. He puts the proposition up to those of his friends and customers that have money to invest. If they respect his judgment and approve the deal, they contribute the required funds. The manager of the syndicate handles all the details such as buying the property, rentals, repairs, managing, accounting, and distribution of profits.

The big advantage of a syndicate is that it enables a person with a few thousand dollars to become part owner of property requiring a down payment of perhaps $100,000 or $150,000. At this level there are few potential buyers and therefore better chances for a bargain.

The syndicate manager Most syndicates are joint ventures, although a few are set up as corporations with stock ownership. In a joint venture, the manager is known as the managing venturer. For his work in setting up the deal he usually gets a free share, perhaps 10%. He may also buy into the syndicate himself as a way of convincing the other investors of his good faith. In addition, the managing venturer, having found the property to be purchased, may act as broker in selling it to the syndicate and thus get a commission. He usually sells the insurance on the building also, so, all in all, the managing venturer is well paid for his services.

The investors in the syndicate are also well paid if—and it is a big if—the manager is shrewd. One syndicate in Washington, D.C., which bought an apartment building, was able to pay its members a cash return of 15% while paying off the mortgage at the same time. Obviously the managing venturer in this case was especially shrewd. Such success undoubtedly is rare. However, yields of 15% including payments on the mortgage are not unusual.

Modernizing older properties The object of the most successful syndicates is usually not just to buy any apartment building or office building and rent it. The goal is to find a building that is currently unprofitable from not being put to its best use, buy it cheap, and convert it to a new and profitable use.

Thus a syndicate might buy an old apartment building with old-fashioned four- or five-room suites, modernize it, and chop each suite in two. It would then contain twice as many units, known as "efficiencies," and the gross rental might be doubled or increased by 50%. One syndicate bought an old out-of-the-way hotel, modernized it, arranged space for stores on the ground floor, and converted the balance into apartments. The building is now making excellent profits. Another syndicate bought an apartment house in a downtown location and converted it into an office building, increasing the rents substantially.

Disadvantages   A syndicate usually is formed to buy one piece of property and thus lacks diversification. Each member has a sizable amount tied up in this single investment, whereas if he owned stock in a real estate investment company or trust (described later), his money would be spread over a number of properties.

Another disadvantage is the syndicate's lack of liquidity. An elaborate legal agreement must be drawn outlining the procedures a member or his estate must use to dispose of his interest. There generally is no organized market for syndicate memberships. When a member of an income-producing syndicate wants to sell out, the other members may pay his original cost. In other cases he may have to sell at a discount.

"Tax free" returns   Here is something else to watch for. Promoters have hit on an intriguing device for paying out tax-free returns to investors. These windfalls are fine when the device is not abused, but in some cases the system undermines the health of the enterprise. It works like this:

The Internal Revenue Service allows the owner of a building to list as an expense (which is tax deductible) a certain amount of depreciation. Thus if a building costs $200,000 and its life is estimated at 20 years, the owner is allowed to set aside on his books one-twentieth of the value, or $10,000 a year, as a depreciation reserve. Theoretically, this amount goes to build up a kitty to replace the building once it wears out or becomes obsolete. In actual practice, however, this depreciation money does not have to be put into a reserve but can be paid out to the owners. It is tax-free at the time of payment simply because it is not a dividend but a partial return of the owners' capital, and it will be taxable as a capital gain once the building is sold.

To many financial men, such a practice is unsound. They contend that if a depreciation reserve is not actually built up to replace a building, but is paid out in dividends, the owners of the building are simply paying back to themselves some of the capital they originally invested. The unsoundness of the practice has been amply proved in recent years. Older buildings have been made obsolete by new construction. And owners who paid out the depreciation money found they had no funds to modernize or replace their properties.

Making a choice Some syndicates require an investment of $10,000 to $30,000 from each member. In others the contributions can be as low as $800 or $1000. If you are interested in such a venture, get in touch with your local real-estate board and find out which agents are in this business. But always remember that the safety and profitableness of a syndicate depend almost entirely on the character and ability of the manager. Before throwing in your lot with any group, talk to others who have already invested in one or more of the syndicates formed by that particular manager. There is no substitute for personal experience. You will find that there is considerable competition to get into a syndicate being formed by a manager with a record of success. Today there are more investors with money than there are opportunities for big profits.

REAL ESTATE INVESTMENT COMPANIES AND TRUSTS

A real estate investment company This is another form of group investment, and it has two advantages over a syndicate. First, the company can invest in a number of properties, thus diversifying the risk. Second, the stock can be purchased in small amounts and easily sold by stockholders without the legal complications of transferring a syndicate membership. The disadvantage, of course, is that the company must pay the corporate income tax while the stockholders must pay their own income tax on dividends. An exception, as with a syndicate, is the tax-free dividend, usually consisting of depreciation money paid out.

A real estate investment trust It combines some of the advantages of both the syndicate and the real estate investment company. If such a trust satisfies certain conditions, one of which is that at least 90% of its net income be paid out to shareholders, it is exempt from the corporate income tax. At the same time, the trust can invest in a wide variety of properties, which gives the shareholder diversification. Stock in the trust usually will be listed on a stock exchange or traded over-the-counter and thus can readily be bought and sold.

A REIT, as such outfits are commonly called, has certain other characteristics. A trust must engage mostly in "passive" operations; that is, it can own buildings, shopping centers, leases and mortgages, it can buy land and build on it, and can develop its own properties for long-term investment, but it cannot manage its own properties, and the income it receives from capital gains is limited to 30% of its gross. This effectively prevents a trust from wheeling and dealing, buying raw land on speculation, and so on.

Management record   The shareholders of a real estate investment trust do not always have the right to elect the trustees who manage the business. Therefore it is particularly important in selecting a trust to check into the competence, experience, and ethics of the management. Here are three examples of trusts, all based in Boston, that have good records. (They are not the only ones by any means.)

❲ Real Estate Investment Trust of America owns properties scattered from the eastern seaboard to California. It has shopping centers, retail stores, office buildings, light manufacturing plants, parking lots, and land for development. The trust and its predecessor trusts have been in existence for over eighty years and have paid a dividend every year. The stock is traded on the American Exchange.

❲ The Bradley Real Estate Trust is another old and respected Boston trust, which owns a variety of commercial properties across the country. The trust has never made a public offering of its stock outside of Massachusetts, but its stock is traded over-the-counter in Boston and may be purchased through Massachusetts securities dealers.

❲ Continental Mortgage Investors is an example of mortgage trust. Its primary business is investing in mortgages and construction loans. It sold stock to the public in 1962 and invested the proceeds largely in FHA-insured and VA-guaranteed mortgages on homes. But its main source of profit is borrowing money from institutions and re-lending it to builders and developers in the form of first-mortgage construction and development loans. Such loans, made for the most part in fast-growing areas of the country, bring a high return because of the risk, which is greater than the risk of owning insured or guar-

anteed home mortgages. But Continental tries to minimize this risk by screening borrowers carefully and keeping a close and continuous check on their operations. Continental stock sells over the counter.

GOING IT ALONE

If you don't want to buy into a group, but feel you have the judgment, capital, and persistence to do your own real estate investing, here are some ideas.

Raw land It has been said that no one ever bought acreage on the outskirts of a growing city and did not make money provided he was willing to wait. There may be exceptions, but that statement is generally true. An oft-quoted rule of thumb for investing in vacant land is to go out a city's main thoroughfare until land is quoted for sale by the acre. Buy and hold until the price of your property can be quoted by the square foot. Another suggestion: property on a thoroughfare linking a main business district to a high-grade residential district. Shrewd businessmen in every city have always purchased land in the path of new express highways or alongside them after they are built. Such property usually increases in value over the years, even though its initial purchase price may seem high.

If you do want to buy land, better stick to commercial possibilities. Residential lots seldom go up as much in value unless they can later be used for commercial buildings or unless they are located in a growing area where all houses are custom built. Since the trend in building is toward mass production and prefabrication, the owner of a single lot in a community may have to wait a long time for the individual to come along who wants to build a home on that particular spot.

In buying vacant property, keep one rule uppermost in mind. It may be a long, long time before you find just the right buyer. So don't load yourself down with a mortgage that you may not be able to carry. And don't use money for a down payment that you may someday need in a hurry.

Lots by mail How would you like to buy some land in Brazil for two dollars an acre, or a bargain-priced lot in the West Indies, Florida, Arizona, or California? Such property is often sold by mail at seemingly low prices, but if you are tempted to send off a check, best advice is Don't. Experience shows that it's always advisable to inspect a piece of property in person and check out the identity of the promoter, the exact location, the value of similar land in the area, the legal status of the property, the financing, the availability of improvements, and the zoning. The lots-by-mail business has been discouraged by various states and the National Better Business Bureau, but it still flourishes in some places. Many of those who went for schemes in the past have been bitterly disappointed. Many lots are now selling at 25% to 50% of their original offering price. And in some cases, the original owners lost their equity.

RENTAL PROPERTY

Why not buy a house and then rent it out? Won't the rental income greatly exceed the payments you will have to make on the mortgage?

Superficially the answer is Yes. Nevertheless, experienced real-estate men believe that a house bought to be rented is not a good investment today. For one thing, the postwar housing shortage is over. So the renter has a wide choice, and competition among houses for rent is increasing. The owner of a house for rent is also in competition with houses for sale on liberal terms.

There are other reasons why buying a single house and renting it may not pay off. The market price of an apartment house is generally based on the income it will produce. Such buildings generally sell for six to ten times the gross annual rentals. The price of a house, however, is not based on its prospective income, but on what home seekers in general are willing to pay for an attractive place to raise their families. Thus you probably will have to pay relatively more for a house as an investment than you would if you joined with others and bought a share of an apartment building.

One other point about a house for renting. There is no such thing as having a 5% or 10% vacancy rate. Your vacancy rate is either 0% or 100%, and when it is the latter, your income is suspended completely.

Lease-back Wouldn't it be wonderful if you happened to own a lot that an oil company wanted to use for a gas station? You might think that such a situation could come about only by chance, but you would be wrong. It is entirely possible for an investor to acquire a property, knowing in advance that an oil company will lease it. This comes about because oil companies today generally want their capital available for expansion, exploration, drilling, and other purposes, not tied up in real estate.

Thus it often happens that when a company picks a site but finds that the owner of the land is interested only in selling, it will look around for an investor who will buy the land, build on it, and lease it to the company. If you happen to be known to the company's local manager as one interested in such investments, you might get the opportunity.

A lease-back arrangement with an oil company is a desirable investment for several reasons. First, you get a ten- to twenty-five-year lease, so you take virtually no risk. Second, lenders have begun to look on such investments with favor and will generally put up 75% to 90% of the money required to build a station. Third, you know in advance exactly what your rental will be. Generally you can expect to get around 6% on the value of the land and 8% on the building.

Some grocery and drug chains also use the lease-back method in building new stores. The size of the investment here is somewhat larger. Whereas a gas station could be built for, say, $30,000 a modern supermarket might cost as much as $150,000 or $200,000. The U. S. Post Office Department also leases sites and buildings for post offices.

In almost every case, lease-back investment opportunities are found by personal contact. You have to be in touch with local representatives of oil companies, drug chains, or grocery chains. Sometimes these companies will retain a broker to find both the site and the investor to buy it and lease it back. Another good contact is the real-estate department of your bank.

Apartment houses Owning and operating a four- or six-family flat or a small apartment house of, say, eighteen units, can be profitable for the small investor, but it is a tricky business. If you don't watch out, you may find yourself with apartments for rent in a part of town that is going downhill. Or a gleaming new modern building may go up across the street and attract many of your tenants.

Small apartment houses sell anywhere from eight to ten times gross rentals. Larger buildings, for which there are fewer prospective buyers, may sometimes be bought for six and a half times gross rentals, but this takes more capital.

SECOND MORTGAGES

Second mortgages and second trusts are treacherous, whether you lend on them or buy them as an investment. A second mortgage or trust is so called because it is secondary or subordinate to the first mortgage or trust.

As an illustration, say Jones is anxious to sell his house for $15,-000 to Smith, who has only $2000 cash. The bank will lend $10,000 on the first mortgage, leaving a balance of $3000 to come from somewhere else. Maybe Smith can borrow it on a second mortgage.

Now, if Smith does get two mortgages and then defaults on either, his house will be sold at auction. If he has missed payments on the first mortgage, the proceeds from the sale first go toward paying off the first mortgagor. Anything left over goes to the holder of the second mortgage. Smith gets what remains. If payments on the second mortgage are in default, the house will be sold and the new buyer will assume the first mortgage. The price may or may not be enough to repay in full the holder of the second mortgage. Thus the holder of the second mortgage is in the riskiest position and is entitled to more interest than the holder of the first. (In case you are worrying about Smith, he doesn't count; he is merely the owner.)

Thirty-five years ago, second and even third and fourth mortgages were common. But they became unpopular when many mortgage holders were wiped out in the depression. Then in 1935 the FHA began insuring first mortgages up to 80% and later 90% of the value of a house, thus combining the function of first and second mortgages. Recently, however, home prices have been trending upward, making second mortgages less risky. And the gap has been widened between the asking price for a house and the amount borrowable on a first mortgage. So second mortgages are back.

The mechanics of it   Although second mortgages are known by various names, assume for clarity that a second mortgage involves two parties, the borrower and the lender, while a second trust involves three, the borrower, the lender, and the trustees. If Smith defaults on a second mortgage, Jones must get a court order to have the house sold. But if Smith defaults on a second trust, Jones notifies the trustees and they sell the house.

There are two kinds of second trusts or mortgages, depending on who makes the original loan. If the seller of the house takes back a second mortgage or trust, the notes are known as deferred purchase money notes. If a third party, such as a mortgage company, makes the loan, the notes are known as money loaned notes. This distinction is important, as will be shown later.

The interest rate on the face of second mortgage or second trust notes might be 6%, 7%, or more. However, hardly any mortgage company will take such notes for less than 9%, 10%, or 11%. Here is how they work it.

Jones takes back a five-year second mortgage of $3000 from Smith at 6%. Then Jones sells the note to a mortgage company at a 15% discount, or for $2550. This means that the first year the mortgage company will get a return of $270 (6% of $3000, plus one-fifth of the $450 discount), or more than 10% on the $2550 investment. Over the life of the mortgage the interest return will average 14%. This is legal even if the state usury law limits interest to 8%, because Smith is still paying only 6% on the $3000 he borrowed.

As a result of this practice, most second trust or mortgage notes are deferred purchase money notes taken back by the seller of the property. Mortgage companies buy such notes and do not generally lend money directly because if they did, it would be money loaned; there would be no discount, and the interest would be limited to the legal maximum. And, of course, they feel that because of the risk they must have more.

Frequently, the seller of a house won't want a second mortgage or trust but will take one anyway in order to make the sale. His intention will be to sell the note immediately. In this case he will naturally try to add the amount of the forthcoming discount to the price of the house, so as to avoid loss to himself. Thus, Jones might offer to sell Smith his $15,000 house for $15,000 cash or for $15,500 if a second mortgage or trust was involved. He would take back a $3500 second mortgage or trust and sell it for $3000, thus getting his $15,000 anyway. Smith, while nominally paying 6% interest on $3500, would really be paying around 10% on the $3000 he needed to buy the house for its true price.

Here are some points to remember about second trusts or mortgages:

When you are a seller, remember that a second mortgage or trust will deprive you of cash you might need as down payment on your next house. If you take a second mortgage or trust, don't expect to sell the notes for face value. Also, don't let the borrower get so far behind on his payments that he will never catch up.

Don't buy second mortgages or trust notes as an investment unless you know something about real estate.

If you do acquire a second trust or mortgage, immediately inform the holder of the first mortgage. Suggest that he notify you in the event he is forced to advertise the house for sale, so you can protect your interest.

PRECAUTIONS

Take nothing for granted. That should be one of your mottoes if you plan to invest in real estate. Even the most seasoned operators in the business are extremely wary. One, for example, has made up a printed questionnaire of over a hundred questions. When considering the purchase of a property, he insists that every one of those questions be answered satisfactorily. If he cannot get the answer to a single question, he passes up the deal, even though all other aspects look favorable.

Take the case of a seventy-year-old doctor and his wife who had saved up $100,000 on which to live in retirement. A real estate broker presented them with what appeared to be an attractive opportunity, an apartment house for sale for $800,000. An existing mortgage of $600,000 was held by a large insurance company, and in addition, the seller was willing to take back a second trust of $100,000. Thus for $100,000 down, the doctor was able to purchase an $800,000 building which presumably would have supported him and his wife indefinitely.

Now the doctor did notice, when considering the purchase, that the first mortgage of $600,000 had less than one year to run. He questioned the broker, but was assured that there would be no trouble in getting a renewal. "What are mortgage companies for?" the broker asked airily. So the deal was closed.

For a few months thereafter the doctor and his wife enjoyed their retirement. But one day a reminder came from the insurance company, saying that the $600,000 mortgage would shortly fall due.

The doctor turned this notice over to his broker, who again stated confidently that it could easily be renewed. A second and more urgent notice arrived. The doctor called his agent, and at this point the agent was worried. "They are all crazy," he said. "They won't renew."

What the doctor didn't know was that the $600,000 mortgage had been taken by the insurance company during the depression as a means of getting rid of a property it had acquired by foreclosure. After twenty years the building had depreciated, and the company felt that $475,000 was the most it cared to lend. If the doctor had been able to raise an additional $125,000 in cash, he could have renewed the mortgage and continued to live on his investment. But he had already used all his resources. He was unable to raise the money and lost the building and all his savings.

Using hindsight, you can easily point out what the doctor should have done. Before he bought the building, he should have gone to the insurance company and asked whether it planned to renew the mortgage. He would have received the correct answer, which was No, and he could then have looked further for a better deal. The moral of the story is, Let the buyer beware. Be sure the broker you deal with is reputable and competent and that all the facts are correctly presented. Then double-check everything yourself. And don't be awed by real estate jargon. Once you learn the technical language, you will find that the ordinary deal is not as complicated as it sounds.

Investigate thoroughly There are three main ways of getting knowledge of and advice on real estate as an investment. First of all, the investor must depend heavily on the counsel of his broker. Therefore, he should take extra pains to ensure that he has a good one. The great majority of brokers are straightforward and ethical and have the best interests of their clients at heart. But a few are concerned only with making a sale and getting the commission.

A new kind of expert in the field is the real estate counselor. For a fee he will give pure advice without acting in the capacity of broker or agent. Since he stands to make no commission on the deal, he is in an excellent position to give advice that is sound and disinterested. However, not many men in the country have enough counseling business to do it exclusively. Most members of the Society of Real Estate Counselors are brokers who will do counseling upon request and, when so doing, will not act as broker in that particular deal.

Second in importance to having the help of a good broker or counselor is having some knowledge yourself of real estate values and legal and financial angles. You can get this by reading the real estate sections of newspapers and talking to brokers, bank officials, and property owners.

Third, and perhaps most important of all, don't sign a contract without checking the details yourself. Look at the property. Ask the tenants whether they intend to stay. Ask the mortgage holder whether he will renew, and, if so, get it in writing. Check on every angle you can think of, and think of as many as you can.

Good advice, some knowledge of the business, and a thorough personal check of every deal—these should be the watchwords. Remember, also, that in real estate your money may be tied up for a long time. Don't use funds you may be needing.

A HOME AS AN INVESTMENT

A carefully selected house bought with the help of a mortgage can do three things for you. It can help you accumulate money by providing a forced savings program. It can make you a profit over the years if you happen to own it during a period of economic expansion, shortages, or inflation. It is one of the few investments that can be used as well as held.

For most people, buying a house represents the biggest financial commitment they will ever make. Therefore, every detail of the transaction is important.

The house should be sound, attractive, usable, and marketable.

The mortgage will probably run for years, so every fraction of a per cent in the interest rate means hundreds of dollars lost or saved.

The monthly payment should not be so large as to be risky or so small as unduly to protract the term of the mortgage and pile up interest.

The price, although sometimes brushed off as unimportant compared to the size of the monthly payment, is obviously very important. Overpaying could result in a substantial loss.

Here are three questions to ask yourself before buying a house:

Is the house attractive and a good buy at the price?

Can I afford to buy it under the financial terms offered?
Will I save money by buying instead of renting?

The neighborhood Choosing a good neighborhood is probably
the first step in choosing a house. Naturally you will consider availability of shopping facilities, schools, churches, and transportation.
But there are other things to consider.

Suburban and rural areas attract many. They provide that "spa-
cious living" out with the trees and bees. They also present their
problems.

Unincorporated communities don't always develop the way the
ads and the real estate salesmen predict. So if you move into such
a community, don't expect miracles. Sewage and water systems may
be a long time reaching you. And when they do, it will cost you
money to connect with them.

Fire protection should be carefully studied. If it is not adequate,
fire insurance may cost as much as $2.50 per $1000 annually, instead
of the $0.90 rate available in many communities with organized, full-
time fire departments.

Cost of transportation is another item that can eat into the savings
you make by living in the suburbs. You may have to drive your
own car to work and pay to park it every day. That soon runs into
money.

Main traffic arteries through better-class residential sections usually
are good guides to follow in picking a suburban homesite. Lots
close to such highways, including those beyond the developed areas,
are likely to have fairly stable values.

Zoning restrictions may be sharply changed as economic pressure
develops in future years. Even if no one puts a glue factory on your
street, you may unhappily discover that your neighborhood is losing
its original residential character. So ask your public planning officials
about the prospects.

Restrictions running with the property may cause unpleasant surprises unless you know about them when you buy. You may suppose
they merely keep the neighbors from doing things like erecting un-
sightly chicken houses in their back yards. But they also may prevent
you from fencing your garden to keep out the neighbor's dog.

The house itself Think ahead about the house you are buying
—five years, ten years ahead. If you have growing children, the ques-

tion of separate bedrooms will come up in due course. Are there likely to be elderly parents or other relatives sharing your home in the future? If so, a first-floor bedroom and bath may be desirable.

The whole question of the livability of any house may be considered in terms of the family's needs. Will it accommodate without friction the hobbies of the individual members, their need for privacy? Is a recreation room a vital requirement?

Settle as many of these questions as you can in family conferences or in your own mind before you start looking at specific houses. It will save you time, perhaps save you from being talked into buying something that doesn't really meet your needs.

For people who build their own houses, structural soundness is largely a question of good specifications and competent supervision to see that they are carried out. Buying an existing house, especially an older one, is a different matter.

The roof line, to take an obvious starting point, should not sag. Such a condition is difficult to correct. Don't let anybody tell you it's a minor matter.

The chimney is important. Some of the extra-wide chimneys being built for single-story ramblers or ranch-type houses have been causing trouble. The only way to check on the chimney draft is to light a fire in the fireplace.

Gutters and downspouts should be checked carefully. Are they rusted through or clogged? Do they drain away from the foundation? Those of copper are more durable than those of galvanized metal. If the metal is painted, Junior's toy magnet will help you identify it. The magnet won't stick to copper.

A copper shield should be between the top of the foundation walls and the sill in termite territory, chiefly in the South. Slender earthen tubes running up the foundation from the ground to the wood framing suggest the presence of termites. Stick a knife blade into suspected beams or joists. If the wood is powdery, buy some other house.

The steel beam or wood girder giving mid-support to the floor joists is the key structural unit in the house. At least eight inches of each end of it should rest on the foundation walls.

Floor joists ought to be at least two inches thick, spaced evenly about sixteen inches apart and bridged about every eight feet of their length with cross braces. The braces stiffen the joists, help distribute heavy loads.

Subflooring is one item on which some builders skimp. It is not visible in the upper rooms, but you can usually check it in the basement. The boards should not be more than eight inches wide, preferably laid diagonally across the joists.

A floor drain in the basement is important. Lack of it sometimes betrays a careless or inferior builder. If the basement has an outside areaway, this should have a separate drain.

Crawl space between the house and any unexcavated portion of the foundation is a must to allow for repairs of pipes, electric wiring and ducts. The crawl space should be at least two and one half feet deep and well ventilated.

Basement leakage can be a major headache. Remember that it is very difficult to do waterproofing effectively from the inside. Wet patches on the foundation and basement walls are danger signs.

Foundation walls ought to be eight inches thick if made of concrete block, poured concrete, or tile, twelve inches thick if brick, and fourteen inches if stone. Vertical cracks in the walls denote settling and often reveal that the concrete footings on which the walls rest are not strong enough. If the house is built on filled land, it may take years for the ground to stabilize. That could mean recurrent cracking of plaster, higher upkeep bills.

Automatic heating systems are the most convenient type. But the important question is whether the furnace is efficient. You may have to check that with a heating specialist.

Adequate hot water storage tanks are essential. For the average family, a thirty-gallon storage tank is the absolute minimum. If the laundry is done at home, a fifty-gallon tank may be needed.

Equipment "economy" may actually prove very costly. Speculative builders often install the cheapest furnace, water heater, and storage tank they can. If there are no written guarantees on this equipment, don't accept it.

Plumbing that makes loud gurgling noises is probably not vented properly. A country sewage system should have a septic tank with a disposal field rather than a cesspool.

Water pressure is often a source of trouble in older houses. Turn on all the faucets in the house; then see if there is pressure enough in an upstairs tap. Examine the water pipe where it enters the house; the diameter should be at least one inch.

Overloaded electrical circuits are dangerous. Ordinary lighting circuits take a fifteen-ampere fuse and are designed for lights or appliances using a total of 1725 watts. Look at the fuse box. If larger fuses have been installed in order to accommodate more lights or appliances, the circuits are overloaded and there is a risk of fire.

Picture windows are all the rage. Even expensive thermal glass does not counteract the tendency of cold air to flow off large glass areas. Moreover, big windows on the street side may drive you frantic, what with lack of privacy, and glare from headlights of passing automobiles.

Insulation of outside walls and roofs is fairly standard in the building of houses now. But insulating material that is pumped into wall spaces may settle. It generally is not as desirable as insulation that is nailed in place.

What should you pay?   As to the price, remember that, generally speaking, the real estate business tends to operate in the interest of the seller wherever there is leeway for any breaks. On residential property it is customary for the salesman's 5% commission to be paid by the seller. So the higher the sales price, the more the salesman makes.

Prospective house buyers usually are unaware that they can hire a real estate agent to work exclusively for them. As an inducement for the agent to negotiate the lowest possible price, a deal could provide for a bonus payment—say $100 for every $500 he succeeds in knocking off the asking price.

Most real estate men will tell you that it is not necessary for a buyer to hire an agent to get a residence. They say that, although the seller pays the commission, they are actually working just as much for the buyer because there can be no sale unless the buyer is pleased too.

Weigh the costs and advantages of each method and use the one which seems best to you.

There's another service available of which many buyers are not aware. Experienced professional appraisers can be hired almost anywhere. They will examine a house, tell you whether it is structurally sound and worth what the owner wants for it. Their fees range from $15 to $35 for each appraisal. But wait until you've got your mind pretty well made up before you call in an appraiser.

CHART 24: MONTHLY PAYMENTS ON $1000

Term	4½%	5%	5½%	6%	6½%
5 years	$18.65	$18.88	$19.11	$19.34	$19.57
6	15.88	16.11	16.34	16.58	16.81
7	13.91	14.14	14.38	14.61	14.85
8	12.43	12.66	12.90	13.15	13.39
9	11.28	11.52	11.76	12.01	12.26
10	10.37	10.61	10.86	11.11	11.36
11	9.62	9.87	10.12	10.37	10.63
12	9.01	9.25	9.51	9.76	10.02
13	8.48	8.74	8.99	9.25	9.52
14	8.04	8.29	8.55	8.82	9.09
15	7.65	7.91	8.18	8.44	8.72
16	7.32	7.58	7.85	8.12	8.40
17	7.03	7.29	7.56	7.84	8.12
18	6.77	7.04	7.31	7.59	7.87
19	6.54	6.81	7.08	7.37	7.65
20	6.33	6.60	6.88	7.17	7.46
21	6.15	6.42	6.70	6.99	7.29
22	5.98	6.26	6.54	6.84	7.13
23	5.83	6.11	6.40	6.69	7.00
24	5.69	5.97	6.27	6.56	6.87
25	5.56	5.85	6.15	6.45	6.76

Does it make any difference when you buy? Of course it does make some difference, but residential real estate prices have been very slow-moving in recent years. If you are thinking of waiting for prices to fall, you might have a long wait. And the long-term trend of prices seems to be up, not down. So unless you are pretty luke-warm about the whole business and would like to look around for a couple of years, don't worry too much about the timing.

Shopping for terms Once you've decided on the house and the price, there remains the problem of paying. To most people that means a mortgage running for fifteen to twenty-five years. It used to be that the borrower paid only interest during the life of the mortgage, no principal. The whole mortgage then would fall due every three or five years and have to be renewed. Sometimes the lender would not renew and the borrower had to scurry around and raise the money somewhere else. Thanks to savings and loan associations and the FHA, most home mortgages written today are self-liquidating. That is, monthly payments include both interest and principal.

You probably will have to deal with a bank, a savings and loan association, a mortgage company, or an insurance company to finance your purchase. Terms and interest rates vary, so shop around. Use the table on page 229 to guide you in relating size and length of mortgage, interest rate, and monthly payment.

Just select the appropriate term and interest rate and then multiply the amount shown by the number of thousands of dollars you expect to borrow. These figures cover both principal and interest. As you repay, a little more of each payment applies to principal and a little less goes for interest.

You can be reasonably sure that reputable professional lending agencies will not permit you to borrow more than your income warrants. But the ordinarily accepted rule is that the purchase price of a house should not exceed twice your income.

Be sure to have a clause in the mortgage permitting prepayment without penalty. That will enable you to pay off a chunk of the principal any time you wish. Some mortgages impose a penalty for prepayment, and that is to be avoided. Note how prepayment can save you money. If you repaid a $10,000 loan at 5% in fifteen years instead of twenty you would save $1605.20 in interest.

Other pointers on financing:

Extras and changes made in the course of construction of a house should be itemized in the purchase contract.

Special assessments for street paving or similar public works often take property owners by surprise. Your local tax office can tell you of such assessments already authorized. The more complete your community is with respect to curbs, gutters, and utilities, the less chance there is that special assessments will be imposed.

Title insurance is a prudent investment. A lawyer can give you a certificate of title, and he accepts responsibility for any outstanding claims he fails to find. But he may die ten years from now. Insurance of the title, costing around $60 per $10,000, protects you in that event, or you may get a title certificate and insurance from a corporation that specializes in this field.

The full cost of owning your house includes more than the monthly payments you make on the mortgage principal and interest. You will also have taxes and insurance, repairs, replacements, utilities, and fuel. As your own landlord, you'll pay all the bills. The total of the annual costs should not exceed one-fourth of your income.

Taxes on your land and house ordinarily should not be more than 2½% of the purchase price. If they are, you should be leery. They will be a regular and recurring burden, so inquire about them at the outset.

Look at it this way. Buying a home makes you save more, so in that way it's a good investment. But it also makes you spend more. To make a decision whether or not to buy, first make a bare bones financial comparison of buying and renting. Then try to weigh the intangible benefits against the extra money you know you will spend.

HANKERING TO BUY A FARM?

Do you have a yen to be a gentleman farmer? Want to buy a place in the country as a haven from the atomic bomb, a hedge against inflation, and maybe as a justification for having some losses to write off on your income tax return?

If so, here is what the experts advise you to do: Go ahead and dream of wide verandas, lush fields, grazing cattle, and an expanding bank account—and then just keep on dreaming. Don't put any money into the idea. If you are city-bred, buying a farm will probably turn out to be simply a romantic way of losing your shirt.

It's true, of course, that you may save your neck by retreating from a crowded industrial area which is likely to be a target for enemy attack. If you want to buy a farm for reasons of sheer self-preservation, and can easily afford to do it, you may as well go ahead and buy one. But if you have to balance your desire for safety against your desire to stay solvent, you had better read on.

A farm, generally speaking, has been a good inflation hedge. In the past thirty years land has increased in value faster than the dollar has declined in value. This does not mean, however, that any farm you buy will do that and also make a net profit.

On that tax deduction point, you may be able to deduct the farm's losses from your income for several years if you are seriously trying to operate your farm as a profitable business. But the Internal Revenue Service knows that no legitimate business operates in the red perennially. Eventually you may be told you are running not a farm but merely an expensive hobby, and your write-offs will be disallowed.

Now, if you are a stubborn optimist who won't take advice and still want to buy that farm, all right. Grab a pencil and your reading glasses, and get ready for a lot of figuring and frustration. Maybe a miracle will happen, and you will turn out to be one of the few city folk who can actually make a farm pay.

First, what is a farm? For the purposes of this discussion, it is a real business in which you invest money and on which you try to make a profit. It's not a fancy country place where you raise a few vegetables and hang up a rustic sign with the word FARM on it.

Buying a farm is like making any other investment. You should know something about it before you start.

One man, a department head in a large company, is getting set for retirement in two years. He is going to buy and operate a farm, so has already started studying. He says that by the time he retires he will know almost as much about farming as he does about his own business. Maybe he will. At least he is beginning with the right idea.

Advice   There is plenty available, free. You won't have any trouble finding sources of information. Next to veterans, farmers get more help from the government than does any other large group. The Department of Agriculture publishes pamphlets, maps, and instruction books galore on every phase of farming, and much of the material is free. In every county there is a man called a county agent who represents both the federal and state agricultural agencies. His sole job is to give free advice and help to farmers. At every state college there is an agricultural extension service that studies agricultural problems and makes the findings available to farmers.

As a starter, write to the U. S. Department of Agriculture, Washington, D.C., for a pamphlet called *Facts for Prospective Farmers.* It gives a long list of sources of information, and it's free. Then go have a talk with your county agent. He probably knows more about the farms in your area than any other single person.

When you begin to look for a farm, keep one thing in mind. You are buying dirt. You can fix up a broken-down barn or a run-down house. You can make a lot of other changes above the surface of the ground. But the soil underneath was built up over the centuries by crumbling rock and tiny deposits of dead grass and leaves. You can't make much of a change in it in your lifetime without spending an awful lot of money. So when you buy a farm, buy good soil. And know it is good.

Soil maps covering two-thirds of the farm counties in the United States are available. The types of soil are shown in colors, and with each map comes a booklet explaining what each type of soil will grow best and about how much it will yield. Some of the newer soil surveys also give suggestions for managing each type of soil.

Get the soil map for your area and study it before you start looking for a farm. You will then know in advance where to look for the kind of land you want. County agents have soil maps. Maps are also available at state colleges and at libraries, or they can be obtained by writing to your congressman or to the Soil Conservation Service, U. S. Department of Agriculture, Washington, D.C.

Other things you want in a farm (make your own check list) are: good neighborhood, good roads, nearby churches, market and shipping points, electricity, phone, school bus, farm help. When you look at a farm for sale, cast an eye on the adjoining farms, too. Note whether your prospective neighbors use good farm practices and conserve their soil. If their land is full of weeds and gullies, yours probably will be, too. If they can't make a go of it, can you?

Farm management It is no accident that farmers in your area concentrate on certain kinds of crops and livestock. By continual experiment generations of farmers have found out what is best suited for each type of land and climate. So be smart. If most prosperous farmers in your area grow corn and hogs, lay off the mink ranches and shade-grown tobacco.

The shortage of farm labor makes it hard to keep a good farm manager and to get hired help. So try to stick to simple farming that requires neither skilled labor nor large numbers of seasonal workers such as fruit and vegetable pickers. A dairy farm, for example, requires skilled farm workers who will stay on the job for a fourteen-hour day, seven days a week. Good dairy hands are scarce.

A cattle farm devoted largely to pasture takes a minimum of labor. Such a farm could have cultivated fields rented out on a one-half share basis, which means that the renter would grow the grain and give you one-half as rent. You would use the grain to carry the cattle over the winter. This type of operation, however, would require a good bit of capital. The breeding herd might well cost as much as the land itself.

The size a farm should be is not measured by whether it contains a certain number of acres, but whether it is an operating unit. The ordinary unit is a farm that can be managed by one farmer and a hired hand or a farmer and his son.

Make it a business proposition. Don't try to run your farm catch as catch can. Hire either a dirt farmer or a management agency to operate it. Here is one arrangement that is common between the owner of a grain farm and his tenant. The owner gets half the grain crops and pays half the production expenses plus all the costs of maintenance of machinery and buildings. The tenant pays a small cash rental for use of hay and pasture land.

On a Great Plains wheat farm, the owner might get from a fifth to a third of the wheat crop but would pay none of the production expenses. In general, if a landlord takes his rent in cash, he gets only one-half to two-thirds of what he would get if he took his rent in crops. And the poorer the land, the smaller the landlord's percentage.

Most tenants or renters won't take as good care of your land as they would of their own. So when you make an agreement, specify the soil conservation measures you want carried out. Probably you will have to pay for these yourself, since the tenant may not see any benefit coming to him.

A farm management agency generally charges 5% of the gross income from the farm—perhaps more if the farm is very small. That will probably amount to 10% of the owner's net income, but in most cases it will be well worth it. Most management agencies not only will operate your farm but will help you buy and stock it.

Financing You can buy a farm at almost any price. But you'll probably get just about what you pay for. When farm income is high, professional farmers working good land are able to get a return of about 8% on their investment. Of course that doesn't apply to the family that buys a run-down piece of pasture at what looks like a bargain. But it does mean that a fertile farm, properly managed, is a good investment.

Borrow money to buy a good farm rather than pay cash for a poor one—that is the advice of agricultural experts. So the next step after finding a farm may be a search for a lender. If you can pay off a mortgage in five years or less, you can probably get a loan from the person who sells you the farm, or from the local bank. In such cases you might pay one-third to one-half down. If you want a long-term loan, there are two possibilities: the local farm loan association or an insurance company.

Farm loan associations are co-operatives authorized many years ago by Congress and originally financed by twelve federal land banks. There are nearly one thousand of these associations owned and run by farmers. They make "land bank" loans ranging from five to forty years.

You don't have to operate your own farm to get a land bank loan. But you must have control of the operation and participate in the management. Loans are limited to 65% of the normal appraised value of a farm. A farm that sells for $30,000 may have a normal, appraised value of only $20,000 and thus be eligible for a land bank loan of not more than $13,000.

Insurance companies lend millions of dollars on farms, and in many parts of the country they meet land bank terms. One advantage of getting a land bank loan or an insurance company loan is that in the process you will get a good, sound appraisal of your farm. You can also get such an appraisal independently by paying a fee to a farm real estate appraiser or a farm management agency.

Farm valuation   How do you know what a farm is worth? You can figure it out yourself by a method known as capitalization of expected net income. This will take some careful figuring and estimating. First you decide what return you think you can get on your investment. You probably won't get it, but you can hope.

Say you want to get a return of 5%. The next step is to figure carefully and realistically the expense, gross income, and net income you can expect from the farm. This will take a good many hours of study and calculation and probably will require the help of an expert such as your county agent. Nevertheless, do it. If you don't, you are being extremely impractical.

The rest of the problem is simple. If you figure you will make a net income of $10 per acre over the long run, divide this by 5% to get a valuation of $200 per acre. Checking back, a 5% return on an investment of $200 is $10 per acre net income.

So if you seriously mean to buy a farm, get every cobweb out of your head, and don't waste time dreaming of country air and home-cured ham. You'll have to work like the devil and use all your ingenuity. If you can make a go of it, you'll have a good investment, a hedge against inflation, a healthful avocation that will keep you outdoors, and probably a safer place to live in this dangerous world. Furthermore, you'll have the last laugh on the experts.

CHAPTER 13

Safety and Income

"Safety" is a deceptive word. Traditionally in the investment field it means putting money into high grade bonds, mortgages, and savings accounts. In those places the dollars themselves are safe in the sense that the owner can be pretty sure of getting them back after a period of time, with interest. Unfortunately, however, those investments do not keep the dollars safe from loss of purchasing power due to inflation and the continual upward creep of prices of goods and services. For this kind of protection, equities such as common stocks and real estate, with their fluctuating values, are supposed to be the answer.

Ideally, in order to get protection both from loss of the dollars themselves and from loss of purchasing power, a fund should consist of both fixed dollar investments and equities. Many money managers not only keep their funds invested in both types, but try to shift into equities when boom and inflation appear likely, and into fixed dollar investments or cash when a recession appears to impend. Theoretically, this is an ideal way to handle money. When the stock market is rising, you own mostly stocks. When the stock market is falling, you own mostly bonds or cash. Or, to use another method, when the stock market seems abnormally high, you shift into bonds and cash. And when the market looks abnormally low, you shift into stocks. Unfortunately, however, this kind of system doesn't work too well in practice because it is so difficult to forecast the trend of the economy or the stock market.

Here is an example of what can happen when you try to outguess the trend of the economy. Back in 1938 the Finance Committee of Vassar College decided to adopt a plan that automatically would cause them to shift their funds into fixed dollar investments when the stock market was abnormally high, and back into stocks when it was abnormally low. The committee studied the Dow-Jones Industrial Average as far back as 1897 to decide on its normal level or median. This they put at 135. The higher the Dow-Jones Average went above 135, the fewer stocks the fund could own. The further below 135 it went, the more stocks it must own. And no stocks could be bought when the average was above 135 and none sold when it was below.

The plan worked all right for the first five or six years while the market was oscillating around the median level, which, incidentally, the Finance Committee adjusted at one time or another to 130, 140, and finally to 155. But along about 1945 an unpredictable thing happened. The market left its "normal" level, never to return (at least it hasn't yet). First it went up to 212, which forced the fund to sell its stocks and go 100% into bonds. Then the market bounced from 193 to 163 a couple of times but never came down far enough to permit the committee to buy back any stocks. Then the unco-operative averages took off, going up, up, up, hitting 200, 300, 400, 500, etc. And during this great bull market the plan, as originally set up, kept saying, "Don't buy, sell." But of course there was nothing to sell, as all stocks should have been sold out long before.

Naturally the Finance Committee didn't stick with the original plan forever. The members were smart enough to see that the whole level of prices had shifted. In 1947 they bought stocks, using new money. And in 1949 they began basing the median level on a projected trend line of the averages which takes into account their long-term upward bias.

Some advocates of formula-timing plans have tied their formulas to an arithmetical trend line based on the Dow-Jones Averages. Others have used a geometrical trend line. Still others have worked out moving averages. One expert has based his formula on the relationship between the current price-to-dividends ratio and that of the ten-year average. As you can see, it is easy enough to decide what ratio of stocks to bonds you want if you know when the market is high, low, and normal. What throws the formula timers is trying to determine in advance what is going to be high, low, and normal.

There are two reasons why the individual investor should be careful about trying to shift his investments back and forth between equities and fixed dollar investments. One is the difficulty of knowing when to shift, as explained above. The other is that most families already have a sizable amount invested in fixed dollars. Life insurance, social security, and most pension plans are of this type. Dollars paid in today will be returned in the form of a predetermined number of dollars sometime in the future. There is no opportunity for growth. So what most families need is an offsetting investment in equities. Nevertheless, for some investors bonds can have a place in the picture. In particular, there are instances where safety of the dollars themselves, rather than growth of principal, is the overriding consideration.

BONDS

Corporate, government, and municipal bonds   These are traded in the open market like stocks. The original buyers don't keep them forever, don't intend to in many cases. Millions of dollars' worth of bonds change hands every day. The price is determined by the law of supply and demand. You buy through your regular broker or through your bank. Commissions on bonds are extremely low. You can buy $10,000 worth of government bonds for a commission of less than $4. The commission on corporate bonds runs a bit higher but not much.

Remember that when you buy a bond the issuer owes you a fixed number of dollars payable on a specific date sometime in the future. The issuer also promises to pay a specific amount of interest per year. If the issuer is a company and it doesn't make good on either of these commitments, the bondholders can force it into receivership. If the issuer is the federal or a local government of the United States, you don't have to worry too much about receivership.

Note the difference between bonds and common stock. When you own stock you own part of the company and there is no promise that your money will be repaid or that you will even get dividends. You are essentially in the same position as is the owner of the corner delicatessen. The company will pay in dividends each year only what it judges it safely can at the time. Sometimes, if business is poor, it won't pay any. Other times it may pay large amounts, 6%, 8%, 10%.

If business booms, stock prices rise because of the prospect of big dividends. Contrariwise, in bad times stockholders don't value their stock as highly because they expect that dividends will decrease. Stock prices thus move up and down pretty far and fast in anticipation of changes in business. Good bonds, however, with their fixed interest rate and promise to return a fixed number of dollars, don't fluctuate so much. And when they do go up or down, it is usually in response to a rather special set of circumstances. Thus bond prices sometimes go down when business is good or up when business is bad.

How bond prices fluctuate   Here is an example of how bond prices can change. Not many years ago when 3½% was a good rate of return on a bond or savings account, the federal government issued a series of 3½% bonds due in 1980. In theory, the buyer of one of these bonds loaned the government $1000. He was to receive 3½% interest, or $35.00 a year, until the bonds matured in 1980. Then he would get his $1000 back. In the meantime, however, the level of interest rates changed. In 1967, for example, the price of these bonds was down below 85, which meant that if the owner sold a bond, he would receive, not $1000 for it, but only $850. It meant, also, that if anyone bought such a bond for $850, he would be receiving, not 3½% interest but more than 5%. The explanation, of course, is that once bonds are issued they are traded on the open market. Their price can go above or below par (the ultimate value of $1000). The $1000 bond may sell for 105 and thus cost $1050, or it may go down to 75 and cost only $750.

Now suppose you buy a $1000 3½% bond for $850. You still get the $35 a year interest—not on $1000 but on $850. That comes to a current yield of a little over 4% ($35 divided by $850). But there's another angle. When the bond finally matures, you will get $1000, or a profit of $150 over what you paid. While this will be considered a capital gain by the Internal Revenue Service, bond dealers generally figure it as part of the "yield to maturity." Sounds funny, doesn't it? The old $1000 3½% bond actually turned out to be—at least in 1967—more like an $850 5% bond.

What makes the bond market go up and down? Why should a promise by the government to pay $1000 in 1980, with 3½% interest in the meantime, sell on the market for $850? The answer is simple. Suppose that some time ago you bought a $1000 3½% bond for $1000. Three and a half per cent was the going interest rate then for a high-grade bond. But in the meantime money has become scarcer. Corporations want to borrow to build new factories, cities want to borrow to build highways and schools, the government wants to sell long-term bonds to replace short-term notes falling due, and to finance a budget deficit. The lender has now got into a strong spot. He can raise his rates. Borrowers must now pay 5% instead of the old rate of 3½%.

What happens to that 3½% bond you bought earlier? Would anyone want to buy it for $1000 when he can buy a newly issued one paying 5%? He wouldn't. Thus if you have to sell your old bond you will take a loss, even though you are guaranteed to get $1000 in 1980. As interest rates go up, the prices of older bonds with lower interest rates go down. By the same token, if business slackens, the monetary authorities may loosen up on credit and let interest rates fall. Then newly issued bonds won't carry the 5% coupon but, say, only 4%. In that case the old 5% bonds will look pretty good and will go to a premium.

Short-term governments If you bought a government bond on the open market that had only a few weeks to run, it naturally would sell pretty close to par. Buying such a bond would be almost like putting money in the bank, only safer. Similarly, bonds due in five years or less usually sell pretty close to par. It takes a very large change in interest rates to change their value substantially. Since there is so little risk of their value changing, they are known as about the most riskless investment there is. And since the buyer doesn't take much risk, he ordinarily can't expect much yield.

Security Investors buy bonds because they are safer and more stable than common stock. The stability, as we have seen, depends somewhat on changes in the level of interest rates in general. But there is another factor that can affect the stability even more and that is how much you can count on getting the full interest and principal when due. In the case of U.S. government bonds, there is no doubt about the issuer's ability and intent to pay. Corporate and municipal bonds are in a somewhat different class. To satisfy the purchaser, many bonds are secured by real property. A railroad may pledge so many miles of track. A manufacturing company may put up its machinery and building. Municipalities pledge future tax collections.

In cases where the interest or principal is not paid on time, the trustee for the issue, usually a bank, will take action in behalf of the bondholders. When a case of default goes to its ultimate conclusion, the pledged property is sold and the proceeds are distributed among the bondholders. This seldom happens in actual practice. The court usually permits the company to reorganize and to replace a defaulted bond issue with a new bond or with a combination of bonds and preferred stock and maybe some common stock.

A good many bonds are issued without any specific security. The issuer gives its word that it will pay, just as you promise to pay when you borrow at the bank on your signature. Such bonds are called debentures and although unsecured are often good investments. Thus the debentures of a strong, profitable company earning enough to pay interest charges several times over might be safer than the first mortgage bonds of a company financially weak and able to meet interest payments only by the skin of its teeth. You don't want to end up owning a property that cannot earn enough to pay the interest on its bonds.

Put it this way. If the ordinary investor wants a speculative security, he might better buy a common stock. If he buys a bond, he presumably wants safety and stability, and therefore he should stick to the highest grades. That means either U.S. government or high-grade corporate bonds or municipals.

Quality To determine the quality of a corporate or municipal bond, the security analyst digs into the history and condition of the issuer. He also examines all features of the bond, including the indenture agreement (the contract between the issuer and the bondholders), the call price (price at which the issuer may call in the bond before maturity), and so on. But most investors don't have the time or the specialized knowledge for this type of test. The best bet for them is the bond ratings published by Moody's and by Standard & Poor's Corp. Moody's rates bonds as Aaa, Aa, A, Baa, etc. Standard & Poor's ratings are AAA, AA, A, BBB, etc. Unless you know exactly what you are doing, stick to the top grades. When you buy a bond, you don't want to have any doubt about the issuer's ability to make good. Usually the higher the yield on a bond, the greater the risk. The lower the yield, the less the risk.

Like everything else, bonds have good and bad features. Your dollars are safe in high-grade bonds, but you have little protection against inflation. And you can lose money, even on bonds that are good. If you had bought government bonds in 1950 or 1951 and sold them in 1966 or 1967, you could have lost as much as 10% or 15% of your investment.

There is another pitfall. If you buy a high-grade corporate bond when interest rates are high, at some future date when interest rates are much lower the company could take advantage of the bond's call provisions, pay you off at a small premium above par, and refund its debt at lower rates. You would lose your high-interest investment and be forced to invest your money somewhere else. The managers of the company are not interested in paying you one fraction of a per cent more than they have to. Any savings in interest redound to the benefit of the common stockholders.

Tax-exempts So-called municipal or tax-exempt bonds are IOU's issued by states, cities, toll roads, and similar revenue-producing public bodies. They promise to repay your money by a certain time and to pay a specific rate of interest. They are regarded as second in quality only to U.S. government bonds. And, the income is completely free of federal income tax and, in some cases, from the income tax levied by the state in which the bond is issued. Municipal bonds fall into four categories. General obligation bonds are backed by the "full faith and credit" and, usually, the unlimited taxing power of the city, state, county, or taxing district. Limited tax bonds are backed by only part of the over-all tax revenue of the jurisdiction that issued them. As an example, bonds might be backed by a state's gasoline taxes or motor vehicle fees. Revenue bonds are secured by revenues from a particular source, such as a toll road, a community water, sewer, or gas department, or even a ferry system. Housing authority bonds are issued by local public housing agencies to pay for building low-rent housing projects. Rents charged in the projects are not enough to pay off the bonds, so every year a federal agency, the Public Housing Administration, makes up any deficit with money granted by Congress.

Generally municipal bonds have a face value of $1000 and are bought and sold in units of five bonds. Thus this type of investment normally means an outlay of $5000. You can sometimes manage to buy a single bond, but it's a little bit risky—you may not be able to sell a single bond except at a sacrifice price if you have to liquidate.

When you buy or sell municipals, you don't pay a commission. The dealer is compensated by his "mark-up"; that is, the difference between what he pays for the bond when he buys it and what he receives for it when he sells it. Dealers often buy bonds and keep them in inventory for months before finding customers for them.

In such cases the mark-up is not easy to ascertain, but it likely will average out at around $2.50 to $3.75 per $1000 bond or $12.50 to $18.75 for $5000 worth.

Not only is the income from municipal bonds free of federal tax, but you don't even have to report that income on your federal tax return. State taxes are somewhat different. In many cases, you do not have to pay state income taxes on the interest from municipal bonds if they were issued in the state in which you file your income tax return. For instance, if you lived in New York, you would not have to pay state taxes on interest from New York state bonds, but you would have to pay state taxes on interest from, say, bonds of Richmond, Va.

Don't be dazzled by the idea of income without taxes, however. There is a catch to it all: Tax-exempt bonds pay markedly lower interest rates than do similar but taxable bonds. The interest is so much lower, in fact, that most people can clear more after taxes from other investments than they can from a municipal bond without taxes. This is because the public bodies that issue municipals clearly do not have to pay as high a rate to compete for funds. They need only match or exceed the small amount that the buyer would clear after taxes on other investments of comparable safety and liquidity. Tax-saving opportunities have the greatest appeal for high-bracket taxpayers, and for them the spread between pretax and after-tax income is sizable. So municipal bonds can often carry interest rates well below the going rates elsewhere and still find buyers. In actual practice, experts don't recommend tax-free bonds to investors unless they are in the 42% bracket or above.

Convertible securities The distinctive quality of a convertible bond, debenture, or preferred stock is that it can be exchanged for common stock. Convertible securities thus resemble convertible automobiles. The car will keep you dry if it rains. But if it is clear, you can put the top down and let in the sun. Similarly, if business is bad, preferred stock and debentures will give you first call on the profits to the extent of a fixed return on your investment before dividends on the common are paid. Or if business booms, you share in the rise in price that may take place in the common. Of course, before you buy either a convertible car or a convertible security, you should assure yourself of the soundness of the merchandise. If there is a drop in the price of the common into which a preferred, for example, is convertible, there may also be a drop in the preferred. But it shouldn't drop as much.

A convertible security can be exchanged for a fixed number of shares of the company's common stock. You make the conversion at your discretion by turning in the bond or preferred stock to the institution acting as the company's conversion agent. There may be a deadline on the conversion right, or in a certain number of years the "conversion ratio" may change so that you stand to get fewer shares than you would have during the security's early life. Many of the securities are "callable"; that is, they can be redeemed by the company before maturity, usually at a small premium such as 3% or 4% over the face amount. The rights of the company and the owner of the security are spelled out in a document called the "indenture." It is vital to get these details before buying a convertible. Convertible bonds and debentures are usually issued in $1000 denominations. Convertible preferred stock most often is sold in $50 or $100 units.

The right to convert a bond, debenture, or preferred stock into common is potentially valuable, and investors usually are expected to accept a somewhat lower rate of interest or dividend on a convertible than on a nonconvertible security. As an illustration, suppose you bought a 4% bond convertible into 20 shares of common stock. If you paid the full face value for the bond and converted at once, you would, in effect, be paying $50 a share for 20 shares of common. When such a bond is issued, chances are the common will be selling somewhat under $50. But say the price of the common stock eventually goes up to $55. You could make a profit of $5 a share by converting the bond into 20 shares of stock and selling the stock for $1100. In practice, however, it would not be necessary to convert because the bond itself would rise to reflect the higher price of the common. Suppose, though, that the common stock declines to $30. The bond also will decline. But it probably will not drop as much because as the bond's price goes down the yield goes up, and the bond becomes an increasingly attractive investment. This illustrates the defensive quality of a convertible security. When the common stock rises substantially, and causes a proportional rise in the convertible security, the convertible loses its defensive value. Thus if you bought an older convertible for 175, the yield, based on this higher price, would be relatively low, and the security would have to decline substantially—perhaps to around 100—before the defensive feature would come into play. So the ideal price for the investor to pay for a convertible security is close to the price he would pay for a security of similar quality that was not convertible. This means that for all practical purposes, convertible securities should be bought when they are close to par and this usually means around the time of first issue.

A convertible security is a hedge. If you knew the market was going up, you would buy common stock. If you knew the market was going down, you would do better to hang onto your cash or buy good bonds. Investing in a convertible is sort of playing both ends against the middle. It's a good idea if it works, and it is working for many investors. They are the ones, however, who have taken time to study each security and get good advice on it before taking the plunge.

Savings bonds   The U.S. savings bond perhaps is the safest dollar investment available. It is nonnegotiable; that is, the owner cannot sell it to another person. If he wants cash he must turn it in to the government for the value stated on the back. Other bonds are traded in the bond market and their values rise and fall daily. But the savings bond, with its predetermined value printed on the back, is removed from the vagaries of the market place. You always know to the penny how much you can get for it.

The two chief types issued by the government are Series E appreciation-type bonds and Series H current-income bonds. Both earn interest at an average annual rate of 4.15% if held to maturity. In addition, the Treasury issues Freedom Shares, which can be purchased only by persons buying E bonds on a regular plan, and which will earn 4.74% interest if held to maturity. Some Series J and K bonds, though no longer issued, continue to earn interest. Here's a rundown on each type.

Series E   Current issues are sold with a seven-year maturity date. However, all E bonds now carry an automatic ten-year extension privilege, and those issued before June 1, 1949, have had two ten-year extensions. All continue to draw interest during the extension periods.

E bonds are now issued in eight denominations—$25, $50, $75, $100, $200, $500, $1000, and $10,000—and are sold at 75% of face value. Interest is added to the value of the bond each six months and at the original maturity date will equal the difference between the purchase price and the face value. The interest rate is low at first—3.02% the first year—and gradually increases to 4.64% during the seventh year; over the whole seven years it averages 4.15%.

The table below gives you a quick check on the status of any bonds you now own and current issues you expect to buy. To find out when they reach face value, add the time given under "original maturity" to the date of purchase.

date of issue	original maturity	life of bond
May 1941–May 1949	10 yrs.	30 yrs.
June 1949–Apr. 1952	10 yrs.	20 yrs.
May 1952–Jan. 1957	9 yrs., 8 mos.	19 yrs., 8 mos.
Feb. 1957–May 1959	8 yrs., 11 mos.	18 yrs., 11 mos.
June 1959–Nov. 1965	7 yrs., 9 mos.	17 yrs., 9 mos.
Dec. 1965–present	7 yrs.	17 yrs.

Although interest on E bonds is subject to federal income tax (but not state or local income taxes), you can defer paying it until the bond has reached maturity or until it is redeemed. This can have the practical effect of allowing you to postpone paying the tax until you retire, when your income tax rates probably will be lower. But you have to defer payment initially. Once you start reporting the interest as annual income, you must continue to do so for the life of the bond, and for any others you purchase unless the Internal Revenue Service gives you permission to change.

If you're purchasing E bonds to finance a child's education, there may be a tax advantage in buying them in his name, then filing a tax return for him reporting the first year's interest. If that interest plus any other earned income he may have amounts to less than $900, there will be no tax and you'll be excused from filing any further returns on bond interest as long as his total annual income is less than $600.

You can buy up to $20,000 face value in E bonds in any calendar year, and you can redeem them any time after an initial two months' holding period. If you do cash them in, remember to redeem the most recently purchased ones first; they're drawing less interest. But don't cash any that are just about to reach the next six-month interest accrual.

Series H The purchase price of H bonds is face value, in denominations of $500, $1000, $5000 or $10,000. Interest, which you must report annually on your federal income tax return (but not state or local ones), is paid to you each six months. You can purchase up to $30,000 in H bonds in any calendar year, and you can redeem them any time after six months at a Federal Reserve bank or branch, or from the Treasurer of the United States. This table tells how long you can expect H bonds to earn interest.

date of issue	original maturity	life of bond
June 1952–Jan. 1957	9 yrs., 8 mos.	19 yrs., 8 mos.
Feb. 1957–May 1959	10 yrs.	20 yrs.
June 1959–present	10 yrs.	10 yrs.

You also can obtain H bonds in exchange for E bonds, or for J bonds within six months after their maturity. The exchange will enable you to defer the federal tax liability on accrued interest on the old E or J bonds until the H bonds are redeemed; but you will have to begin paying tax annually on the H bond interest. H bonds you receive in exchange are not subject to the $30,000 annual limit on holdings. You can make the exchange only if your E or J bonds have a minimum redemption value of $500.

Freedom Shares   Formally titled United States Savings Notes, the shares will be issued through April 30, 1969, or until the end of the war in Vietnam if it extends past the 1969 date. Shares are sold in denominations of $25, $50, $75, and $100 at 81% of face value and mature in four and a half years. You can buy them only with the simultaneous purchase on a one-for-one basis of Series E bonds via a regular payroll savings plan or bond-a-month plan. The face value of the E bond can be larger, but not smaller, than that of the Freedom Share.

maturity value:	$25.00	$50.00	$75.00	$100.00
issue price:	20.25	40.50	60.75	81.00
period after issue date	redemption values during each half-year period			
1 to 1½ yrs.	$21.07	$42.14	$63.21	$ 84.28
1½ to 2 yrs.	21.53	43.06	64.59	86.12
2 to 2½ yrs.	22.03	44.06	66.09	88.12
2½ to 3 yrs.	22.56	45.12	67.68	90.24
3 to 3½ yrs.	23.14	46.28	69.42	92.56
3½ to 4 yrs.	23.74	47.48	71.22	94.96
4 to 4½ yrs.	24.36	48.72	73.08	97.44
4½ yrs.	25.00	50.00	75.00	100.00

You can buy only $1350 in Freedom Shares in any one year, and you must hold them for at least a year before redemption. Tax on the interest must be handled in the same way you handle your tax on E bonds. The preceding table gives redemption values over the four-and-a-half-year period.

Series J and K   Of the bonds no longer on sale, only J and K continue to earn interest, and not all of those do. Both were issued between May 1952 and April 1957 for 12-year terms, at an annual interest rate of 2.76% if held to maturity. Final issues cease to draw interest on April 1, 1969. About $25,000,000 worth, those issued before mid-1955, already have done so. If you're holding any of these, it's important to check the maturity date (just add 12 years to the date of purchase) to take advantage of the H-bond exchange privilege.

Redemption values of U.S. savings bonds are good, of course, no matter how long after maturity you hold them. And you're assured of replacement if they're lost, stolen, or destroyed. But there's little point in holding a bond that no longer earns interest—A through D "baby bonds" and F and G war bonds.

INCOME

One of the best ways to get a high yield from your investments is to buy good growth stocks and hold them. While such stocks pay relatively small dividends based on the current price, the dividends tend to rise each year so that in a few years the yield will be quite high based on the original investment. Herbert P. Buetow, formerly president of Minnesota Mining & Manufacturing Company, has explained it this way. "What appears at first glance to be a conservative dividend policy may prove in the long run to be most rewarding for the stock owner. Any company dedicated to growth, but disinclined toward borrowing money or diluting its stock, must retain a substantial part of its earnings to provide funds for expansion of facilities and activities. This policy of 'postponed dividends' ultimately leads to appreciation of the stock as well as to greater dividends by stimulating sales and profits. Dividend policies of growth companies should not be measured in terms of a percentage of the current market value of the stock. Instead, current dividends should be expressed in terms of a percentage of the market value of the stock five or ten years earlier. A current Minnesota Mining & Manufacturing dividend may look conservative based on the current price of 3M stock but it represents a return of 17% to the investor who bought 3M stock ten years ago."

So remember that while, in recent years, good bonds have been yielding more than common stocks, yet with a bond you are frozen into a fixed interest return while in the growth stock your yield can increase indefinitely and eventually far outstrip the income from the bond.

Retired people, widows, and others may have a need for more income than their investments yield. In such cases the income can be supplemented by drawing down principal. The most primitive way to arrange this would be for an investor to decide to pay himself a certain percentage, say 6%, on his investments each year. When dividends failed to make up this return, he could sell the least favored of his stocks, pay himself the necessary amount in cash, and reinvest the balance.

Withdrawal plans   There are, however, more sophisticated ways of handling this problem. One of the most intriguing is the withdrawal plans offered by most mutual funds. You may have accumulated an investment in mutual fund shares, or you can purchase a sufficient number of shares to start such a plan. You sign an agreement with the fund by which it undertakes to send you a check regularly each month. The money that makes up the check-a-month comes from two sources: dividends earned by your investment and, if there are not enough dividends to make up the full amount, from selling off just enough of your shares or fractions of shares to provide the balance. The rest of the money remains fully invested and fully diversified. Capital gains distributions can be plowed back into buying more shares in the fund. About the only requirement is that at the time you start a plan you must have a minimum sum invested in the mutual fund—most commonly $10,000.

There are many kinds of withdrawal plans, but basically they can all be lumped into two main categories—"fixed payment" and "variable payment" plans. In a fixed payment (or "constant dollar") program, you decide ahead of time how many dollars you want to have coming in each month—and that's what you get. Some plans of this type set a maximum annual withdrawal rate—usually 6% of the value of your shares the day the plan took effect. On $10,000 this amounts to an annual withdrawal of $600, so the maximum monthly check you could arrange for would be $50. As a rule, a fixed-payment arrangement is handiest in cases when you must depend on a given, regular source of supplementary cash to help make ends meet.

On the other hand, if your check from the mutual fund is mostly the frosting on the cake, you might look into a variable-payment type program, one which expands, dollarwise, when the market is up, and contracts when it slumps. You might arrange, for example, to sell off a given number of shares in your mutual fund each month. Under such a program, you'd get more dollars when share prices were high, fewer when prices dropped. Still another variable-payment plan would tie the size of your regular check to a percentage of current value of your holdings.

With either plan, you could conceivably run out of money at some point. But if the market continues in the long-term upward trend it has followed over the last fifteen years and your withdrawals are not excessive, there's a better-than-even chance your money will outlast you. In fact, there could be some left over to go into your estate.

But note the "if." As in all stock market investments, there is an element of risk. The course of prices is unpredictable. Although the long-term trend probably is up, steep intermediate downturns could make your investment shrink and perhaps eventually vanish.

As it happens, recent years have been pretty good ones. A lump sum invested in any of several mutual funds would have been worth more than its original value by the end of almost any recent ten-year period, even if you had been making modest withdrawals all along.

Although these programs are particularly suited to people thinking of retirement, this is not their only use. Any mutual fund shareholder can start a plan whenever he wants and for whatever purpose he wants. For instance, one was recently set up to handle an educational fund for a young man about to begin four years of college plus medical school.

You can always suspend or cancel a program. If you're going to be away, you can have your checks made out to a third party or deposited directly in your bank account. Detailed statements are sent out regularly to help you keep track of how you stand and how much you owe in taxes. Bookkeeping costs are absorbed by the mutual fund in most, but not all, cases.

Keep in mind, if you consider a withdrawal plan, that the type of fund you pick has a direct bearing on how your fortunes will fare. A fund specializing in growth stocks may do extremely well during good times, but it might also take more of a beating in hard times than a more conservative balanced-type fund, which carries a sizable chunk of its investments in comparatively safe bonds or preferred stocks. And remember, too, that picking a top-notch fund is considerably more important than settling for a so-so company just because it happens to have an appealing withdrawal plan.

How about a formal withdrawal plan using, instead of a mutual fund, a portfolio of your own stocks? It's possible that you could set up such a plan with your bank. At least one bank, the Lincoln Rochester Trust Co., of Rochester, New York, offers this kind of service. Here is how it works.

You open a "spending power account" and turn over to the bank shares of common stock in any one of thirty blue-chip companies. At the same time, you instruct the bank to begin paying you a fixed monthly income. The bank will liquidate enough full and fractional shares each month to pay the income. It will also reinvest all dividends in additional shares. (And, if the value of the shares rises in the future, as it has in the past, you might even be able to collect your income without depleting your capital.)

It is interesting to note what would have happened to a hypothetical spending power account opened in 1956 with $10,000 worth of Eastman Kodak common stock. The owner could have drawn down $100 a month for ten years and at the end of 1965 his stock still would have been worth $33,200. There's no assurance, of course, that any future ten-year period will resemble that of 1956–65.

A spending power account isn't cheap. You need a minimum of $10,000 worth of stock. Minimum withdrawal is $50. Withdrawals may be made monthly or quarterly. For deposits up to $25,000 there is a 4% acceptance fee, on larger amounts a somewhat smaller one. There is also a 2% fee on each withdrawal, a 2% terminating fee and brokerage fees.

Here are the eligible stocks: American Cyanamid; A T & T; Chrysler; Consolidated Edison; Dow Chemical; DuPont; Eastman Kodak; Ford; General Electric; General Foods; General Motors; General Telephone; Gulf Oil; IBM; International Harvester; Minnesota Mining; Mobil Oil; National Dairy; Pacific Gas and Electric; Pfizer; Procter & Gamble; RCA; Sears, Roebuck; Standard Oil of Cal.; Standard Oil of N.J.; Texaco; Union Carbide; U. S. Steel; Westinghouse; Xerox.

Annuities   One trouble with withdrawal plans is that you can't be sure you won't outlive your money. There is, of course, a way to guarantee that your money, in the form of monthly income, will last as long as you live. The vehicle for such an arrangement is an annuity. Most annuities are sold by life insurance companies. But insurance and annuities are two different things. When you buy insurance, you give the company a series of payments in return for its promise to pay a specific sum to your beneficiary if you die. When you buy an annuity, you pay the company a specific sum in return for its promise to give you a series of payments as long as you live. The annuity is designed primarily to protect you, not your dependents.

Actually, you can pay for the annuity either in a lump sum or in installments. Your money is invested mostly in fixed-dollar investments, such as bonds or mortgages, and earns interest. Then, when annuity payments begin, your investment plus interest is paid back to you periodically at a guaranteed rate that would theoretically exhaust your investment at the end of your life expectancy. But you keep on collecting even if you live longer. Your funds, keep in mind, are pooled with those of other annuitants. And the money left in the kitty by people who die earlier is used to pay incomes for those who live longer.

You can arrange to have your income paid monthly, quarterly, semiannually, or annually. Monthly payments are most common.

Annuities fall into two general classes. One type starts paying an income immediately after it's bought for a lump sum. The other, known as a deferred annuity, guarantees an income to start sometime in the future. You'd typically pay for it in installments, though a few companies will let you pay for a deferred annuity with a lump sum.

What if you die before you're slated to collect? In most cases, your beneficiary would receive a death benefit equal to the cash value of the annuity at the time of your death or the sum of the premiums paid, whichever is larger. If you surrender your contract before maturity, you'd collect the cash value.

You can also buy a combination insurance policy and annuity that provides more death protection during preretirement years while you're still paying for the annuity. That's called a retirement income policy.

You can choose to collect an annuity in one of five principal ways. (In each case, though, you receive an income as long as you live.)

Straight life annuity. This is known as a "pure" annuity. All payments stop at your death. If you die shortly after the annuity starts, you will have gotten back only a small portion of your investment. But if you live longer than expected, you collect more than the purchase price plus interest.

Life annuity with installments certain. If you die before a specified number of years, ten, for example, the payments continue to a beneficiary for the rest of the guarantee period.

Installment refund annuity. If you die before you have received as much as you paid in, your beneficiary keeps collecting until total payments equal your investment.

Cash refund annuity. Your beneficiary collects in a lump sum if you die before recovering the original investment.

Joint and survivor annuity. Two people—usually a husband and wife—receive an income as long as either one lives.

Which way is best? Because a straight life annuity offers no guarantee that you will recover all or most of your investment, it is the least expensive. It furnishes the largest income for a given price. Thus it is suitable for the person who needs maximum income and either has no dependents or has taken care of them through other means.

Perhaps you dislike the prospect of losing much of your investment if you die soon after your income begins. You might buy a refund or installments-certain annuity—if the income is adequate for your needs. (The argument for one of these annuities is stronger if you're in poor health.) But consider instead buying the less expensive straight life annuity and investing the difference elsewhere to pass on to your heirs. In that case you'd still leave something even if you outlived the guarantee period of a refund annuity.

Are you counting on an annuity to support you and your wife? The joint and survivor annuity then makes sense. But if your wife is much younger than you, the payments may be too low for your needs.

The price of an annuity is figured on the amount of income it promises to pay. You can look at the price tag from two angles: how much income you get for a given premium, or how big a premium you must pay to buy a given income. You'll find typical rates on pages 256 and 257. Notice how costs vary with:

Age. The older you are when you start to collect, the lower the cost. That's because your investment is returned over a shorter life expectancy. With a deferred annuity, the younger you are when you sign up, the less your annual premium will be. That's because your cost is spread over a longer paying period.

Sex. At the same age, women pay more than men for the same income. That's because women, on the average, live longer and collect more.

Income plan. A straight life annuity, as noted above, is the cheapest. The more generous the guarantee, the greater the cost.

An annuity, basically, is an investment. True, it's a particular kind of investment. Nevertheless, you've got to compare annuities with such things as stocks and bonds, bank savings, etc., to pick out the advantages and drawbacks. The chief advantages are:

1. You're freed of the job of money management. No need to worry over investments—what and when to buy, what and when to sell.

2. Annuities are the safest way to obtain a retirement income. (If you're uninsurable, they may be the only way.) You get guaranteed payments that can't be reduced by depression.

3. You can never outlive your capital. You might develop your own system for tapping both principal and interest to finance retirement. But are you sure the capital will hold out as you grow older?

4. A deferred annuity, paid for in installments, makes it easier to save for old age and more difficult to dip into your savings.

5. There may be tax advantages. Your annuity premiums draw interest during your working years, but you pay no income tax on the interest until you actually collect it. By then your tax bracket may be much lower.

But annuities also have their disadvantages:

1. You use up your capital and leave little if any for your heirs.

2. You earn a relatively low rate of interest on your investment.

3. Your investment value or income will not increase if inflation erodes the dollar's value. The dollars are safe; the purchasing power is not.

4. Once annuity payments begin, you can't get at your investment

in an emergency. An annuity, as a rule, has no cash or loan value after you start collecting.

THE COST OF ANNUITIES

Annuity rates are usually quoted in one of two ways: The amount of income you get per $100 or $1000 of premium. Or the amount you pay per unit, usually $10, of monthly income. Check the costs below, quoted by a typical insurance company. Yearly dividends on the deferred annual premium annuity, if left with the company, might substantially increase the guaranteed monthly income.

CHART 25: THE COST OF ANNUITIES

Immediate single premium annuity (income to begin at once)

Age Male	each $1000 buys this monthly income			each $10 of monthly income costs		
	Straight life	10 years certain	Installment refund	Straight life	10 years certain	Installment refund
50	5.08	5.02	4.87	1968	1992	2055
55	5.65	5.52	5.31	1771	1811	1883
60	6.40	6.15	5.88	1562	1626	1700
65	7.44	6.91	6.61	1344	1447	1512
70	8.85	7.75	7.53	1130	1291	1328
Age Female						
50	4.62	4.60	4.52	2166	2175	2212
55	5.08	5.04	4.92	1970	1986	2032
60	5.70	5.61	5.44	1755	1784	1840
65	6.55	6.33	6.10	1527	1579	1640
70	7.66	7.16	6.91	1305	1397	1448
75	9.21	8.05	7.93	1086	1243	1261

Inflation-proof annuities   The trouble with the conventional annuity is that, once you begin receiving payments, they are fixed at the same amount for life. Rising prices could make that monthly income woefully inadequate after only a few years. To meet this objection, insurance companies have come up with what is known as a variable annuity. Theoretically, a variable annuity is close to the ideal retirement plan. It guarantees to pay you an income as long as you live. The size of the income is not fixed, as with a con-

Chart 26: THE COST OF ANNUITIES

Deferred annual premium annuity (for men age 65 when income starts*)

Age at Issue	each $100 a year buys this monthly income			each $10 of monthly income costs this much a year		
	Straight life	10 years certain	Installment refund	Straight life	10 years certain	Installment refund
30	34.44	31.33	28.38	29.04	31.92	35.23
35	27.49	25.01	22.65	36.38	39.98	44.15
40	21.35	19.42	17.59	46.84	51.49	56.85
45	15.92	14.49	13.12	62.81	69.01	76.22
50	11.12	10.12	9.17	89.93	98.81	109.05
55	6.88	6.26	5.67	145.35	159.74	176.37

* A woman would receive 15% to 20% less in annuity income per $100 of annual premium than a man of comparable age at issue.
NB: Rate and income quotations are basic manual figures. Actual quotations are varied by policy fee and state premium taxes.

ventional annuity, but is designed to increase if prices increase and thus give protection against inflation.

The principle involved has been tested. For many years college professors and others in 1500 institutions have participated in a retirement plan (called TIAA-CREF) that offers them both a variable annuity and a fixed-dollar annuity. They have been happy with the results.

Well, then, why isn't everyone rushing to buy variable annuities? Why aren't more retired people living off them?

For one thing, despite TIAA-CREF's record and the fact that several small variable-annuity companies have been in business for five or ten years, there still hasn't been a great deal of experience with them and they are thus approached with caution by many people. There are no figures even approaching the wealth of long-haul data available to the buyer or seller of other investments, conventional annuities, life insurance.

An ordinary annuity pays you a fixed number of dollars per month for life. Thus at age 65 you could hand an insurance company about $50,000 and receive a contract guaranteeing you a monthly lifetime income of $350. Month after month, rain or shine, you would receive that $350 regardless of economic conditions, the cost of living, or how long you lived.

But you know that for many years prices have been rising and the value of the dollar declining. As a result, you may be leery of a fixed income. That $350 a month looks fine now, but it could be inadequate in fifteen or twenty years.

So instead of $350 a month, suppose you elected to receive each month one share of common stock now worth about $350 a share. You plan to sell it and use the proceeds as your income for the month. Now the value of stocks, on the average, has risen faster than the cost of living. So when prices rose, you would expect to get more for your share and thus be able to buy what you needed even at higher prices. For example, over the past ten years the price of IBM has grown at the average rate of 19% a year compounded. If it continued to grow at even half that rate, the income of a person receiving a share a month would be well protected against inflation.

A variable annuity does not pay you off in shares of stock, but the idea is very similar. Instead of promising you a certain number of dollars a month, as a conventional annuity does, your contract promises you a certain number of "units" a month. Each unit represents a proportionate share in a large portfolio of selected stocks. Every month the company will send you an amount of money equal to what your units are worth that month. Here is how the system works:

Suppose you sign up to buy a variable annuity with monthly payments during preretirement years for an income to start when you reach 65. When you send in your payment, you will be credited with "accumulation units" representing a stake in the investment portfolio. If the portfolio is then worth, say, $100,000,000 and there are a million accumulation units outstanding, a $200 payment by you (forgetting expenses for the moment) would get you two accumulation units. If the fund's value went up to $120,000,000, your $200 would pay for only 1⅔ units; if it fell to $80,000,000, your $200 would buy 2½ units. Over the years, dividends and profits from the fund would be reinvested, and you would get your share in extra accumulation units.

Now comes age 65. You stop buying accumulation units and you start receiving "annuity units." The number of units you will get each month is fixed at that point and will never change. But the value of each unit will change with the value of the company's investments. For each annuity unit, like an accumulation unit, represents a proportionate stake in the fund. Thus you will never know in advance exactly what your retirement income will be. You will naturally hope, though, that any variation will be upward, especially when prices are rising.

Once you get beyond the variable-value feature, you'll find that the structure of variable annuities closely resembles that of fixed-dollar annuities. You can buy one some years before retirement, with the income to start at a later date (a deferred annuity). Or you can choose to buy one at the time you retire, with the income to start at once (an immediate annuity).

You then have a choice of how you pay. An immediate annuity is paid for in a single, large lump sum. Thus it is also known as a single-premium annuity. A deferred annuity can be bought with a lump sum, too. Or you can buy it with regular monthly or quarterly payments until retirement (an installment annuity).

You will also have the usual choice of pay-out plans. You can elect a straight life annuity—it will pay as long as you live and then stop, no matter whether you live only a few years or decades. You can elect a joint-and-last-survivor annuity—it will pay until the last of a pair of beneficiaries (usually husband and wife) dies. You can elect a payments-certain plan—it will pay for a minimum of, say, ten or twenty years even though you yourself die sooner, but will continue for your lifetime if you live longer. The number of annuity units you will receive each month differs with each type of pay-out plan.

You can cancel a contract before the income period starts. You will get back whatever the value of your share in the fund is at the time you terminate, which may be more or less than you put in. You can usually borrow against this value, too. As with conventional annuities, however, you can't ordinarily cancel and get a cash value back after you have started receiving your monthly income, nor does the contract have a loan value then.

This is all well and good, but everything seems to ride on the assumption that common stocks will keep going up. All stocks don't go up, of course, even over the long pull. And those that do rise sometimes having sinking spells. For example, IBM, used in the illustration earlier, fell sharply a couple of times during the last ten years, even though it was growing 19% a year "on the average."

Of course, a variable annuity is backed by a broad selection of common stocks. Therefore, the monthly income of annuitants moves pretty closely with stock prices as a whole. The long-range trend of stock prices as a whole has been steadily upward, and this trend appears to be continuing.

But even the stock market itself can go through some pretty wild gyrations. Furthermore, no one can rule out 100% the possibility of a protracted slump in the economy and, as a result, the market.

This is why most people and professional groups who use variable annuities team them up with a fixed-dollar annuity. In the TIAA-CREF plan for colleges, in fact, a participant must have at least a part of his contribution put into a fixed annuity.

The fixed annuity carries on even during stock market declines. If there should be a depressed period of falling prices, its dollars would be worth more. Meanwhile the variable annuity provides the kick that keeps the team ahead in what looks like a never-ending race with the cost of living.

There is also a kind of annuity that is a mixture, partly variable and partly fixed-dollar. It is variable during the "pay-in" period—after deduction of expenses, the installments you pay during preretirement years are invested in stocks and the value of your accumulation follows the level of stock prices. The pay-out, however, is in the form of a fixed-dollar annuity—the same number of dollars each month for life. Such a contract is generally not considered to be a variable annuity. For one thing, the whole point of a variable annuity is inflation protection during the retirement years, which the hybrid contract does not give. Secondly, such an arrangement is easily set up on a do-it-yourself basis: invest in stocks or mutual fund shares during preretirement years, use the resulting fund to buy a conventional annuity at retirement.

As you can see, there are many ways to provide safety of your dollars and income from them. The big question is, What kind of safety do you need most? If you can expect to live for a good many years, the biggest threat to your money probably comes from inflation. So you probably should have a good portion of your money in equities such as good growth stocks or sound real estate. And money so invested and kept invested over the years, eventually should provide a good income—more income, in fact, than you would get if you started out with income as your object.

CHAPTER 14

Trust Funds

A trust fund is a safe place to put assets and where flexible arrangements can be made for the disposition of the income. By definition, a trust is an arrangement whereby one person has the legal ownership of property but holds or manages it for the benefit of someone else. Here are the parties who are involved in such an arrangement.

Definitions   First, there is the trustee. He is the legal owner who manages the property for someone else's benefit. He does not own it in the everyday sense of the word. He can do with the property only what the person who gave it to him has empowered him to do. He must dispose of the income from it and, sooner or later, the property itself, as instructed. He is accountable at law for mismanagement or failure to carry out instructions properly.

Actually the trustee is likely to be not a person but an institution: a bank or a trust company. And there may be more than one. Many trusts are administered by cotrustees such as a bank and an individual.

Next comes someone who appears in the definition only by inference. He is the fellow who owned the property originally and gave it to the trustee. He may have any of a number of titles—commonly creator, grantor, or testator. He can, if he wants, name himself among those to benefit from the trust, directing the trustee, for example, to pay the income to him while he lives and then to his wife.

Finally, there is the person or group of persons or, perhaps, the charity or institution that is to receive the income and, eventually, the property itself. These are beneficiaries. Those who get money from the trust only while they live are life income beneficiaries. Those who get the principal of the trust when it is broken up are remaindermen.

So much for people. Two things round out the five elements that comprise a trust: the property itself and the set of instructions given to the trustee.

Your lawyer and banker will call the property placed in trust the principal, res or corpus of the trust. Almost any kind of property can be put in trust: real estate, insurance policies, patents, cash, stocks, etc.

The directions you give the trustee are the trust terms and are ordinarily set forth in a legal document called the trust agreement or, under certain circumstances, in your will. Some of the terms are fixed by law and public policy.

These terms will be examined at some length later. For now, simply note that they will outline the duties and powers of the trustee, say how long the property is to remain in trust, tell what shall and shall not be done with income and principal, and specify the rights of the beneficiaries.

Put all of these five elements back together again and translate them into an example. Mr. Green, preparing for retirement, assembles $75,000, garnered from the sale of his home, the cash value of his insurance, and his savings. He creates a trust, with his bank serving as trustee. The bank's trust department agrees to invest the money and to collect interest and dividends. Mr. Green is to receive this income quarterly as long as he lives, and then it is to go to Mrs. Green in the same manner as long as she lives. After her death the bank is to reinvest the income and divide the total accumulation among grandchildren as they reach the age of twenty-one.

As you can see, the trustee undertakes quite a job—investing, reinvesting, collecting income, parceling it out on schedule, keeping records, preparing tax information, keeping track of the grandchildren. Moreover, although the trustee does not by any means guarantee a fixed income or the absolute safety of the capital, he is legally responsible for managing the fund carefully and prudently.

Fees   A trustee doesn't take all this on for the fun of it. He receives a fee. The amount varies with many factors, including state law. It may be a percentage of the income from the trust or a percentage of the principal or both. There ordinarily is a minimum charge when the trust is so small that it yields inadequate compensation on a percentage basis.

As a rule of thumb, fees, however computed, usually come to

about ½ of 1% annually of the value of the principal. On a large trust a sliding scale is commonly involved in the computation, and the charge might be proportionately lower; on a very small trust the minimum charge commonly comes into play, and it might be proportionately higher.

Basic types of trust Two basic types of trusts are available:

One is called a "living trust." It means a trust that you create during your lifetime, getting your lawyer to draw up an agreement and signing over some of your property.

The other kind is a "testamentary trust," also known as a "trust under will." Here you get your lawyer to incorporate the terms and the nominations of trustees and beneficiaries into your will. After your death the property is transferred to a trustee by your executor when he settles your estate.

Another kind of trust is sometimes treated as a third basic type, though it is really a subspecies. This is the life insurance trust, one in which insurance policies and the proceeds from them form the principal. It is a form of living trust. You draw up the agreement and make the trust the beneficiary of your life insurance. At your death the policies pay into the trust fund, which from then on operates just like any other trust. Sometimes the creator of such a trust continues to pay the premiums on the policies involved. Sometimes he puts into the trust, in addition to the policies, cash or income-producing property, which the trustee uses to pay premiums and keep the policies in force.

When you create a testamentary trust, you can't change your mind after it has started to operate, because you will be dead at the time. But when you create a living trust, you can leave yourself free to reconsider. You can make it a revocable trust by reserving the right to withdraw some or all of the property. Or you can make it an irrevocable trust by yielding all such rights.

Obviously you want to think twice about making a trust irrevocable. One man put everything into an irrevocable trust, reserving to himself only a retirement income. When he later encountered a long illness, with heavy medical and convalescence costs, he couldn't touch the funds he needed to meet the emergency.

What a trust can do Here is a rundown of some of the things that must be or can be provided for.

❲ *Income payment:* The trustee can be told to hand over all income as he gets it or to make payments monthly, quarterly, or annually. He can accumulate income for a time, as in a trust fund being built up to provide a college education. The trustee can be empowered to pay income only at his discretion. He can make payments on someone's behalf—college bills, medical expenses, insurance premiums.

❲ *Payments from principal:* Suppose you leave money in trust, income to your wife and principal to the kids at her death. Can she withdraw some of the principal, too, if she needs it? You can fix it either way. You can guard against emergencies or higher living costs by authorizing her to call for principal; or you can preserve the principal at all costs by forbidding her to. Or you can compromise by allowing withdrawals for stated purposes, within limits, or at the discretion of the trustee.

❲ *Duration:* You must specify how long the property is to remain in trust before being distributed. The duration will be measured by lives, not by a period of years—that is, the property will be marked for distribution not after ten or twenty years but, in most states, within twenty-one years after the death of any number of designated living persons. Any lawyer or trust officer will be glad to explain why this is so, but you will be sorry you asked. It involves something called the Rule Against Perpetuities, which, to put it mildly, can be complicated.

❲ *Power of appointment:* Instead of saying who gets the principal at the end, you can delegate someone else to choose later. Example: A man leaves a trust for his wife during her lifetime, to be divided among their children at her death. Should the money be shared evenly or will some deserve or need more than others? How many will be living? Rather than try to guess, he might stipulate that the money be divided as the mother directs in her will.

❲ *Investments:* State laws limit what your trustee may do with the funds you give him. In most states he has reasonably broad discretion. In others he is limited to a "legal list" of securities, which is often restricted wholly or largely to such items as government bonds and gilt-edged utility bonds. You, however, can give him more or less leeway than the law prescribes. In a living trust you can reserve a voice in investment decisions for yourself.

❲ *Protective provisions:* You can incorporate special provisions to protect what you feel are the best interests of beneficiaries. A spendthrift trust places a beneficiary's money beyond the reach of creditors.

Benefits can be contingent on something happening or not happening. A man might leave money in trust for a son's widow but provide that his grandchildren get it instead if she remarries.

That doesn't cover all trust terms. Nor does it delve into the legal problems they present. It does explain and illustrate the common ones.

Note the variety, enabling you to adapt a trust to all sorts of circumstances and objectives. Note that most are concerned with putting a sum of money to work for one purpose while preserving the sum itself for another purpose—a basic idea of the trust. Finally, note how you can use the options to make a trust very rigid or very flexible.

In general, trust experts urge flexibility—broad investment authority, discretionary powers, ways to tap principal. You just can't foresee every contingency. Here are cases of too rigid trusts cited as evidence.

Early in the century a couple of successful businessmen gave trustees explicit instructions that they knew from experience would ensure sound, no-nonsense investment for all time. One said to invest his money only in first mortgages on Brooklyn real estate. Another specified the bonds of streetcar companies only.

Another man left money in trust for his son. To make the trust an incentive to his son's ambition rather than a drag on it, he decreed that payments from it were to match, dollar for dollar, the son's earnings. The more he earned, the more trust income. The less he earned, the less trust income. This scheme was greatly admired at the time. But the son contracted tuberculosis and was unable to earn a cent.

Ways to use a trust See whether any of these eight reasons for using a trust fund apply to your family.

1. To make up for lack of financial skill or interest. By using a trust fund, you hire a professional to do the job. Mr. A. knows his wife is completely unequipped to invest skillfully the small sum he will leave. She might be overspeculative in her investments or overcautious. A trustee manages for her. Mr. B has little experience and less interest in handling invested capital. His small retirement fund is in a revocable trust for himself and his wife later.

2. For convenience. A trust can turn an irregular income into a regular one, eliminate record keeping and the bother of reviewing and reinvesting. And income continues at death instead of being cut

off while an estate is settled. Mr. C works a trust into his retirement plans simply so that he, and his wife after him, may relax and look forward to a monthly check in the mail. Mr. D, who supports a dependent sister, places a sum in trust with the income to go to her directly and thereby saves both of them bother and embarrassment.

3. To guard against waste. Money in trust can be partly or wholly safe from a beneficiary who would be likely to lose it or fritter it away. Mr. E was concerned over his wife's tendency to buy things "we simply must have" but that he couldn't afford. He left his money in trust. Mr. F had confidence in his daughter but not her husband. A trust gave his daughter the use of the money but kept it from his son-in-law.

4. To protect someone who is disabled or incompetent or a minor. The trust does the job they cannot. Mr. G wanted to leave money directly to a grandson but put it in trust until the grandson was old enough to handle it himself. Mr. H trusteed property for his own benefit, so that if in advanced age he became physically or mentally unable to manage for himself, there would be someone to look out for him.

5. To train and observe an individual or group slated to take over financial or business management later. A revocable living trust gives the creator a chance to do so. Mr. I wanted his two sons to carry on his business, first as trustees of controlling stock that would pay an income to his widow, and later as outright owners. He gave them control of the business as trustees of a living trust to gain experience and display their ability under his guidance.

6. For tax economies. Trusts can sometimes reduce income and estate taxes. The economies are usually of significance only to fairly well-off people, however, and should be worked out only with great care and in terms of the individual case. The man who gave his sister the income from trusteed securities may have removed that income from his own top tax bracket and placed it in her lower one. Mr. J is leaving $300,000 to his wife, who will leave it to their children. His estate will be taxed on $150,000, hers on $300,000. If half is put in trust, only $150,000 will be taxed at each stage.

7. To insure a future gift. This is another way of saying that a trust preserves capital. Mrs. K wants her sister to enjoy the income from real estate that Mrs. K owns, but she is chiefly intent on leaving the property itself to her son. A trust achieves both goals. Mr. L uses an insurance trust to provide an extra inheritance for his grandchildren.

He establishes a living trust to pay premiums on an insurance policy on his son's life. The grandchildren will eventually inherit insurance proceeds plus capital.

8. For flexibility in the future use and disposition of money. A trust is a way around too early or too rigid decisions. Take Mr. M, who provides that if his wife dies before him or with him, his life insurance proceeds will not be split arbitrarily among his children but will go into a trust, where the money can be used in the children's behalf at varying times, in varying ways, and in varying shares.

In appraising the utility of a trust, you should always, of course, consider alternative ways of achieving your objectives. Trusts have advantages and disadvantages. Two alternatives are outright ownership of the property and life insurance settlement options. Compare these courses with a trust.

Outright ownership gives full control over the property, eliminates trustee fees, allows complete freedom in investment and reinvestment, and may produce higher returns and greater capital gains. On the other hand, it leaves the burden and bother of management, makes funds vulnerable to loss and misuse. You cannot put conditions or limits on the use or disposal of the money. You can provide for one beneficiary but not a series of them. The results obtainable from the trust will depend on the financial abilities of the trustee. They may be good, or not so good.

Life insurance options and annuities offer a guaranteed lifetime income, guaranteed safety of principal, no trustee fees, and a unique system for the planned and orderly withdrawal of principal. Within limits you can impose restrictions on the use of the money. On the other hand, they do not have the flexibility of trust provisions, can include no discretionary powers, offer no chance of capital appreciation (except in the case of the variable annuity), and produce a lower return than an average trust. The interest element in an insurance-option plan works out to around 3%; an average trust will net, after fees, 4%—more or less, depending on the size and terms. Moreover, under settlement options your money is often scattered among several companies instead of being concentrated in a unified fund.

Common trust funds The common trust fund is a recent and somewhat spectacular development in the banking field that has brought trusts down within the reach of average folks. Briefly, a common trust fund is a method whereby a bank combines the funds of small trusts into one single investment unit and thus obtains greater diversification for the trusts and operating economies for themselves, which are passed along as lower fees.

If you walked into a certain big Eastern trust company and established a $20,000 trust, the fee would come to $275 a year under the standard system of trust management, which requires that the principal of each trust be kept entirely separate from the funds of every other trust. Moreover, the bank might have trouble maintaining average income, diversification, and growth while balancing safety, yield, and liquidity in a fund of that size. If it did manage to produce the average 4% return, your beneficiaries would net only about 2½%.

But if you authorized your trustee to use the bank's common trust fund, the fee would drop to $105 a year. You could reasonably expect a net income for your beneficiaries of 3½% and somewhat more capital appreciation.

In another bank, of course, your charges might be different. But a return of 4% on your money and a 3½% net to your beneficiaries would be close to a national average. How are funds invested? At one extreme are funds invested exclusively in bonds; at the other are funds exclusively in common stocks. However a typical discretionary fund (which the majority are) might very easily be close to 50% common stocks, 12% preferred stocks, about 15% corporate bonds, 20% U.S. government obligations, and the rest scattered.

A few short years ago, before the spread of common trust funds, estate planners had a rule of thumb that a trust need be considered only when a man's assets began to exceed $50,000. Now, however, it can be practical for a man with only a $10,000 life insurance policy.

Do not, by the way, confuse a common trust fund with a mutual fund. It is easily done, but they actually are very different. The latter is a device by which a number of individuals pool their money for staight investment purposes. A common trust fund is a vehicle that a bank uses to invest money that it is administering as trustee. Your money can't find its way into a common trust fund unless you have a "true fiduciary purpose"—that is, unless you are thinking in terms of such objectives as are outlined on the preceding pages. That is why, for example, banks are flatly prohibited from publicizing the yields earned by their common trust funds. They will quote current performance to a prospective creator—but to advertise yields would give the impression that such funds were investment plans, which they are not.

But you may well have, perhaps to your surprise, a true fiduciary purpose. You may want to plan your life insurance under a more flexible program than options permit. You may want to preserve some hard-earned savings for another generation while you and your wife spend the income in retirement. You may want to make a gift to a grandchild or assure your heirs control of a family business.

Should these or any of the other objectives that a trust can win sound familiar, pay a call on your lawyer or your bank's trust department.

They will examine your problem, explain how a trust can or cannot solve it, and fill you in on all the details. You just might walk out with one of the most valuable financial tools you have ever owned.

CHAPTER 15

Speculating

Speculation, according to the dictionary, is to engage in commercial operation that involves risk of loss, especially with an implication of rashness. Some gifted people speculate successfully. Bernard Baruch was a famous speculator and a successful one. But he never thought that the ordinary person had a Chinaman's chance at it. John Maynard Keynes, as will be shown later, made a fortune speculating in commodities. But he was one of the world's most brilliant analysts and economists. Most people, according to psychoanalysts, speculate because they have a compulsion to lose. So the ordinary investor should take warning. He can speculate easily enough. Perhaps if he devotes hours a day to studying statistics and if he has an instinct for sensing market trends, he can make a go of it. But he should realize at the start that all the odds are against him. He is competing with shrewd men who spend their time on the floors of the exchanges or in the commodity pits and rings, who are steeped in knowledge of the market place, who catch each bit of news seconds after it hits the wires. Some of these experts even use computers to analyze the most intricate statistics on production, supply, and demand. So speculation definitely is not recommended. But for those who are interested, here are some of the ways that it is done.

SHORT SELLING

In the old days many a fortune was made by selling short. Such famous figures as Joseph P. Kennedy, father of President Kennedy, and Bernard M. Baruch used the technique. After the excessive speculation of the Twenties, however, the New York Stock Exchange and the United States Securities and Exchange Commission adopted regulations that wiped out the opportunities for "bear" raids on the market. Today, short selling is still possible, but it is so hedged by restrictions that it is rather sparingly used, even by speculators on the floor of the exchange. Nevertheless, anyone still can sell short if he wants to.

To most people short selling is a kind of upside down way of trying to make money. If a speculator bought 100 shares of stock at 20 and later sold it at 30, he would make $1000 less commissions. But let's suppose, now, that he sells it first at 30, then buys it later at 20. He still would make $1000 less commissions. In the second case, he would have borrowed the stock through his broker, sold the borrowed stock at 30, then later bought it back at 20 and returned it to the borrower.

In the old days when the stock market was much more volatile and when stocks surged up and down more rapidly, short selling was popular. In fact, speculators on the floor of the exchange sometimes ganged up on a stock, sold it short, drove the price down, and "covered" their short positions at much lower levels, making a pot of money in the process.

It is doubtful, however, whether the small individual investor ever consistently made money selling short. To do so, he would have to guess correctly that the stock he borrowed and sold would, in fact, go down. If it went up, instead, he would be in a serious predicament. In the first place, when he borrowed the stock he would have had to put up as security to the lender all the proceeds from the sale. If the stock later went up, the short seller would have to increase his deposit with the lender by an amount equivalent to the increase in his stock's value. If the stock kept going up, the day might come when the lender would want his stock back. In this case, the borrower would have to buy shares in the open market, take a loss, and close out the deal.

Prudent short sellers, if there are any such people, sometimes hedge their short sales by use of a stop-loss order. Thus if a speculator sold a stock short at 30, he might put in a stop-loss buy order at 32. Thus if things went wrong and the stock began to rise, 100 shares would automatically be purchased for him at 32 and he would stand to lose only two points.

Short selling is a particular form of short-term trading that should be attempted only by the most sophisticated market operator. The ordinary investor cannot use it successfully.

COMMODITY FUTURES TRADING

"Have you heard the one about the country boy who wandered into the Coffee Exchange, blinked his eyes, scratched his chin, tugged at his ear and, upon leaving, learned that he had made $7000?" So ran an ad some years ago in a financial newspaper. It went on to describe commodity futures markets as "the fastest trading markets in the world—where you operate on as little as 10% margin—where fortunes have been made and lost in a matter of months."

Basically, this description is true. As a young man, John Maynard Keynes, author of the famous Keynesian theory of economics, was determined to be financially independent and never to "relapse into salaried drudgery." So shortly after World War I he began speculating, first in foreign exchange. He sold German marks and bought U.S. dollars. But early in 1920 the dollar began to decline and the mark rose, and Keynes soon found he had lost £13,000.

He borrowed enough to keep going and plunged into the commodity futures market, trading heavily on very small margins in lead, tin, copper, zinc, rubber, wheat, sugar, linseed oil, and jute futures. Within four years he had made £58,000. During most of his life he continued to speculate in commodities and stocks, finally accumulating a £500,000 fortune.

Keynes, of course, was a genius. Unfortunately, the ordinary speculator in commodity futures may well have the opposite experience. A Department of Agriculture study some years ago indicated that three times as many small speculators lost money as made it. Still, the lure of quick riches is strong. Every large brokerage house has its contingent of men, and even women, who are trying to outguess the weather and the professional commodity traders in New York, Chicago, Minneapolis, and Kansas City. Here are the mechanics of it and the way the speculators figure their chances of success.

Hedging vs. speculation Suppose in early spring you overheard a wheat farmer say, "I've just planted my crop and I see that wheat is currently selling at $2 a bushel. I'd be happy to get that price for my crop when I harvest it next September."

At this point you might say to yourself, "This might be a good deal. The long-range weather forecast is for a hot, dry summer. Congress may raise the support price of wheat. By September the going price may be considerably above $2." So you say to the farmer, "Tell you what. I'll contract to take 5000 bushels next September at $2 a bushel. And I'll give you 10% down to show good faith."

If you and the farmer made this kind of deal, you would, in effect, have bought a September wheat future and he would have sold one. Every day thousands of transactions of this kind are made. Only instead of farmers and speculators meeting face to face, they give their orders to brokers who send them by wire to traders on the floor of one of the commodity exchanges. There the orders are filled much as are orders to buy or sell stocks on the New York Stock Exchange.

Visit the Chicago Board of Trade and from the visitors' gallery you will see the pits, or trading areas, where contracts for wheat, corn, oats, rye, soybeans, and lard are constantly being bought and sold by quick signals of hand and finger. In Minneapolis there is the Grain Exchange, in Kansas City, the Board of Trade. In New York and Chicago there are the two Mercantile Exchanges, where egg and potato futures are bought and sold. At the New York Commodity Exchange it's hides, lead, rubber, copper, and zinc.

There are only two reasons why a person would buy or sell a commodity future. One is to speculate; the other is to avoid speculation, in other words, to hedge. The farmer in the example just cited was a hedger. He knew wheat was $2 a bushel right then, and he wanted to establish the price for his crop once and for all without having to worry about future fluctuations.

Other examples of hedging: In January a chain of grocery stores wants to buy 100 carloads of flour to be delivered June 1. It asks a flour mill to quote a firm price. Now the miller does not want to buy all that wheat in January and store it until June. But in order to quote a firm price on the flour, he must know the cost of raw material, as well as overhead and profit. This means he must immediately establish the price he will pay for his wheat. He can do this by buying wheat futures. Who will sell them to him? Some speculator who thinks wheat is due to go down so that by June he can buy the futures back for less and make a profit.

When a rubber manufacturer buys raw rubber, he may sell an equivalent amount of rubber futures. Since he thus buys and sells rubber at the same time, he guards himself against a loss in case the price of rubber, and rubber goods, changes while his raw material is in inventory or in process of manufacture. Once the finished goods are sold, he will cancel his hedge by buying futures. If, in the meantime, rubber has gone up, he will pay more for his futures, but he also will receive a higher price for his rubber products. Or, if rubber has gone down, he may have to sell his products for less than planned, but also he will buy back his futures for less and hence make an offsetting profit.

You can see that the speculator, by taking the other end of the deal from the hedger, is providing a public service. But that, of course, is not why the speculator is in the market. He buys and sells for only one reason, to make a profit.

Can he do it? Yes, say the brokers who handle such accounts, the speculator can profit if he has the capital, the nerve, and the will to follow certain rules of the game. But, at best, it's a risky business.

Rules of the game Here is how the brokers reason. In commodity futures trading, margins are very low, 5% to 10%. So while the risks are great, so are the potential profits. If a speculator buys on a 10% margin and the price rises 10%, he doubles his money. If he buys on a 5% margin and the price rises 10%, he triples his money. And while the speculator must pay close attention to daily movements, there are not so many basic variables to watch as there are in the stock market.

The two main ingredients of the commodity market are supply and demand. And the figures on these are public information. There can't be any inside dope. Crop reports are jealously guarded against leaks until they are made public, and, once public, they are available to everyone. So are statistics on carry-over, exports, stocks under government loan, and so on.

Then there are certain basic seasonal trends. Over the years, wheat prices, for example, tend to be lowest at harvest time in July and August and on the average gradually move up during the fall and winter until the new wheat comes in. Soybean prices usually hit their lows in the first two weeks in October.

Lord Keynes asserted that futures prices tend to rise 10% per year on the average. Professor Paul Cootner, of Massachusetts Institute of Technology, once made a study of the years 1954 to 1959 to determine what would have happened if, in June of each year, a speculator had bought a wheat contract calling for delivery in the subsequent May. A May wheat contract bought in June 1954 would have appreciated 9% by the time its delivery date came around in May 1955. The same future bought in subsequent years would have appreciated as follows: 11% in 1956, 1% in 1957, and 10% in 1958. But in 1959 it would have fallen 6%. The average annual appreciation would have been 5%.

Considering that the speculator could have bought such a contract on a 5% margin, you might assume that, if he had averaged out, he could have doubled his money. This assumption would be dangerous, however. For one thing, prices rise and fall from day to day, and the margin trader could easily have been wiped out on a series of temporary declines. Also, if he were pyramiding his profits, he would have been wiped out in 1959 anyway.

Just the same, brokers have certain rules of thumb that they think guard against some of these dangers. In the first place, no one should even think of speculating in commodity futures unless he is prepared to take losses. Some losses are almost inevitable. But the theory is that if losses are always cut short and gains allowed to run, a speculator can make money even if he is right only 35% of the time.

Most brokers recommend that whenever a speculator takes a position in a commodity future he immediately put in a stop-loss order. If he buys a wheat future for $2 a bushel, for example, he should put in a stop-loss order 2 cents below the market. Then if wheat falls to $1.98, he will automatically be sold out and his loss limited to only 2 or 2½ cents. If he sells a future short, he should put in a stop-loss order 2 cents above the market so that if wheat rises, instead of falling, he will again be sold out before he has lost much more than 2 cents.

In this way the speculator should attempt to cut his losses short. But if by chance he catches a broad trend, then he should let his profits run. Thus if a speculator bought wheat futures at $2 and wheat began to rise, going to $2.10, he should not take a profit but should move his stop-loss order up to $2.08. Then if the upward trend continued, to say to $2.20, he could move the stop loss to $2.18 and so on.

But what happens to the speculator who buys wheat at $2 and is sold out at $1.97 or $1.98? If he has bought one future, or 5000 bushels, on a 5% margin, he has put up only $500, but has lost $100 or $150. If he tries it again, he may have the same luck. In fact, it may take several tries before he catches his trend. In the meantime, his capital is impaired.

That is why the larger and more conservative brokerage houses will accept as commodity trading customers only those who they think understand the risks and can afford to take them. And unless a new customer has a stock account (and on the average over half of them do), he usually must open his account with a deposit of at least $1000. Brokers generally shy away from women as customers. The reason given: Most women can't stand to take losses.

Trading in commodity futures is not expensive as far as costs and commissions go. The commission in and out for a 5000-bushel wheat contract is only $18. It figures out that a three-eighth-cent rise in the price will compensate for the commission. Everything above that is gravy, at least on paper.

A good bit of free information is available to the commodity trader. The larger brokerage houses provide a wire service giving hourly price quotations and figures on stocks on hand, crop estimates, and so on. Various advisory services also are on file in brokerage offices, or may be purchased on a subscription basis from the publishers, giving outlook and opinion on all commodity futures prices. Some brokers provide a free handbook giving an informal course in how to trade intelligently in futures.

As you see, it's easy to get into the futures market. Margin is small. Commissions are modest. And the same information is available to everyone. Then why don't more people make money at it? Here are the answers from account executives of several leading brokerage houses.

The risks The average trader won't make money in the long run because once he makes a few profits he begins to think he's an expert and doesn't bother taking the proper precautions, such as putting in stop-loss orders on every trade. Also, most people who trade in commodities also have previously traded in common stocks. They can't get used to the idea of cutting losses short. If the market goes against them, they tend to hold on and become stubborn. They apply stock market logic, which is that a good stock eventually is bound to come back. But this doesn't apply to commodities. The May wheat future can go inexorably down right until May. And at that point the owner must either sell and take his loss or take delivery of 5000 bushels and make payment to the seller in full.

Amateur commodity traders have other faults. They are basically optimists and tend to take the long side of the market most of the time. In practice, according to the experts, a trader should be short about half the time.

Some years ago a group of Maine potato farmers got interested in the potato futures market. In theory, their role should have been that of hedgers. If the price was good when they planted their crop, you might expect them to sell futures and fix their year's income. Instead, many of them got overenthusiastic and actually bought futures. This meant, in effect, that the potato farmers had two crops to worry about instead of one.

Taking small gains is another pitfall. The successful trader must have nerves of steel and allow his profits to run. If he chickens out and takes small profits, they will be eaten up by the inevitable small losses.

And even though the information is available to everyone, the unexpected can easily happen. In the spring of 1960, eggs were firm, and the Department of Agriculture implied a short supply. But chicken farmers are not dumb. When they received this word, they simply reversed their usual practice. Instead of culling out their old hens, they let them live and keep on laying. As a result, September egg futures fell from around 38 cents a dozen to 30. And since there are 15,000 dozen eggs in a futures contract, every price drop of 1 cent meant a loss to the futures holder of $150 per contract.

Yes, it's fun to read about the country boy who wandered into the Coffee Exchange, blinked his eyes, scratched his chin, tugged at his ear, and made $7000. That's a good old Wall Street joke. But here's another story, a true one.

An unsophisticated speculator bought a couple of coffee futures contracts, putting up $1500 margin. The market turned against him and he decided to sell, but he couldn't the first day because coffee was down the allowable daily limit on the first transaction and there were no more trades that day. He put his sell order in the next day, and again futures were down the limit on the first sale and trading stopped. This went on for five days. By the time his position was liquidated, he had lost his $1500 plus nearly $10,000 more.

And that's no joke.

BUYING STOCKS ON MARGIN

You can buy a house with 20% down, a car with 25% down, a washing machine with nothing down, but if you want to make an investment for the future by buying common stocks, you have to put somewhere between 50% and 100% down. In most recent years the figure has been 70%. In this necessary and fair? Or are the authorities still terrified by the specter of 1929, when low stock margins admittedly gave impetus to the downward market spiral and the crash?

To these questions one or two others might be added. Should the ordinary person buy on margin? What are the advantages and disadvantages of this kind of purchase?

Initial vs. maintenance margins   To cope with the subject, get firmly in mind the meaning of certain stock market jargon. The "initial margin" is the percentage of the purchase price that the customer pays when he buys a stock. If he buys a share at 100, he must put up under recent requirements 70%, or $70, and the broker can lend him $30. Once the stock is purchased, however, the margin begins to change as the market price of the stock goes up or down. It then becomes the "maintenance margin."

Suppose, for example, that the stock, purchased for $100, were to rise to 140. At this point the loan still would be $30, so the customer's equity would be $110 ($140 market value minus $30 loan), or 79% of the stock's value. The margin, then, would be 79%. On the other hand, suppose the price of the stock were to decline to 65. The loan still would be $30, so the customer's equity would be $35 ($65 market value minus $30 loan), or only 54% of the stock's value. So the margin would be 54%.

One reason it is important to keep these distinctions in mind is that the Federal Reserve Board regulates only the initial margin. Thereafter, the margin that the customer must maintain is determined by the brokerage house and the rules of the New York Stock Exchange. As a matter of fact, the maintenance margins that most brokerage houses and the New York Stock Exchange require are far below the 70% level required by the Federal Reserve Board at the time of purchase.

According to New York Stock Exchange rules, margins must be maintained at 25% or above. In other words, as far as the stock exchange is concerned, the customer's equity can decline to 25% of the market value of the stock.

Most brokerage houses, however, are a little stricter and insist that margins must not fall below 33⅓%. Thus in the example, the customer's stock, which he purchased at 100, putting up $70, could fall in price only to 45 before he would receive a "margin call." The value of the stock would be $45, the customer would owe $30 on it, leaving his equity at $15, or 33⅓% of the market price.

To sum up—under Federal Reserve Board regulations, in effect in recent years, a customer could buy stock by putting up 70% of the purchase price. Thereafter, under most brokerage house rules, the stock could decline 55% before the customer would be called for more margin. The margin at any time may be computed by this formula:

$$\text{margin equals} \frac{\text{market value minus loan}}{\text{market value}}$$

Margin calls   What happens when the price falls to a point where a margin call comes? The customer can do one of several things.

First, he can put up more money, thereby decreasing the loan and increasing his equity and hence the margin. To keep his margin at 33⅓%, he must put up two-thirds of a point for every point his stock falls below the minimum margin level. To check this in the example above, suppose the stock fell to 44.

$$33⅓\% \text{ equals} \frac{44 \text{ minus the new loan}}{44}$$

Solving the formula shows that the new loan must be $29.333, which means the original $30 loan must be decreased by 67 cents, or two-thirds of a point. Actually, if the stock falls below the 33⅓% margin level, the broker is more likely to ask for an increase in the margin of two or three points, bringing it up to 35% or 36%, to provide a little leeway.

The second alternative the customer has, of course, is to sell the stock, pay off the loan, and take his equity in cash. In the Roaring Twenties, when so many speculators were purchasing stocks on 10% and 20% margins, there was a popular saying, "Sell on the first margin call." This was another way of saying, "Cut losses short and let profits run." In those days, with small margins, a call would come after a rather small decline in the price of the stock. Under rules in effect in most recent years, a stock could decline 55% before touching off a margin call, so the old rule is not applicable.

A third alternative to the customer who receives a margin call is to buy more stock. This is a method of raising his margin since out of every dollar he pays for such stock he must put up, under recent rules, 70 cents in cash. Say the customer buys at 100, putting up $70 and borrowing $30. His stock falls to 44 and he receives a call for more margin. If he buys $1.82 worth of stock, putting up 70%, or $1.275, in cash and borrowing an additional $0.545, his margin then would be

$$\frac{\$45.82 \ (\text{market value}) \ \text{minus} \ \$30.545 \ (\text{loan})}{\$45.82 \ (\text{market value})}$$

or 33⅓%.

Pyramiding So much for margin calls. Now take the more optimistic possibility. What if instead of going down the price of the customer's stock goes up? In this case, his equity and margin rise, and he can actually buy more stock without putting up any more cash. This is known as pyramiding. Assume that when the stock reached 120, the customer sold out, took his larger equity and used it to repurchase on a 70% margin. After paying off his $30 loan, he would receive $90 (disregarding commissions). Using this as his 70% margin, he could buy $128.57 worth of stock ($90 is 70% of $128.57). He would then owe $38.57 (30% of $128.57).

In actual practice it is not necessary for the customer to sell, take out his equity, and repurchase. He can acquire the additional $8.57 worth of stock by a paper transaction. If the customer pyramided once and the stock continued to rise, he could pyramid again. The table on this page shows a succession of pyramids. It is assumed that each time the market value rises 20% the margin is readjusted back to 70%.

PYRAMIDING ON MARGIN

	additional stock acquired by borrowing	market value	loan	customer's equity	margin
Initial Purchase		$100.00	$30.00	$70.00	70%
First 20% Price Rise		120.00	30.00	90.00	75%
First Pyramid	$8.57	128.57	38.57	90.00	70%
Second 20% Price Rise		154.28	38.57	115.71	75%
Second Pyramid	11.02	165.30	49.59	115.71	70%
Third 20% Price Rise		198.36	49.59	148.77	75%
Third Pyramid	14.17	212.53	63.76	148.77	70%

Note that with pyramiding the three 20% price rises would raise the customer's equity from $70 to $90 to $115.71 and finally to

$148.77. If at the start he had invested his $70 outright, without borrowing, the three 20% price rises would have raised his equity from $70 to $84 to $100.80 and finally to $120.96. You see the theoretical advantage of pyramiding.

Margins for investment A customer can, of course, use margins for investment. One way is to allow the dividends from the stock to liquidate the loan. Assume that you buy a stock paying a dividend of 6¾%. You borrow 30% of the cost at 5% interest. If you let the dividends pay off the loan, you will own your stock free and clear in around five years. This is because you receive dividends on your total investment but pay interest only on 30%. The magic of compounding does the rest.

Margin trading depends on borrowing, and borrowing costs money. The interest charged by brokers can run over 6%, although it might be higher for small accounts and lower for large and especially favored customers. The interest is payable only on the loan, which is only part of the market value of the stock. A stock theoretically might yield enough to cover the interest on the loan and even pay a net return.

For example, suppose a stock yielding 6% is bought on a 70% margin at an interest cost of 5¾%. For every $100 worth of stock owned, the customer receives $6 and pays 5¾% on $30, or $1.73. His net income, then, is $4.27. But remember, he has put up only $70 of his own money. So this $4.27 income gives him a percentage yield of 6.1% on $70. And the interest paid is deductible from income for tax purposes.

On stocks paying higher dividends, the advantage of owning on margin is greater. Thus if the stock paid 7%, the customer would receive $5.27 ($7 minus $1.73 interest cost) on a $70 investment, or 7½%. An 8% stock would yield nearly 9%, and a 9% stock nearly 10½%.

Dangers The stock market crash of 1929 was not caused by margin trading, but low margins undoubtedly made it worse. After each of the awful days of the panic, Black Thursday (October 24, 1929), Black Tuesday (October 29) and the others, lights burned all night in Wall Street as clerks, fighting to catch up on their paper work, sent out thousands and thousands of telegrams calling for more margin. The customers who could not put up the cash were sold out forthwith, adding to the terrible downward pressure on prices.

The crash brought to light the two great perils of low margins. First, many a small trader, using margins as a means to speculate, suffered a total loss of his savings, whereas if he had bought stocks outright, he might have salvaged something. In fact, if he could have held on, he or his heirs might have done very well, as many stocks today are selling at several times their 1929 high. Second, the pressure of forced liquidation contributed to the panic, which had such a depressing effect on business as a whole.

After the crash Congress undertook to prevent a repetition. Some experts wanted to abolish margin trading altogether, but this was overruled on the grounds that it would impair the liquidity of the great securities markets. Others wanted to have the privilege of trading on margin reserved for investors with accounts of $10,-000 or more. This idea also was rejected.

In the end, it was decided that the problem could be solved by regulating initial margins. The Federal Reserve Board, in its discretion, can move the level upward or downward. Since 1934, when it received this responsibility, the board has changed the requirement many times, having set it as low as 40% in the late thirties and as high as 100% during the short boom of 1946. The board takes some satisfaction from the fact that no sudden drop in stock prices in recent years has developed into a downward spiral.

Brokerage houses themselves have a rule that to some extent deters the small investor from speculating on borrowed money. A margin account cannot be opened without a deposit of at least $2000. And according to the New York Stock Exchange, 80% of all margin accounts are held by people with incomes over $10,000.

Whether any individual should buy on margin is a question only he himself can answer. The theoretical advantages of buying on margin in a rising market have been shown. The disadvantage is that margins usually are a tool of the trader. And trading seldom works for the ordinary investor. His best bet is to buy top quality stocks with a future and hold them.

If a man buys a house or a car or a washing machine with a small down payment, he gradually pays off the debt and eventually owns his purchase free and clear. Installment buying actually is a way of saving. But the trader who buys on margin seldom pays off his debt in installments. Whether he is ahead or behind, he is likely to liquidate his loan by selling the stock. And in either case he is a good prospect for another hot tip on a sure winner. Successful investors didn't make their fortunes in this way.

PUTS AND CALLS

Once upon a time, four office workers employed in a large Eastern city ran into a broker they knew who asked, "Say, do you fellows want to make some money?"

There is only one answer to that question, and one of the group gave it, "How?"

"Buy some United Fruit," the broker said. "I can't tell you the reason right now. It's confidential. But take my advice. Buy a hundred shares." He hurried on.

This cryptic recommendation was discussed at lunch. United Fruit at that time was selling for 23½. It had sold over the past year or two as high as 45. In any event, a hundred shares would cost $2350 plus commissions, a sum beyond the capabilities of the four friends. But one of them had an idea. "Let's buy a call on it. Then if the guy is right, we'll make some money. If not, we can't lose much."

How a call works This idea was adopted, and by the following day a call had been purchased for $350, or $87.50 apiece, good for six months and ten days, exercisable at a price of 23¾. In other words, for $350 the group had acquired an option to buy 100 shares of United Fruit at a price of 23¾ per share at any time during the ensuing six months.

The profit and loss prospects were as follows. The most the group could lose was $350. And they would lose it only if the stock declined and did not recover to 23¾ during the life of the call. In that case, the call would be allowed to expire. But if the stock went up, then the group stood to make $100 for every point it rose. However, the first 3½ points, or $350 of profit, would go to offset the cost of the call. Thus if the stock rose from 23¾ to 27¼, or say 28 to cover commissions also, the group could count on breaking even. All it would have to do would be to sell 100 shares at 28, then exercise the call and buy 100 shares at 23¾. But if the stock went above 28, then the group really would stand to make a clear profit of $100 for every point of rise.

As it turned out, the company showed signs of invigorated management, and the stock rose to 29 during the summer. But then it sagged off, and on September 18, when the call expired, it was 25⅞. The group got back $175 (cost of stock $2375 less two dividends, $2350. Sale $2587 less two commissions, $2525. Difference, $175.) Nevertheless the members were not dismayed. They had had the chance of making several hundred dollars apiece.

A put   This example, an actual one, shows one way of using a call. A put is the opposite of a call. When you buy a put, you acquire the right to sell 100 shares of stock at a fixed price at any time during a given period.

Suppose, for example, you owned 100 shares of a stock that you had bought originally at 50 and that now was selling at 70. You might want to keep your stock in hopes it would go higher. On the other hand, you would like to put a floor under your profit. So you might buy a put for, say, $500. If the stock continued on up, you would let the put expire and your ultimate profit would be reduced by $500. If the stock went down, you would exercise the put by requiring the man at the other end of the deal to buy the stock from you at 70. In effect, you would then have sold it at 65 (70 minus the 5 points for the put).

How to buy a put or call   Puts and calls, as you can see, are simply options to buy or sell. They have been used by traders for hundreds of years, but nonprofessional investors seldom have taken the trouble to understand them. In recent years, however, the public has shown a growing interest, and dozens of put and call options are offered for sale each day in the financial pages of newspapers. Buying such an option, however, is not the usual way of acquiring one.

If you wanted to buy a call on 100 shares of XYZ stock (puts and calls are seldom sold on less than 100 shares) you would not bother to shop through the newspaper ads but would go directly to your broker. He, in turn, would get in touch with a put and call broker in New York. There are only a few of these, but each one has a stable of clients who own many stocks and who are ready to sell, or "write," options on any of them at a price.

A typical option writer owns a large portfolio of the most commonly traded stocks. From experience he knows he can make money by standing ready at all times to sell any stock he owns for, say, three, four, or five points above the current price, or by buying more stock for, say, three, four, or five points below the current price. Therefore at any time he will write an option on any 100-share block of stock he owns, charging a price equivalent to three, four, or five points, depending on the length of the option, whether the stock is high-, low-, or medium-priced and whether its price has been stable or volatile.

By shopping around, your broker eventually would be able to buy you the kind of option you wanted, provided the stock was that of a large company, widely owned. In such a case you would be buying a newly written option, exercisable at the market price at time of purchase. It could be made to run for 30 days, 60 days, 90 days, or 6 months and 10 days, the extra 10 days in the last case being to ensure the buyer that any profit would be a long-term capital gain.

Prices vary, but the average cost of a 6-months, 10-days call, for example, would be 14% of the total value of the stock. If you bought a call and sometime later decided to exercise it, you could sell it back to the put and call dealer direct, or you could actually acquire the 100 shares and sell them in the market. The result would be the same, and in either case you would pay the regular New York Stock Exchange commission on the sale of 100 shares.

Once you own a put or call, you can sell it at any time during its life. If you sold it well in advance of its expiration date, it might be resold by the dealer. The "special" put and call options advertised in the daily papers are such resales. While newly written puts and calls usually are exercisable at the then market price of the stock, those up for resale must carry the original price, which may be above or below the market price of the stock at the time of resale. The sale price of the option will have been adjusted to cover the difference.

How profitable? Now for the crucial question. Can you make money trading in puts and calls? Theoretically, yes. But in actual practice, the chances are against the nonprofessional. The U. S. Securities and Exchange Commission once concluded an exhaustive study of puts and calls. Here are a few of its conclusions:

❡ The buyers of puts and calls generally are individuals, mostly small investors. Calls are more commonly bought than puts.

❡ Approximately 43% of calls are exercised. The rest are allowed to expire.

❡ Of the 43% exercised, about one-half (21½% of the total) are exercised at a loss, the owner getting back, on the average, 40% of his cost and losing 60%.

❡ On the 21½% of calls exercised at a profit, the profit averages 150%.

Translated into briefer language, the above would seem to say that, if you are a small investor and are considering buying a call, the chances are about four to one against your making money at it. But if you beat the odds and do make a profit, it might run as high as 150%.

CHARTS AND GRAPHS

There are two basic ways of selecting stocks and gauging the course of the stock market. One is known as the fundamental approach. It calls for a study of business conditions, of the relative position of industries, of the earnings of companies, and quality of management. It attempts to evaluate, to discover merits, weaknesses, potentials. This is the approach that has been stressed in this book.

The other method is known as the technical approach. Its premise is that stock prices themselves, as they move along from day to day, weave a pattern and tell a story of events to come. The technician, through his price charts, watches the interminable battle between buyers and sellers. He senses the rise and fall of investor confidence. From the actions of prices, he believes he can spot the time when supply or demand is winning out, and a stock, or the market as a whole, is about to break out and go higher—or lower.

Use of the technical approach is not recommended for the individual. For one thing, it requires a great deal of statistical work, more than the ordinary person can handle. And while most professional technicians use their charts to forecast the longer-term price movements, most amateur technicians are prone to use charts to try for short-term profits. This calls for trading in and out of the market, which seldom works for the ordinary investor.

Nevertheless, the technical approach is of interest. At its best, and when combined with the fundamental approach, it can be revealing—sometimes startlingly so. And today, when it has become harder and harder to find bargains in the market, some big institutional investors, the managers of large funds, are paying a good deal of attention to the charts and prognostications of the really competent technicians.

Point and figure   A point and figure chart shows only one thing, price movement. It neither shows volume of trading nor takes into account time in the usual sense. Time, says the chartist, is merely a measure of change. Therefore, unless the price of a stock changes by, say, one point, no entry is made on the chart even though weeks and months may go by.

Look at the chart below. It is based on one-point units and shows price movement of a stock that was first charted at 20. Once the chartist posted an X opposite the figure 20, he was interested in two things only—whether the stock sold at or above 21 or whether it sold at or below 19.

CHART 27: POINT AND FIGURE

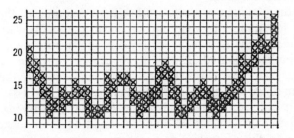

This stock subsequently sold at 19, so an X was made in the 19 square just under the previous posting at 20. This X established a down trend and, as long as this down trend remained in effect, all subsequent postings were made in the same column. In this case the down trend continued until a price of 17 was reached. The stock then reversed one point by selling at 18 and the chartist moved over into the next column to post 18.

Once this 18 posting had been made, a sale at 19 or 17 would establish a trend. The next recordable sale was 17 and the trend carried down to 15 in the second column. Subsequent fluctuations produced the pattern shown.

There are variations of this method—for example, the one-point unit, three-point reversal chart. In this case a reversal in trend is posted only if it extends three boxes up from the previous low or down from the previous high.

What does the chartist learn from his intricate pattern of X's? Chiefly he pays attention to "congestion areas." These are irregular horizontal bands in which the X's waver up and down but their main direction is sideways. These areas represent periods of accumulation by investors (perhaps insiders) who have confidence that the stock will go up, or distribution by holders of the stock who have reason to believe that it will go down. Eventually, once the sideways movement is over, the stock will break out either up or down.

The technician often can identify these periods of accumulation or distribution, although congestion areas take many forms and it requires experience and reference to other technical data to tell whether a given area represents a top or a base. In the most easily identifiable case, the end of a period of accumulation is signaled by some recognizable formation; for example, the bottom of each column of X's is a little higher than the previous one. This indicates a breakout on the up side.

Once the direction of the move has been determined, the chartist attempts to estimate how far up, or down, the stock will go. This vertical movement is thought to depend on the horizontal width of the accumulation period. Thus if the accumulation period in a one-point unit chart had covered fifteen horizontal squares, the upward movement might be estimated at fifteen points.

As you can see, the technician uses his charts to try to measure the great intangible force of investor confidence that makes stocks sell at seven times earnings at one time and twenty times earnings at another. How do you measure the force that can push the price of a stock sharply up or down even though the company's financial situation would seem not to have changed?

Market charts   The technician uses many charts. One shows the breadth of the market, in other words, the share volume of advancing stocks and the share volume of declining stocks traded daily on the New York Stock Exchange. Another shows the number of stocks traded that advanced in price versus those that declined. When volume is increasing and advances exceed declines, the market presumably is in for a rise.

Another intriguing way by which technicians attempt to measure confidence is by means of Barron's Confidence Index, published each week by *Barron's National Business and Financial Weekly.* There is a school of thought that the upward and downward movements of this index precede those of the Dow-Jones Industrial Average by two to four months.

The Confidence Index is based on the assumption that professional bond traders can sense the coming changes in business conditions some weeks earlier than traders in stocks. The index measures the shifts back and forth between demand for high-grade, relatively safe bonds, and run-of-the-mill and hence more speculative bonds. If bond traders have confidence in the business outlook, they tend to buy speculative, high-yielding bonds. But if the outlook appears to demand caution, these traders shift into bonds of higher grade.

The Dow Theory You may have heard of the Dow Theory. It is based on the great law of action and reaction which says that things do not move up or down in a straight line. A movement starts, gains momentum, and goes too far. Then a reaction sets in. When this reaction is completed, the primary movement starts again. Once more there is a reaction. Thus in a bull market stock prices seesaw upward. In a bear market they fluctuate downward. These wavelike motions are perhaps rough and irregular, but the technician attempts to gauge them.

One of the oldest attempts to interpret these undulating movements of the stock market was the Dow Theory, originated some sixty-five years ago by Charles H. Dow, first editor of *The Wall Street Journal,* and his successor, William P. Hamilton, and further developed by a financial writer, Robert Rhea. These observers of the Wall Street scene believed that the stock market was a relentless forecaster of business conditions. The market gives its bloodless verdict, say the Dow theorists, because businessmen are the chief buyers and sellers of stocks and each contributes what he knows about business. The market thus sifts and averages what all businessmen think about the future.

The Dow theorist, watching the continually moving lines of his industrial and railroad averages, thinks of himself as an observer on the beach watching the ocean. He measures the waves to determine whether the tide is coming in or going out.

The tides, or broad bull or bear movements, last several years. The ripples are the daily fluctuations and have no meaning. The waves that tell the tale are the short swings lasting for several weeks or months. If each new wave rolls up the beach a little higher than the last, and recedes not quite so far, there is a bull market. But at some point a wave will not go as high as the preceding one. It will also recede further. This might indicate that the tide had turned and a bear market begun.

The Dow theorist doesn't hope to catch the exact turn of the market. He knows that major trends run for several years. He expects to be late and doesn't mind as long as he's right. In October 1929, Hamilton wrote a famous editorial in *The Wall Street Journal* entitled "A Turn in the Tide." It stated that a bear market was definitely under way. Jeers came from Wall Street because the industrials had already fallen 75 points and the rails 21. But, by 1933, industrials had dropped another 264 points and rails another 154 points.

Today the Dow Theory is considered by many to be somewhat archaic. But the technicians believe that the great law of action and reaction still operates.

Dangers of charting   There are a great number of other indexes and charts that attempt to forecast price movements, measure intrinsic value, and gauge investor confidence. Almost every brokerage house has a chartist on its staff.

The great danger in all these charts and theories, of course, is that the layman tends to see in them the open-sesame to riches, the lazy man's easy road to wealth. But they are far from that. Even the technicians handle these tricky tools with the greatest circumspection. The late Edmund Tabell, of Walston & Co., who worked with charts for over thirty years, admitted to around 30% of misses. And he used his charts, not in a vacuum, but as a check and a supplement to the fundamental approach to investment values.

"The layman who makes investment decisions based on fifteen minutes of chart work a day," he once said, "is simply playing financial Russian roulette."

Odd-lot statistics as forecasters of the market   The public is always wrong. This old Wall Street adage can't actually be proved to be true or untrue. But, as in many old adages, there seems to be just enough truth in it to make it worth pondering.

Put another way, the adage says that the little guy is always pessimistic at the bottom and rampantly optimistic at the top. He sits suspiciously on the sidelines during a long bull market. As prices go higher, he realizes that he is missing the boat so he plunges desperately in just at the point when the professionals decide the rise is over and quietly sell out.

Then the coin turns over and the other side appears. The little guy holds his stock and watches it go down and down. In the beginning he won't believe he is wrong, and therefore won't sell out and take a small loss. No, he will ride the market down until at last he gives up in disgust and sells out at a big loss. This, according to the theory, marks the end of the decline, the point at which the smart professionals move in and buy. Then the cycle repeats itself with the little guy sitting on the sidelines watching the market rise again.

The proof of the pudding is supposed to lie in the "odd lot" transactions on the New York Stock Exchange, shown each day on the financial pages of newspapers. An odd lot is a block of stock of less than 100 shares. Most big investors buy and sell in round lots, i.e., blocks of 100 shares, while most small investors, having less money to work with, generally buy in odd lots of 10, 20, 50 shares, and the like.

The odd-lot figures reveal more than do the round-lot figures. Round-lot transactions are matched on the floor of the stock exchange, and there must be exactly as many sales as purchases. Therefore round-lot transactions give no clue as to whether the trading is being initiated predominantly by buyers or sellers. But when a small investor puts in an order for an odd lot, the odd-lot dealer who receives the order either makes the sale out of his own inventory or, if necessary, buys a round lot, sells part of it, and puts what's left over into inventory. In the same way, when a small investor wants to sell an odd lot, the dealer buys it in and adds it to inventory. Odd-lot transactions, therefore, are recorded either as buy orders or sell orders and thus are about the only available measures of what the public is doing.

Now for the $64 question. Do the odd-lot figures really show that the public usually buys at the top and sells at the bottom? Unfortunately the statistics can be interpreted in different ways. Some of the shrewdest Wall Streeters believe that odd-lot transactions may have been useful market indicators in earlier periods when margins were low and there was a great deal of speculation. In those days, buying by the public meant that stock was passing into weak hands. Today, however, the small investor often is a young man with a family who buys sound stocks for the long term and hangs onto them. Nevertheless, many analysts believe that if either odd-lot purchases or sales, or particularly odd-lot short sales, took a very sharp jump or drop, they would sit up and take notice.

And some of the simon-pure chartists go a great deal further. They believe that the odd-lot figures do give an advance tip on market declines and rises. Actually, it may be that the actions of the steady, investor type of odd-lotter do not reveal anything special about the market, while the actions of the emotional, speculative odd-lotter do give a warning worth heeding. In other words, sudden jumps or drops in odd-lot transactions may indicate that the public is getting impulsive and emotional and thereby contributing to instability.

What's the significance of all this? Probably it's twofold. First, you may want to keep an eye on the odd-lot figures with the idea that there's a germ of truth to the theory that the public is usually wrong. Second, and more important, you should use the figures to keep your own perspective. Investors are like a flock of sheep: they tend to surge in one direction. This causes prices to go up too far in bull markets and down too far in bear markets. In the corrections that inevitably follow, those who bought at the top or sold at the bottom get hurt.

Perhaps the best way to handle your investments is to buy sound stocks at regular intervals, thus averaging out the price. But if you want to try to time your purchases, then better keep an eye on the odd-lot figures so you won't be infected with the spirit of the mob. After all, you don't want to help prove the old adage that you, as a small investor, are always wrong.

CHAPTER 16

An Investment Philosophy

Everybody can't be rich, but almost everybody could be better off. Managing money successfully requires neither genius nor drudgery. Mainly you need perspective on your own affairs. You must be able to discern the broad groupings: your income, expenditures, savings, and net worth. To do this, get out of the tangle of financial tree trunks up onto a hill where you can look down on the outline of the woods. Make yourself a hardheaded set of over-all records. Anyone who does this with care should be able to adjust outgo to income and arrange a small surplus.

That surplus can mean the difference between peace of mind and constant fret and worry. In the words of Mr. Micawber, annual income twenty pounds, annual expenditure nineteen pounds, nineteen shillings, sixpence, result happiness; annual income twenty pounds, annual expenditure twenty pounds, no shillings, sixpence, result misery.

Once you have savings, you can think of investments. That is better than trying to work it the other way. For most families these savings should be channeled first into life insurance and an emergency fund, then possibly into a house. Monetary reforms have made life a lot safer, but they still haven't eliminated the danger of death, depression, or loss of job. Only when there is money above and beyond these protective needs should it go all or partly into stocks. Once you have got your head above water and have some spare cash that is really "cash to spare," then you ought to be able to make a little money. Others have done it without specialized training. But you probably have noticed that this book gives no pat formula. There is no foolproof method. For every person and for every period of time, the road winds a different way. What was smart ten years ago may not be smart today. What the Joneses get away with may be the worst thing for you.

This book has tried to describe some of the lore, the rules of thumb, the tricks of the trade that have proved useful to other travelers. Perhaps the surest way to succeed is to use the brains and self-reliance that nature gave you. Make your own decisions. Don't go with the crowd because history shows that when it comes to investments the crowd usually gets stuck in the end.

This is a time of great opportunity. The free-enterprise system is not just a campaign speech phrase. It exists and gives every American the real precious freedom to earn money, to keep it, and to use it as he sees fit. On the one hand you can buy security, the most convenient and safest there is. On the other hand you can buy a stake in a dynamic, expanding America. Certainly that is a combination that our ancestors would have given plenty to own. In the "good old days" such security and chances at profits came only to the few. Today they are available to anyone who has the imagination and energy to grasp them. Recognizing that fact is half the battle.

Index